GOON

T0197966

GOON

Memoir of a Minor League
Hockey Enforcer

Second edition

Doug Smith
with Adam Frattasio

McFarland & Company, Inc., Publishers
Jefferson, North Carolina

All photographs are from the authors' collections.

This is a revised and updated edition of *Goon: The True Story of an Unlikely Journey into Minor League Hockey* (Baltimore: PublishAmerica, 2002).

LIBRARY OF CONGRESS CATALOGUING-IN-PUBLICATION DATA

Names: Smith, Doug, 1964– author. | Frattasio, Adam, 1962– author.
Title: Goon : memoir of a minor league hockey enforcer / Doug Smith with Adam Frattasio.
Description: 2d ed. | Jefferson, North Carolina : McFarland & Company, Inc., Publishers, 2017. | Includes bibliographical references and index.
Identifiers: LCCN 2017048645 | ISBN 9781476671680 (softcover : acid free paper) ∞
Subjects: LCSH: Smith, Doug, 1964– | Violence in sports—United States. | Hockey players—United States—Biography.
Classification: LCC GV848.5.S65 A3 2017 | DDC 796.962092 [B] —dc23
LC record available at https://lccn.loc.gov/2017048645

BRITISH LIBRARY CATALOGUING DATA ARE AVAILABLE

ISBN (print) 978-1-4766-7168-0
ISBN (ebook) 978-1-4766-3031-1

Front cover: Doug Smith sporting a black eye as a member of the Moncton Hawks hockey team during the 1993–1994 AHL season (author's collection)

Printed in the United States of America

McFarland & Company, Inc., Publishers
Box 611, Jefferson, North Carolina 28640
www.mcfarlandpub.com

To all those who don't have everything it takes,
but do it anyway.

Table of Contents

Acknowledgments

All of the events, characters, names, and nicknames depicted in this book are factual with deference to my memory and the recollection of others. The one slight exception made in the interest of literary ease was "Gator," which is a composite character covering the actions of co-author Adam Frattasio and his brother, Jon "Fin" Frattasio.

I owe many of my experiences in the pro hockey world to the friendship and selflessness of Sean "Commander" Coady, who took me under his wing and opened doors that would otherwise have remained locked.

Eugene "Geno" Binda was also kind enough to take a flyer out and help me realize my goal to work in a pro hockey game as a linesman. I had a dream of getting into a fight with a player while wearing the zebra shirt, but I suppose it was a good thing I left the profession before giving Binda that kind of black eye.

Former Hanover High School hockey players Paul Keating and Brian Hennessey offered themselves up to me as personal punching bags during my early days of practice on rented ice. While there were many folks who provided their services as sparring partners, this pair allowed me to hit them full force. Sorry, guys.

Before Mike "Kuzzy" Kuzmich joined Steve Plaskon on the ice, where both worked to convince Brian Carroll to bring me back down to the Carolina Thunderbirds for my rookie season, he took the tedious time back home to teach me such skating basics as leaning into a turn and crossing over. What an embarrassment.

I also bow to NHL scout Paul Merritt. I don't know what the hell he was thinking when he recommended me to the Thunderbirds for a tryout, but I thank him nonetheless. I likewise salute player agents Brian Cook and Jay Fee, men of their words who not only didn't throw away my name and phone number but used them to get me into a few different uniforms over the years.

After I had established myself as an aspiring minor-leaguer, the manager of the Quincy Youth Hockey Arena, Bev Reinhart, gave Frank Derwin a nod of approval to open the rink for me every weekday morning so I could work on my skating free of charge and without anybody around to laugh at me. Pro shop steward Bill "Red" Skinner sharpened my skates gratis and supplied me with everything else I happened to need.

Allegiance should be paid to all youth groups, programs, and operators for their largely volunteer and thankless efforts. My particular kudos goes to the Hanover Police Boys' Club, retired detective Thomas Hayes, and former chief of police the late John Lingley. Their passionate work to build and sustain the Boys' Club since its incorporation in 1977 has helped guide many Hanover children and keep them busy over the years. My involvement with the Boys' Club and the police officers I came into contact with there are the reasons I am a police officer today.

Robert Sylvia, long-time coach of the Quincy High hockey team and a member of the Massachusetts High School Coaches' Hall of Fame, had the nerve to put me on his summer roster for play in the Pro-Am Hockey League. I can only imagine how many people snickered and sneered at him for that move, which led to my first season as a pro in the East Coast Hockey League.

Robert's brother, Jim Sylvia, another no-brainer choice for the state's Hall of Fame, also cut firmly across the grain when he took me on as his assistant coach for the Hanover High School hockey team in 1990. I don't dare admit to having much of anything to do with it, but I had a grand old time standing on the bench in the Fleet Center cheering my Hanover Indians on to three state championships during my 20 years wearing the blue and gold.

Any new kid on the block needs a helping hand to fit in and Donna Fowler volunteered to be my surrogate mom for a while when I first settled into Winston-Salem with the T-Birds. Likewise, Patrick "Hoppy" Dunn and his dad, Cecil, opened their home and hearts to me during my stay in New Brunswick with the Miramichi Gagnon Packers. While I was there, Bernie Williams filled my gullet on a regular basis at the good old Hi-Lo Tavern. I am so grateful and fortunate to have visited one last time, to see my friend Hoppy, "The Voice of Miramichi," for a roast in his honor a year before his untimely passing. See you again down the road, pal.

Substantial color and insight for the book was provided through in-person, long-distance telephone, and Internet conversations with Bill and Lisa Whitfield, Brock Kelly, Greg Neish, Brian Carroll, Greg Batters, Grant "The Otter" Ottenbreit, Jacques "The Mailman" Mailhot, Scott Allen, Rock Derganc, Dave Gushue, Chris Hampton, Ira Rubenstein, Wayne Bernard, Darwin McCutcheon, Bev Bawn, Jukka Suutari, Bruce Wensink, Ryan VandenBussche, Nick Vitucci, Richie Lovell, and sadly, the late Darren Miciak, who passed away far too soon on January 4, 2013, at the age of 47. Their contributions reinforced, added, brought a different perspective to, or otherwise shook free information that had previously remained dormant or swamped in the further recesses of my mind.

A huge thank you to Brian Fisher of JPI Communications, Inc., out of Dieppe, New Brunswick, who was good enough to grant a request I made of him before my first AHL game in Moncton. He went above and beyond with his video camera by keying on me during my first period shifts and in the process very clearly and professionally captured my ample beating at the stone fists of Frank "The Animal" Bialowas.

Because Adam and I are basically a pair of dumb jocks with severe limitations on the use of proper English grammar, Doug Flynn, a Syracuse University graduate and former Boston Bruins beat writer, was invaluable as an initial editor.

Additional research for this book, including histories of various Double-A hockey leagues and literally all of the statistical references—no, you don't understand, I mean *literally all of the statistical references*—were made possible by Ralph Slate's incredible Internet Hockey Database (www.hockeydb.com/). It is the most inclusive and thorough work of its kind on the planet and an easy way for any hockey nut to kill four or five hours.

Many former players inspired me before and during my journey into minor-league hockey, but Paul Stewart always stood as my model of a guy who substituted heart and grit for what he may have lacked in ability. My pal John Olsen's 1982 interview with Paul "Le Chat" Stewart is one I have memorized word for word.

Many locals followed my travails with interest and enthusiasm, but few matched the fervor of Pat and Denise MacFarlane, Jen Marchetti, Ken "Captain Kenway" Dickinson, Scott Mottau, Noel Frattasio, Seth Frattasio, Christian Frattasio, Bob Miot, Mike Brenton, Dan Flaherty, and the old crew at the Boys' Club. Journalists Judy Enright, Denise Falbo, and Paul Harber chipped in with nice newsprint stories about my journey while I was playing.

I thank my mom, Helen, my sister, Pam, and my late dad, Douglas, an old-time tough guy who first taught me how to hold up my fists. While they may not have fully understood what I was trying to accomplish on the ice, they exercised a rare trait maybe only a loving, caring family unit could practice—they shut their mouths and allowed a grown boy to do his thing.

It is difficult to find the correct word or phrase that can aptly describe my feelings about the movies adapted from my experiences in hockey. I suppose that "fucking incredible" might suffice. I am thankful to everybody responsible for creating these new cult-classic hockey films, and from my rear-view mirror nobody more than executive producer Jesse Shapira and working partner David Gross, who were able to realize their own unlikely dream of making a real Hollywood movie through the world of hockey fighting.

And finally, along the way I managed to get the former Sharon Parsons to marry me, and help her create two beautiful daughters, Vanessa and Victoria. Nearly three decades since I first dropped the gloves for the Carolina Thunderbirds have gone by like the blink of an eye, and somehow I completed the transition from a wandering vagabond to a somewhat stable human being with a family, career, and the proverbial white-picket fence. As far as I'm concerned, I continue to live a dream come true.

Preface

Warm streams of blood pumped from a deep gash carved into my brow. I squinted as the blood cascaded down and filled my left eye. As I skated toward the Moncton Hawks' bench with my head bobbed I watched my blood spit and splatter onto the ice, adding to a trail that began at a spot in front of the St. John's Maple Leaf net, where yet another of my dreams came true.

I had been cut many times before, but never with a punch as hard and square as the right uppercut Frank Bialowas had used to rip me open. The blood in my eye stung while I continued toward the gate that would lead me to the Hawks' dressing room. I wanted to look into a mirror to make sure my eye was still there. It was one of the most glorious moments of my life.

That was my first fight in the American Hockey League, the second-best hockey league in the world. While it was an accomplishment shared by thousands, few of them had laced up their first pair of skates at the over-ripe age of 19, as I did.

I made my debut in the American League as a goon, a decidedly vulgar term for players whose primary role on a team is to be a policeman on the ice. Goons serve to protect and bolster the confidence of their less physical, more talented teammates in response to abuse from opposing ruffians during a game. In Webster's Dictionary, "goon" is described as "a man hired to terrorize or eliminate opponents." That's what I did.

Most players who fall into this category of player don't care to be labeled a goon, as they feel the moniker is demeaning and trivializes their athletic ability. They instead prefer the less repellent designations of enforcer, grinder, physical player, or maybe at best—checking forward.

I didn't mind being known as a goon because that's exactly what I was; a fighter on skates who would stick up for teammates or otherwise menace and intimidate the opposition. I never dared fancy myself a traditional hockey player because I didn't possess the prerequisite skills that

1

included quality skating, vision, and puck-handling abilities. My primary job was to seek out the toughest guy on the other team and challenge him to fight.

Whether I won or lost didn't particularly matter, because just the concept of being there ready and willing to do battle made a powerful statement. If the other club's goon had any thoughts of roughing up and intimidating my teammates, he was going to have to go through me to do it, and we'd fight all game long if need be to get my point across.

Some may wonder what the hell kind of satisfaction I gained from such a strange and seemingly thankless position on a team, but I never doubted the initial reason why I undertook my unlikely journey into professional hockey. The chance to play a sport at the professional level was the baited hook, plain and simple, and I swallowed it whole.

I didn't pursue organized youth sports growing up and I was never a member of any high school athletic team. After missing out on much of the experiences of Little League and watching with a measure of envy while others played out their glories on high school and college teams, I jumped at the chance for redemption that professional hockey appeared to offer. I decided to carve out my own niche in sports with this odd role of hockey goon and take back every athletic opportunity I had squandered.

From the 1988–89 through 1997–98 seasons I was paid to *play* for seven different teams in four different hockey leagues, never veering from my original course. While I was credited with four assists during my limited time on the ice, the 404 penalty minutes I accrued during my 60-game "career" as a goon remain my true statistical prize.

However, as precious a possession as those penalty minutes are to me, only rarely during or after my playing days did anyone interested in my experiences inquire about my stats. They clearly weren't interested in the one-dimensional, black-and-white picture sketched by mere numbers.

Friends and acquaintances instead demanded color commentary. They wondered if the hockey fights were real or if they were staged like wrestling on television. They wanted to know exactly what two guys would say to each other on a face-off before dropping their gloves, and they asked if a coach ever specifically pointed somebody out and ordered me to fight him. They asked if I ever lost, if I was ever hurt, and how much I was paid. They wanted to know who the toughest guys were, what my opponents thought of me, and what my teammates thought of me—especially the ones I had to fight off for a job during training camp. They wanted to know about the bench-clearing brawls, where I lived, what I ate, the women, and if the long bus rides were really as horrible as the vintage tales described.

As I look back at my experiences, it's funny, but I shared many of those same questions before embarking upon my unlikely journey into minor league hockey...

From the Coauthor

I first came upon Doug Smith when I was a senior in high school. He was an anonymous freshman, one of a sea of awkward pubescent boys trying to fit in while remaining cautiously in the shadows, content to observe and learn from the relative safety of shore, wary of jumping into the faster-moving waters of the upperclassmen-dominated social stream.

I like to think I am observant, that I notice things missed by others, but more than likely we all have personal moments of awareness that are shared and also unique. In that respect I am proud to say that I am probably the only one who noticed the unremarkable Doug. He was the kid with bright blue eyes I thought lived somewhere within the vicinity of my neighborhood and may have been on my school bus, who remained pressed silently against the hallway wall offering an appreciative grin while watching the hijinks performed by me and my fellow class clowns after lunch.

It wasn't for another four years that I formally met Doug, after he started hanging around with one of my younger brothers. He was the kid I remembered against the wall, the same bright blue eyes, and while he was still a bit guarded, he managed to transform himself into a physically imposing figure after taking up weightlifting and boxing.

Beginning with the dismantling of bullies and personal tormentors within the high school, Doug became a local tough guy. Every generation has one—the toughest guy in town. He wasn't a bully or a big mouth or a braggart—actually quite the opposite—but he was certainly a guy with a genuine mean streak who earned the reputation as someone not to be trifled with, *at all*—unless you were looking for trouble or had a strange desire to be knocked out.

As for any colorful local character, I could recount many Doug Smith stories—part fact and part fiction—leaving the absolute truth in the air like a volleyball to be batted back and forth. However, there are three little stories I will leave with you that encompass the portion of Doug's persona that helped create this book. It is of passing interest to note that two of these tales orig-

5

inated before, and then one after Doug had taken a job as a police officer and generally stopped squaring off with people on the street or ice.

I had a bit part to play in my first scenario, skating midnight hockey at Babson College with a bunch of guys in their thirties. A 19-year-old Doug, who still hadn't tried on a pair of skates at this point, brought a couple of my younger brothers along to watch and they all took up at the end of our bench making themselves useful filling water bottles and operating the gate for the players.

On the other team was a little guy, in his early 30s, maybe 5-foot-5 and 140 pounds, running around slashing and hacking people. He got into it with my roommate, Kenway, a beginning skater who wasn't looking for any trouble. My 14-year-old brother yelled at the guy, who then skated over to give him some shit. Doug stood up, there were a few, and I mean a very few words, before Doug reached over the boards and knocked the little guy out with one straight right. All of the other project managers and computer programmers and school teachers and insurance salesmen stopped playing and skated over. They derided and yelled at Doug and told him to pick on somebody his own size. Not one with a flair for getting into a war of words, Doug quietly left the bench area, much to the victorious delight of the attacking hoard of paper-pushing nerds and weekend warriors.

Problem was, Doug never really left. He just parked himself behind the Plexiglas at the end of the rink, and every time one of the big mouths skated by, Doug looked at him square in the eyes and just as squarely pounded a fist into his opposing palm. After a short time the now nervous group of guys skated over to me and asked what was going on.

While I hadn't talked to Doug, I knew. I told them that Doug was waiting until the game was over, and that he was going to beat up every single guy who had a problem with and something to say about what he did. Each and every one of the guys was mortified. Their faces sunk as if told they had cancer. They pleaded with me to make things right, to call off the attack. No problem. I skated over and diffused Doug like an old bomb unearthed in London. He stuck around in case anybody grew a set of nuts, but nobody developed any second thoughts.

I was also witness to my second story—starting out as a passenger in Doug's car waiting our turn through the indomitable four-way traffic jam that is the daily summer intersection of Queen Anne's Corner in Hingham. "Look at this asshole," said Doug, his gaze fixed on the rear-view mirror, watching a couple guys on Harleys weave their way through two lanes of tightly-packed traffic for a spot at the front of the line. Doug would have none of it for himself, so as the motorcycles approached he quickly and very deliberately angled his car to effectively cut off any additional pathway. The guys were wearing vests, showing their colors, but I can't remember what club they were with. In any case, they got off their bikes and challenged us. I got out and squared off with the first guy, but in a matter of seconds Doug bowled me over from behind to take the guy on himself. I just stood there with the other guy, in a standoff, watching the fight unfold.

It was over fairly quickly—about 30 seconds. Doug pounded the guy to the ground and got back in his car as if he had just mailed a letter at the post office. But not everything was quite over.

A few days later, the head of the local chapter of the bike club that the two guys belonged to came into the Boys' Club. He wanted Doug to know that there would be no retaliation; that the fight was fair and Doug would get a "free pass" for this one. Doug put on that half-aggravated, half-amused face of his. Free pass? Doug said that if he, the guy he beat up, or anybody else in the chapter had the inclination, they could come down and fight him right there at the Boys' Club. I was horrified. I couldn't believe that Doug was instigating this guy. Why couldn't he just be a little gracious and slide away unscathed from the situation? After all, he would still come out the winner.

But it wasn't in Doug's DNA to be intimidated, *he* was the intimidator, and he put the ball right back into the bikers' court. Thank goodness the guy backed off a bit and reiterated that he wasn't looking for a fight. He said that he just didn't want to hear about it. I got the feeling that the guy Doug beat up had been a pretty tough member of the chapter, and the leader just didn't want the story going around. With that the guy left, along with the last that ever came of it—thank goodness.

Now here's my personal favorite, a story told to me by another cop who witnessed the event.

There was a dispatch at the police station one late weekend night for brewing trouble at a local dive. A few cops, including Doug, arrived at the bar to confront a drunk and unruly crowd. While the other cops tried their conversational best to corral the belligerent hell raisers, Doug surveyed the area like an old western gunslinger and quickly surmised the reality of the situation. He strolled into the middle of the ring and soon, one by one, the crowd stopped arguing and began paying attention to the big cop who so very obviously placed himself before them. Unlike so many years before, when the tentative high school freshman was content to remain silent and hidden within the protection of the anonymous crowd, Doug now worked to attract an audience. After his bright blue eyes noticed he had everybody's attention, Doug slowly and very deliberately reached across into his shirt pocket and pulled out a glob of molded rubber, which he held between the thumb and index finger of his meaty right hand. Just as slowly and deliberately he placed the mouth piece securely between his teeth, shook his arms loose and asked, "Who's first?" The once rowdy but now a bit more sobered crowd thought for a few moments, thought better of it, calmed down and began to disperse.

I don't use the words "hero" or "heroic" lightly, and I wouldn't use them for Doug. For me, those words should be stored in a secure vault and taken out only periodically to enshrine war veterans, or the likes of civilians Arland Williams, Jr., and Lenny Skutnik (go ahead, look them up). But in a completely literary sense, from what I have come to understand, the classic "American Hero" is a flawed person who goes on to commit certain acts of bravery or heroism. I think the flawed part allows regular folks, like me, to more easily relate to a person not perched upon an unattainable pedestal. Like most of us, Doug has his flaws, some real whoppers. I suppose this helps to make him more grounded and relatable and more like the rest of us.

The stories I've recounted are meant to illustrate very particular attributes of my friend's character and inner mettle—hopefully more for the better than worse—which I thought were actually captured by the screenwriters and Seann William Scott, somewhat, in the movies. In any case, that is the *real* "Goon," the guy I know and regard as a brother, and who some of you have now come to know as Doug "The Thug" Smith.

1

Reborn in the Boys' Club

I was a runt growing up in Quincy, a small municipality that shares a short border with the southeastern corner of Boston. I was the kid in the neighborhood who was singled out and picked on.

My dad had been a light-heavyweight amateur boxer and taught me how to box in order to defend myself from the neighborhood bullies. Whether it was bare-knuckle horseplay in the kitchen or more formal instruction with eight-ounce gloves in the backyard, my dad strove to teach his only son not to be anybody's fool.

While I managed to play a bit of Little League baseball growing up, I didn't have the structure at home to encourage full immersion into the sport, or any other organized athletic activity. But for Gator, whom I befriended when my family moved a bit south to the upper-middle class town of Hanover, sports were an almost fanatical obsession and permanent way of life.

Gator played baseball and hockey in college, and also competed as a bodybuilder and powerlifter. Many of his eight siblings followed his lead to lift weights, play baseball, hockey, football, field hockey, and softball through high school and college. When all was said and done, highlights of the family's final tally included three collegiate baseball captains, a Division 1 College All-American field hockey distinction, and a Collegiate All-American powerlifting honor.

Stepping in line with Gator's family, I fell in with an athletic crowd in Hanover, where our second home became the Hanover Police Boys' Club, a community gym where I lifted weights, hit the heavy bag, and sparred with local amateur and professional boxers.

Our area was rich in boxing lore, with the nearby city of Brockton being the birthplace of the great Rocky Marciano and the adopted hometown of Marvelous Marvin Hagler. I trained as a boxer at first just to stay in shape, but before long I began to enter amateur bouts. Hagler actually moved to Hanover while he was the world middleweight champion and I was honored to spar with him while both of us prepared for fights. On a whim I entered

Tough guy in the making.

the Massachusetts Golden Gloves Tournament, and despite a broken nose suffered during training with Hagler's half-brother, Robbie Sims, I reached the heavyweight final, where I lost a split decision.

I first began watching televised National Hockey League games at the Boys' Club as well. Gator, who would have been considered more of a feisty little goal scorer when he played hockey, enjoyed the fights in the pro game more than anything else, and owned a large collection of hockey fight videotapes that chronicled on-ice battles since the early 1970s. The more games and fight videos I watched, the more intrigued I became.

The key to what I was doing, and about to do on the ice, revolved around my unusual desire to fight not only in the ring, but also at functions, parties, and later as a nightclub bouncer. I wasn't a bully and never picked on other kids—maybe because of the hard lessons I learned growing up—but if there was a fight to be had I wanted it.

Most of the time I didn't fight out of anger, which is a trait that helped me succeed as a fighter. The simple fact was that I enjoyed the competitive challenge of a one-on-one fight. If I got wind that a kid with a tough reputation was at a party or playing basketball at the town courts, I'd go there and challenge him to a fistfight. I usually fought with no feelings of animosity or malice toward my opponent, and win or lose I would usually shake the kid's hand and thank him for the duel.

If I had lived in the world portrayed in the movie *Hard Times*, I surely would have been the character played by Charles Bronson, who scoured depressed towns during the 1930s to engage local champs in bare-knuckled fights for cash. What I didn't necessarily yearn for was to be a traditional boxer. Fighting as a disciplined boxer was too robotic for me, there were too many rules. Also, the intensity and shear amount of training far outweighed the relatively brief time spent in the ring, banging it out during a match once every few months or so.

But I saw an attractive opportunity for myself in professional hockey. Pro hockey was the only team sport that tolerated fighting. Certainly there were penalties that kept a leash on fisticuffs, but fighting was nevertheless part of the fabric of the game complete with its own etiquette and strategy.

There had always been fighting in the game. As far back as the 1920s and 1930s such players as Eddie Shore and Red Horner, both members of the National Hockey League's Hall of Fame, forged their reputations as tough bastards who wouldn't hesitate to drop their gloves in an attempt to intimidate opponents or protect their teammates.

To explain this concept of an "enforcer" or "protector" in the world of hockey, think about a skittish 14-year-old boy entering high school as a freshman. There are many older, bigger kids in the school and the little 14-year-old is, by nature and survival, a bit apprehensive, nervous, and yes, intimidated by his surroundings. This intimidation would likely occur even if the boy wasn't being bullied. The boy would probably keep a low profile. He would be smart to avoid the bathroom, or other places he may find himself alone and at the mercy of ruthless upperclassmen hell bent on stretching his underwear up and over his head.

Now picture that same 14-year-old entering high school with a senior brother who also happens to be the 6-foot-5, 280-pound starting tackle on the football team. Do you think the 14-year-old is going to get picked on by other students? Is it possible that the 14-year-old will feel a bit more secure among his new surroundings, stand a little taller, walk around the building with a more confident stride because his big brother casts a long, dark, intimidating shadow, and will kick the shit out of anybody who looks at his little brother cross-eyed?

This is the positive, enabling effect a tough guy in hockey has on his teammates. Knowing there is somebody there willing and able to address the bully on the other side lifts a burden of nerves from narrow shoulders and allows more freedom to go into the corner after a puck, or use the bathroom whenever there is a need to go.

Eddie Shore and Red Horner brought these traits to their clubs. They were superbly talented hockey players who took on an additional tough-guy role to further help their teams win. This duality flourished with yet another Hall of Famer, Gordie Howe, the Detroit Red Wings star who won what was billed as the Heavyweight Championship of the NHL with his highly publicized and devastating victory over a much bloodied New York Ranger, Lou Fontinato, during a game at Madison Square Garden in 1959.[1] Whether a coincidence or not, it should not be lost that the Red Wings made it to the Stanley Cup Championship Finals eleven times and won four Cups during Howe's unmatched 25-year tenure as the club's leading thumper. After Howe left the club in 1971, it would be 24 years before the Wings reached another championship final playoff series, and 26 years before sipping from the Cup again in 1997.

Not to be outdone by the intimidating effectiveness of Gordie Howe, the Montreal Canadiens jumped into the fray and employed a high-profile enforcer of their own, as John Ferguson carried the fighting torch for Les Habitants though the 1960s. He was in turn matched up in a fistic rivalry with Boston Bruins toughie "Terrible" Teddy Green. During his first NHL game in 1963, Ferguson took on Green in the old Boston Garden and scored a three-punch victory, which brought with it the league's heavyweight title until he retired after the 1970–71 season with five Stanley Cup rings.[2]

Despite the success of the Wings and Canadiens during this period, it would be a difficult point to argue that a team could only win a championship if it employed the toughest player in the league. It would be easier to point out that tough guys certainly helped, but a good goalie, defense, and a few players who could put the puck into the net made up the bulk of championship squads. And it must be noted that, while Ferguson and Green weren't Hall of Famers, they were much more than just fist men. Ferguson averaged 18 goals a season and Green played in two all-star games to go along with his two Stanley Cups as a Boston Bruins defenseman.

However, when it came to the impact of tough guys and fighting in the NHL, everything changed with one terrible sucker punch and the eventual creation of Dave "The Hammer" Schultz, who punched his way into the league with the Philadelphia Flyers during the 1972–73 season.

* * *

There are moments in athletics when changes of rules, equipment innovations, or the emergence of a particular player produces a significant impact on an entire sport. During the infancy of baseball, the job description of the pitcher called for him to facilitate the batters' hitting of the ball. Each batter indicated to the pitcher exactly where he wanted the ball to be thrown and the pitcher would try his best to place it there, truly attempting to put the ball on the proverbial silver platter. When this rule was changed in favor of the pitcher being allowed to do everything in his power to deny the batter a hit, the game was forever transformed. Babe Ruth followed and indoctrinated baseball with the home run. Jackie Robinson broke the color line to make the game more talent-laden and competitive, and in the late 1960s the pitcher's mound was lowered to return a competitive edge to the hitter and increase offensive production. Larger, streamlined gloves along with technological advances in bat and ball design, as well as performance-enhancing drugs, have also played a part in transforming baseball and its coveted records over the years.

Before Sammy Baugh signed on with the Washington Redskins in 1937, the National Football League labored in semi-obscurity with a slow and monotonous, bang-'em-up pace dictated on the near total reliance of a grinding running game. But "Slingin' Sammy" came along as the catalyst that helped catapult the NFL into modern times with his desire and ability to throw the forward pass, and football has never looked back. Pushing further away from football's prehistoric days was the use of improved protective gear from head to toe. Then Hall of Fame Cleveland Browns running back Jim Brown came along to usher in the physical standards of modern-day players with his dual gift of talented size and speed.

It took racial integration to transform basketball into the dynamic sport it is today, and one need only review a single Wonder Bread–white National Basketball Association contest from the 1950s to appreciate how colorful the game has become. Such agents of change as Wilt Chamberlain, who forcefully unveiled the athletic big man, and Julius "Dr. J" Erving, who taught players how to fly, combined with innovations like the shot clock and three-point arc to revolutionize basketball.

Hockey has likewise enjoyed defining moments throughout its history that have changed how the game is played. From Jacques Plante donning a goalie mask in 1959 and the introduction of curved sticks and ultra-lightweight pads, to the revolutionary dynamics of Bobby Orr—who turned hockey onto its head by meshing the defense with the offense—players, rules, and equipment have come along to dictate new direction.

While nobody can sanely argue that Dave Schultz had an impact on hockey equal to that of Orr or Wayne Gretzky, his emergence with the Flyers introduced for the first time in the history of the NHL a player whose primary focus on the ice was to beat up others.

The door to the era of the modern hockey goon was cracked open on April 13, 1968, during a Stanley Cup Quarterfinals game between two brand-new NHL franchises, the host Philadelphia Flyers and visiting St. Louis Blues. During a fight on the ice, 31-year-old Flyers forward Claude LaForge, a 5-foot-8, 160-pound lightly penalized journeyman, was innocently milling around the fray when he was blindsided with a roundhouse left to the face delivered by nasty 6-foot-1, 210-pound Blues defenseman Jean Noel Picard. Ed Snider, owner of the Flyers, recounted the scene during a filmed interview years later.

> **Ed Snider:** "I'll never forget, there was a fight in the Spectrum in which Noel Picard sucker punched Claude LaForge … and he just came from behind and he went down in a pool of blood. I wasn't used to that type of thing, and I basically made up my mind at that time and told my people we may not be able to come up with the great players and great shooters and real great talents because we were an expansion club and it was going to take us a while, but we could come up with guys that could beat up other guys if that was what was necessary. I don't ever want a Philadelphia Flyer team intimidated, ever, ever again."[3]

It appears as though Snider's resolve came a little too late for LaForge, a victim of being in the wrong place at the wrong time who was never the same player after the Picard incident. Before the savage attack he had bounced around the minors for years, spending spotted time in the Big Leagues with the Montreal Canadiens and Detroit Red Wings. After two years away from the NHL he appeared to catch an enormous break at the ripe old age of 31 by latching on for the full 1967–68 season with the brand-new Flyers expansion team. But he'd only play two more games with the Flyers after the punch, spending five more years toiling away in the minors before retiring at the age of 36.

As Snider intimated, it even took a little while to get his marquee goon, but when Dave Schultz finally arrived on the scene with the Flyers he led the league in penalty minutes during each of his first three seasons, and logged what is still an NHL record 472 minutes in the penalty box during the 1974–75 campaign. And while Schultz enjoyed the adoring home crowds and even the castigation from opposing fans, his hard-won piles of penalty minutes were earned in a familiar, noble pursuit of protection and retaliation.

> **Dave Schultz:** "If you want to try to intimidate one of the better-skating players, more skilled, you better turn around because I was coming after you. Somebody had to do it, and I did it."[4]

It was that simple, and that attitude was not lost on the rest of the league, especially when the Flyers overtook the once dominant Canadiens and Bruins to win two consecutive Stanley Cup championships while Schultz was in the lineup acting as a protectorate and intimidating force.

There are no better examples of the copycat phenomenon than in sport, and the NHL is a working model of the rule. What the Flyers, otherwise known then as the "Broad Street Bullies," did to produce a championship-caliber team was to simply amplify the blueprint of the rival "Big Bad Bruins," who had built a club that could fight and skate well enough to win a pair of Cups themselves a few years earlier. After the Flyers' success, other teams jumped on board and employed their own versions of Schultz to pour cement down the backbone of their rosters.

Make no mistake, it's hardly a coincidence that one year after Schultz broke into the NHL, the expansion New York Islanders brought up 5-foot-9 terror Garry Howatt, who celebrated his first full season in the league by setting an NHL single-season record for fights with 26. Not to be outdone by Howatt, Schultz matched that figure the following year, and then fought 27 times with 405 penalty minutes in 1977–78. Improving upon the trend, Montreal's Chris Nilan was the first to reach the 30-fight plateau in 1984. Paul Laus holds claim to the current mark of 39 fights set in 1997 as a member of the Florida Panthers.

Before Schultz came along, the most penalty minutes logged during a single NHL season were 291 by Chicago Black Hawks defenseman Keith Magnuson during his 1970–71 effort. Schultz bested that mark with 348 minutes during his sophomore year before hitting the unfathomable figure of 472, which remains the league standard.

What Schultz had been able to pull off wasn't lost on any number of aspiring players who may have been able to bring aggressiveness but little else to the professional hockey table. These players usually found themselves on the bubble of making a club during training camp before being cut loose because they didn't possess the skating or puck-handling skills to succeed at the higher level.

But with Schultz being celebrated for his style of play, and competing teams rushing to fortify their own stock with such bare-knuckle prowess, the floodgates—though some would say the sewers—opened and there poured out the likes of legendary wild man Steve Durbano, who came through with 370 penalty minutes during the 1975–76 season while splitting time between the Kansas City Scouts and Pittsburgh Penguins. Talented and tough Dave "Tiger" Williams logged 338 minutes in the box the following winter as a member of the Toronto Maple Leafs. Terry O'Reilly, who some would argue spent as much time falling as skating on the ice, broke in with Boston during the 1971–'72 season, taking over for Teddy Green as the Bruins top enforcer into the mid–1980s.

Since Schultz first broke the 300-minute barrier during the 73–74 season, 46 different NHL players have amassed at least 300 penalty minutes 75 times during the 36 years through the 2009–2010 season—not including three more times by Mr. Schultz himself.

It would be a mistake and downright unfair to stop here after painting a portrait of Dave Schultz with the short brush of a barbaric beast. While Schultz is justly accepted as the father of the modern-day hockey goon, he also had the considerable ability to skate in 608 NHL games. If that fact doesn't place him in select company, he scored 20 goals during the 1973–74 season—the first year the Philadelphia Flyers won the Stanley Cup. There are literally rosters full of past and present NHL players, tough guys and accomplished skill players alike, who do not boast a 20-goal season in the world's best hockey league.

Would the Flyers have won the Stanley Cup without Schultz? It is difficult to say one way or the other. But the Broad Street Bullies' persona of a team that could skate and fight better than all others over a two-year span, before other teams could catch up, was built around Schultz and one of the players he helped to protect, high-scoring marquee center Bobby Clarke.

Maybe it would be easier to ponder whether or not teams came into Philadelphia's Spectrum with less fire in their bellies. Did opposing players enter the Flyers' ice den with less desire in their hearts and less jump in their legs knowing they were going to either get challenged or the hell beat out of them by Schultz and a compliment of hooligans that included Don "Big Bird" Saleski, Andre "Moose" Dupont, and Bob "Hound Dog" Kelly? I say that visitors did, on the whole, play a less aggressive, more passive game when visiting Philadelphia. Furthermore, until the other teams in the league came up to snuff with their own crop of matching tough guys, they weren't thrilled to host the Broad Street Bullies in their own barns, either.

Whichever way one decides to come down on these questions, the bottom line is that Dave Schultz recognized a route of escape from a career of long bus rides and third-rate motels as a minor-league journeyman. He decided he didn't have the ability to fulfill his dream of making it to the NHL and sticking around for an appreciable amount of time as a scoring force so he chose to fight. Because of his desire, ability, and hard work he became much more than just a head shot on the browning pages of a memorabilia collector's Richmond Robins media guide. No, Dave Schultz remains "The Hammer," a two-time Stanley Cup winner and one of the toughest sons of bitches to ever play at the highest level of the game.

Hockey fighting evolved even further during the 1980s when the role of enforcer became more established as a clear-cut position on a team through the process of specialization. No longer was it necessary that a fighter be required to play on a set line or log a regular shift during a game. But for a few notable exceptions, the days of a John Wensink skating a wing on the Bruins' power play and scoring 28 goals were over. In his place came such designated thumpers and hit men as Shane Churla, Rob Ray, and Stu Grimson, forwards who never individually scored more than eight goals in an entire season despite logging a combined 37 years in the NHL. They would be sent out to "play" on a selective basis when their team needed a little pick-me-up or an opponent needed to be straightened out.

With this role of goon clearly defined for me, I was further enticed by the fact I wouldn't have to fight three two-minute rounds as I had to during my amateur boxing matches. The thought of fighting in a 20- or 30-second blast of energy within a controlled atmosphere on the ice was far more palatable and presented an exciting challenge.

Another interesting aspect of hockey fighting was that the decision didn't appear to result in a zero-sum outcome as it usually did in the boxing ring, where one person's win corresponded to the opponent's total loss. While there is usually a distinct winner and loser of a hockey fight, a guy could lose three fights during a game but his efforts could still go a long way toward helping his team ultimately win the contest. The simple concept of a guy being there on the ice or sitting ready on the bench willing to answer the bell and stand up for his teammates if the going got rough could go a long way toward winning or losing the game.

Gator and I poured over hockey fight film. We studied the manner in which fights started, how players dropped their sticks and gloves, how they squared off, where they grabbed each other's shirts and positioned their heads while trading shots. We recognized which players punched and who preferred to wrestle, who was able to throw punches with either hand, who threw lethal bombs and who jack-hammered a quick succession of nagging punches. Boston's Lyndon Byers had a dangerous uppercut, and Vancouver's Ron Delorme threw his punches straight over the top. Delorme could also absorb big Dave Semenko's hardest shots to the face and not go down. Tim Hunter switched hands effortlessly, and the great Terry O'Reilly would have been even more effective if he had the balance of his teammate, Stan Jonathan who, when he had enough of trading punches, grabbed the bottom of his opponent's pants, pulled up and pile-drove him to the ice.

We broke hockey fighting down to an art, and a good hockey fighter is indeed an artist of his trade. The untrained eye may see a fight break out for no apparent reason to mar or interrupt an otherwise enjoyable game, but we watched for style, for purpose, for reason.

Any number of hockey fight scenarios can find two tough guys on the ice at the same time. Throughout a game one of them may have terrorized the smaller, more talented players on the other team, who would in turn become intimidated and gun shy. The good players stopped carrying the puck or chasing after it along the boards or into corners for fear of being checked or manhandled. They now played with less intent and desire, limiting their effectiveness and hindering the overall performance of their club. In this situation it is clear that somebody has to stand up as a protector, and that is the dual job of the enforcer, who acts as a savior as well as mayhem maker.

An enforcer as mayhem maker can run around hammering the other team's talent, and he can also drop his gloves as his club's savior, effectively telling his mirror image on the other team, "If you screw around with my teammates you're going to have to deal with me." In both instances the message has been sent.

Long-time enforcer and Stanley Cup winner Dave Brown conveyed this point very succinctly when explaining his role with the Philadelphia Flyers: "If there's a problem on the ice, I go out and fix the problem."[5] And the rest of the team reaps the benefits.

"Every player on our team felt a little bit more safe with him on the ice with us," said 5-foot-10, 170-pound NHL center Pierre-Marc Bouchard about his former teammate, 6-foot-7, 260-pound enforcer Derek "The Boogeyman" Boogaard, who died tragically at the age of 28 from a lethal cocktail of pain killers and alcohol.[6]

Along with this job of bodyguard, the goon may also initiate a fight with an opponent for the simple intention of lighting a fire under the sagging asses of his underperforming teammates, who may for any number of reasons be playing in a coma. The fight, hopefully, wakes up his sleeping team with a jolt, as if to say, "I'm doing my part, I'm kicking ass, now it's time for you guys to do your job!"

What I've offered here is the strategic, honorable, and very noble job description of a goon. But during my time on the work site I discovered that an enforcer's role is also incorporated into the game for its sheer entertainment value. In fact, because fans enjoyed the on-ice battles so much, some fighters were actively encouraged to drop their gloves on a regular basis and even paid a cash bonus for each fight they had.

One established NHL enforcer told me that when he balked at being sent to a downtrodden city during the early years of his minor-league career and instead planned on falling back on his college degree, the coach offered him a $100 bonus per fight along with his regular salary. He bit at the proposition and a few years later was making half-a-million a year doing the same job in the NHL.

There has been some suspicion that hockey fights are staged, or worse, faked on the level of professional wrestling. I recall a fight between the NHL Heavyweight Champion at the time, Georges Laraque, and up-and-comer Raitis Ivanans, who was looking for an opportunity to prove himself and his worth to his Los Angeles Kings. Laraque was wearing a microphone for television, and when he approached the faceoff with Ivanans waiting for him, panting like a dog, the world heard Laraque ask, "You want to?" Ivanans, off camera, obviously jumped at the chance, prompting the classy Laraque to reply, "Good luck, man." The behemoths then checked in with a pretty lively battle, each man trying to knock the other's block off.[7]

Afterward, a couple of college journalism majors working as broadcasters on the television show *The NHL on TSN* ranted hysterically, one calling the perceived set-up "embarrassing," while the other called the fight a "waste of time for fans in the building." They were especially incensed that the two combatants weren't necessarily angry at one another before the fight. This is the major problem with non-players who attempt to wrap their wits around the concept of hockey enforcers. The role is too complex for them to have a real clue. So it was wonderful to then watch Pierre McGuire and Keith Jones, who have both been on NHL benches, disagree with the young lads and put them back in their playpens.[8] In the words of former NHL tough guy and referee Paul Stewart, "It's akin to a nun professing what it's like to be a whore; unless you've done it, you really don't know what the hell you're talking about."

I didn't play a lot, but I was a flat-out goon and I can attest that hockey fights are choreographed only to the extent that the general unspoken rule allows for tough guys to fight other tough guys. We all knew what our job was, and if I came onto the ice and the other tough guy was there as well, it didn't matter whether I was particularly angry at him, he was just the guy I had to challenge, and he knew I wasn't there to sell him a magazine subscription.

Sure, there were times on a faceoff when I asked a guy if he wanted to go; sometimes he'd say yes, and other times no. For me it was about professional courtesy. There were times the guy would say he had a bad hand, or that he was nursing a sore shoulder or another ailment. At that point we'd decide not to fight, but there would also be a mutual understanding that the injured tough guy wasn't then going to run around without a leash barking and nipping at my teammates. I would even share glances with an opposing tough guy as we skated around our respective ends during warm-ups. Maybe we would nod to each other, effectively acknowledging we'd fight at some point during the game. If you wish to call all of this "staged" then so be it. To me it was about not being a fucking ignoramus.

I would imagine there are times when an NFL linebacker might glare at a quarterback from across the line of scrimmage and yell, "I'm going to rip your fucking head off." So if the linebacker happens to follow through on the next play and sack the quarterback, maybe even rip his helmet off in the process, is that a staged play? I also recall the tale of a storied Major League base stealer who would at times nod to a superior catcher before he attempted a stolen base. He did it out of gamesmanship, professional courtesy, the game-within-the-game. Everybody in the stadium knew the guy was likely to attempt a steal, and to the catcher's credit he wouldn't call for a pitch out. The very public battle was actually quite personal, just between them, with all spontaneity and surprise taken out of the equation because there really wasn't any spontaneity or surprise at work to begin with.

When I asked a guy if he wanted to fight on the ice, it also wasn't like I'd say, "Okay, I'll throw three rights, then I'll miss wild and you catch me with a left and I'll fall down." No, as tough guys we recognized the fact we had to fight each other. We also, in general, respected our opponent, and rarely fought in anger, but when I tangled I tried to win, which generally followed that I threw my punches with bad intentions.

As far as hockey fights emerging from the natural ebb and flow of the game, we can't pretend our roles and actions on the ice are spontaneous when everything we ultimately do is inevitable. Anybody with even half a clue skating on the ice, sitting on the benches and in the stands recognizes the role players and the anticipation of a fight as soon as the potential combatants are out at the same time, and when a challenge has been accepted few punches are pulled and even fewer fans leave for beer. Call me crazy, but I will guess that the vast majority of fans would not say their time in the stadium is wasted by a fight.

Ultimately, what the talking heads don't and can't seem to understand is the basic fact that a goon's primary job is to just be there, willing to fight and stand up for his teammates. It isn't important that he get angry or keep his intentions a secret. In fact, I think it's probably more intimidating and effective to growl or otherwise announce that you're chomping at the bit to drop the gloves. That simple fact alone may keep the game purring along without the need to have two guys fight.

Staged fights and real or fake punches aside, it has also been my experience that rarely are combatants seriously injured during a hockey fight. Certainly skate blades have sliced players during wrestling scrums, and there have been countless broken noses, black eyes, missing teeth, stitches, separated shoulders, broken hands, and facial scars to serve as badges of courage for most enforcers. But because hockey fights are so tightly framed within the protective shell of three on-ice officials, watchful teammates, and an average fight life span of about 30 seconds, the ugly aspects found in the uncontrolled arena of a street fight are avoided.

Even with hockey fights put in the proper perspective, there have been bouts that made such an impact on players as to make them think seriously about quitting the game. Alan May did such a number on Jeff Chychrun's face in the minors that he had to rethink his desire to stick around to make his mark in the NHL. The same was true with his teammate, Craig Berube, who after making it up with the Philadelphia Flyers was so roundly beat up by Boston's Jay Miller and Lyndon Byers that he considered quitting the game right then and there. After some soul searching, Berube refocused his career plans and went on to play more NHL games than Miller and Byers combined.

After a vicious stick fight during the 1969 pre-season between St. Louis Blues Wayne Maki and Boston's Ted Green, which left Green near death and later with a steel plate in his head, maybe the worst outcome of a modern day fight in the NHL occurred during the 1988–89 season when Red Wings heavyweight Joe Kocur broke the cheek and orbital bones of New York Islanders forward Brad Dalgarno, who had to sit out an entire year to recover from his injuries.

These are examples of high-profile players under the Big League spotlight. It is anybody's guess just how many players gave in to their doubts and fears and walked away from their dream of playing junior or pro hockey. Bruce Wensink related a story of how his brother, former NHL enforcer John Wensink, used intimidation to end the hopes of some aspiring hockey players.

Bruce Wensink: "John was a pretty cold guy growing up. I know he ended a lot of guys' thoughts about playing Junior-A Hockey. One guy who coached my daughter practiced for years on his outdoor rink and on traveling teams in Cornwall to try out for the Cornwall Royals. In an inter-squad game John smashed his face into the glass and he thought this hockey thing was no fun so he quit. My daughter's other coach was watching this from the bench and thought he didn't want to make this team either."

Fear wasn't my enemy. If nothing else I was a tough, rawboned kid without much fear of others, so undaunted, unaware, and without a care or concern about the inner workings of the hockey fight game that would eventually unfold before me, my friends and I staged countless hours of hockey fight scenarios in the aerobics room of the Boys' Club. We bought replica jerseys of our favorite NHL goons at the Boston Garden pro shop, and we'd also bring hockey gloves and sticks into the gym to practice tossing our equipment far enough away so as not to "skate" over them and trip as we squared off and performed the sizing-up dance. These practice fights were controlled confrontations, and when two of us got down to fighting the others stopped what they were doing to play referee, ready to jump in and stop the battle when one took a clear advantage over the other.

The Boys' Club and living rooms of our homes eventually gave way to street hockey games, which lasted only until Gator gave me a pointed shove and made eye contact. When that happened, our street turned into Boston Garden, where Gator was Jay Miller and I was Philly's big, bad Dave Brown.

Silly as it may seem, hockey fighting became an obsession with me, and a skirmish could break out anywhere or anytime. Once while Gator and I were in the supermarket, I was beside the long meat bin and Gator thought it looked too much like the boards of a hockey rink to pass up, so he rode me into it and grabbed my right sleeve, signaling me to start trading punches with him, much to the horror of a capacity crowd of soccer moms at the deli counter that particular Saturday afternoon.

Another time while stopped at a red light, we started exchanging punches while seated in the car. Gator unconsciously lifted his foot off the brake and rolled into the car in front of us. That guy, who had been watching us in his rear-view mirror, yelled that if we want to fight just go in the park. Soon we'd sort of take his suggestion.

I suppose that if I had gone to college after graduating from high school I would have had far less time on my hands for this kind of nonsense. But with nothing to study and no impressive job on the horizon, my experimental hockey steps continued unimpeded, and before long I put on my first pair of skates.

Hacketts Pond was across the street from my house and became my first on-ice proving ground. Gator and I fought for a winter season on Hacketts' frozen sheet before we moved on the next year to the more spacious Jacobs Pond a few miles down the road. Jacobs was nearer ground level with a shoreline as close to the road as good lodge seats at the old Boston Garden. Not only did casual skaters get a kick out of our fighting practice, but passersby in cars couldn't help but slow down for a peak, kind of like a quick preview while motoring past a drive-in movie.

I graduated from the ponds to skating sessions with Gator and other friends on inexpensive midnight ice we'd rent at local rinks on the weekend.

Just like the street hockey games, which began with impressive puck control, play-making and back-checking, tired legs brought a measure of boredom. When the game unraveled we devoted the balance of our ice time to fighting.

For a long while Gator toyed with me on the ice. Though he was much smaller, his strength and superior balance allowed him to put me at his mercy. While he shook me like a rag doll with his left hand he pummeled me with a combination of right overhands and uppercuts until he simply couldn't hold me up any longer and I crumpled to the ice.

But the playing field slowly began to level out the more I skated and the better my balance became. Soon I was able to concentrate on much more than just not falling down. With my legs firmly planted beneath me I began to work on some of the things he was trying to teach me, like the best ways and places to hold onto his jersey. I experimented on the effectiveness of grabbing his shirt at the shoulder, back of the neck, inside the elbow or lower at the wrist, and with a sturdier base I could measure more effective punches.

With improved technique and balance I found a strong advantage; as a trained boxer not only did I have little fear of being punched in the face, but

Practice fighting with Gator (left) at Babson College.

with 250 pounds behind my heavy shots soon even Gator stopped challenging me on a regular basis.

Yearning to play some real hockey, I plunked down $200 I didn't have to join a team in an adult recreational league out of Boston. Nobody there was prepared to deal with a 6-foot-1, 250-pound goofball like me who was just looking for an opportunity to fight. I am sure the president of the organization would have just as soon be rid of me as well, but the program was a profitable business for him and he wasn't interested in giving me a refund. So I terrorized all the players on the other teams, and the few who wanted to do something about it found, I am sure to their displeasure, that I was far too willing to drop the gloves. I spent an inordinate amount of time sitting on the bench, in the penalty box, and in the stands rather than on the ice, but at least I was able to get my feet wet, so to speak. Come the following year, however, it was obvious I brought along more than $200 worth of aggravation and I was asked not to return.

With compromised skating ability, no hockey sense, and a growing reputation as somebody you didn't want soiling your ice, I needed some special help for the pieces to fall into place in order to play professional hockey. The biggest piece early on was getting a chance to play in the local summer Pro-Am Hockey League a few towns over.

The Pro-Am attracted current and former college players as well as a diverse group of pros from all of the minor-league ranks. There were also some established NHL players on board such as Joe Mullen, Mathieu Schneider, and Eric Desjardins, and tough guys such as Lyndon Byers, Curt Walker, Chris Nilan, Nick Fotiu, and Nevin Markwart. It wasn't difficult to get the NHLers to play because many of them vacationed on Cape Cod and needed a venue to stay in shape for the upcoming season.

I may have been the only one in the league who didn't have at least college playing experience, but a friend of mine coached one of the teams and put me on his roster to give me a taste of some high-octane hockey. I believe it may also have been the case that my buddy was so sick of listening to me ramble on about wanting to play pro hockey that he figured the Pro-Am would discourage me from pursuing the fantasy any longer.

During this time I was also fortunate to meet a local guy known as "Commander" during his playing days. Commander grew up in a neighboring town, had played Division 1 college hockey, and enjoyed a brief minor-league career as an undersized yet fearless fighter in the highest rungs of the minors. After retiring as a player, Commander eventually worked his way up to lofty positions in the personnel departments of a few NHL hockey teams. My friendship with Commander would become instrumental in not only developing my "craft," but also opening doors of opportunity later.

As I had done in the Boston adult league, I quickly became the scourge of the Pro-Am with my physical style of play, and it didn't take long before everyone figured out that my singular purpose for being there was to fight. This concept didn't sit well with likely all of the other guys in the league who played for the sole purpose of staying in shape for their upcoming college season or pro training camp.

I challenged every big kid on the ice and every guy who seemed to play tough, but most of them skated away from me without a reaction or as if they couldn't be bothered. Others swore and derided me. I plodded on.

I knew I could make a name for myself if I fought Lyndon Byers, the kid from Saskatchewan who was a wildly popular enforcer with the Boston Bruins. I wouldn't mind popping him from a personal standpoint as well because he acted like jerk and blew me off when I tried to talk to him outside the rink. At that point in his career, Byers was an unmarried, good-looking pro athlete making decent money in a town that worshipped him. My guess is that the only people outside his circle he was interested in talking to were pretty women, and he probably thought I was some cellar dweller looking for an autograph.

During the pre-game skate before my first game against Byers, a teammate of his, Billy O'Dwyer, who also played with him on the Bruins, approached me and said he knew what I was up to and to leave Byers alone. I told him to mind his own business. I caught up to Byers and casually skated alongside him. I told him I was a big fan of his, which was true despite what I thought of him personally, and politely asked him if he wouldn't mind giving me a break and engage in a fight.

Byers flatly said, "No," and skated away.

Though disappointed at what I knew stood as an earth-shaking opportunity flushed down the toilet, I never questioned Byers' decision. He had already fought all the biggest names in the sport so he certainly wasn't afraid of a complete nobody like me. There was no upside in it for him. At best he would've knocked me out cold with one of his patented uppercuts, or at worst broken a hand on my helmet or face and jeopardized his career. In either case there was nothing for him to gain and everything to lose—never mind the outlying possibility that I could connect with a lucky punch and put him down.

But my fortunes changed abruptly with Bill Whitfield.

Previously, my only real on-ice fights were against recreational skaters during pick-up games and former high school wash-ups in the Boston adult league. Those opponents had little desire or ability to fight and did so only after my constant prodding. All of those fights lasted only a few seconds as

I wasn't able to throw many punches before either falling to the ice from lack of balance, or dropping like a felled tree on top of my victim.

Whitfield, a powerful weightlifter built like a dumpster, was an altogether different challenge. He was a former Division 1 collegian out of Northeastern University who had come off an exceptional season his first year pro, where he established himself as a two-way all-star defenseman with the Virginia Lancers of the ill-fated All-American League.

The big guy had checked one of my teammates hard behind the play and I seized upon the chance to challenge him as both teams headed up ice and we were alone in his end. Whitfield quickly obliged, to my pleasant surprise, and we fought near his blue line.

I had never before been in a straight-out, toe-to-toe punch fest on the ice against a quality opponent, and while this was something like many of the fights I had with Gator on the ponds, Gator was never trying to knock me out. Lacking experience I dropped my head, which allowed Whitfield a degree of leverage. My punches flailed wild while he kept his head up and directed his shots with more accuracy. I eventually landed on top of Whitfield to end the battle, but I felt as though I lost. Another mistake I made was not having my jersey tied down, which enabled Whitfield to pull my shirt over my head. Not only was I blind during the fight, but I also looked disheveled and defeated when it was all over.

I skated about the ice lost for a few moments not knowing what else to do but adjust my equipment. I contemplated my next move as Whitfield's bench howled at me. They were so happy their guy beat-up the goon who was terrorizing the league. I thought I would leap headfirst into their bench and take out as many of them as I could, but instead settled down and headed off to the locker room and a two-game suspension.

Bill Whitfield: "Greg Pratt, who I played with in college, came up to me during warm-ups and said, 'That guy is eyeballing you,' so I knew Doug was coming. It was during the first period, we were alone in my end and I said to him, 'Do you want to go?,' and the next thing you know we're throwing them. It was actually one of the best fights I ever had. I remember switching hands, it went real well. Anyway, we both got kicked off the ice and I wasn't too happy. It had just taken me an hour to drive to the rink and now after just a couple of shifts I have to go right back home. So I'm in the locker room naked, I've got a towel around me, and all of a sudden the door opens and it's Doug. I'm thinking, 'Oh shit, I've got to fight this kid again.' But he came over, shook my hand and thanked me. He said he really enjoyed fighting me."

Through my defeat came victory, however, as Buffalo Sabres scout Paul Merritt was at the game and saw the fight. I first met Paul a little while back and peppered him with questions about how to get invited to a pro tryout strictly as a fighter. Apparently he was impressed by my willingness to fight Whitfield and he set the wheels in motion for my tryout with the Carolina Thunderbirds, who were about to begin a third incarnation as a founding member of the new East Coast Hockey League.

Merritt gave Thunderbirds coach and general manager Brian Carroll a phone call. He told him I was a horrible hockey player but was willing to fight anybody and that I might be worth a look. I also knew John Torchetti, a Boston-area kid and one of the better players on previous Thunderbirds teams. He talked me up to Carroll and I received an invitation to camp. The bottom line was that the Thunderbirds had absolutely nothing to lose bringing me in—as long as I paid my own way to Winston-Salem, North Carolina.

2

My First Training Camp

While the East Coast Hockey League was just starting out it was hardly a new concept. The circuit was part of an ever-evolving group of lower minor leagues that played at a level at least two steps below the NHL. Borrowing a term from minor-league baseball, the new ECHL became part of "Double-A" hockey lore.

The original AA Hockey invention appears to have been the Eastern Hockey League, which operated from 1933 through 1973 with such Eastern Seaboard teams as the Boston Olympics, Atlantic City Sea Gulls, Long Island Ducks, and Nashville Dixie Flyers. In 1967 the Eastern League was the kind of a place a 22-year-old defenseman with an engineering degree out of Cornell could make a top salary of $140 a week—and an extra $20 if he would also drive the team bus. The problem was, unless a player had the obvious talent to climb the minor-league ladder or was viewed as a viable prospect with an NHL future, that $140, paid only during the six-month season, wasn't enough to sustain the desire of an industrious young man with designs on a substantial career, marriage, and raising a family. So for many players, the stay in AA Hockey was a short one.

The Eastern League split along north and south borders to form both the Southern League and North American League from 1973 through 1977. The two factions melded into the Northeastern League for a year before giving way to another go-around for the Eastern League. After three seasons of teams emerging and folding, as well as money being lifted from the league's coffers, surviving Eastern League team owners banded to form the Atlantic Coast Hockey League. The Carolina Thunderbirds established themselves in Winston-Salem for the 1982–83 ACHL season.

While you could be given a waterbed as a bonus for scoring a hat trick playing for the Mohawk-Valley Stars, the Atlantic Coast League ended up being all wet, and the New York Slapshots stood as the poster child for this drowning operation.

The Slapshots' owners must have thought they made a big score early

28

on when they hired legendary NHL tough-guy Dave Schultz as the team's coach. The team did receive a goodly amount of print and television attention because of Schultz, who also served a term as league commissioner, but the team's owners had failed to lock down a rink in which to play home games. In desperation, the Slapshots played all of their home games on the road in Vinton, Virginia, at the LancerLot Arena, which also happened to be the home rink of the rival Virginia Lancers.

The Slapshots poured through 44 different players during that tenuous first year, but appeared to be on firmer ground when they began the following season based out of Troy, New York. After six games, however, the troubled franchise ceased operations and merged with Mohawk-Valley, leaving the league with just four teams.

In 1987 the entire Atlantic Coast League took the Slapshots' lead and merged with the doomed All-American League, which formed from the ashes of yet another shaky AA fold, the small-time Continental League. If you have a headache, take a few aspirin before continuing.

After slogging through one season there, the Thunderbirds, owned by local businessman Bill Coffey, jumped the sinking All-American ship along with the Virginia Lancers and a Pennsylvania franchise located in Johnstown, which were both owned by Henry Brabham. This exodus would eventually lead to the formation of the East Coast Hockey League.

The pair set out on a three-day van trip in the summer of 1988 to scout cities and arenas for potential franchises. Brabham saw what he liked in Erie, Pennsylvania, and created the Panthers. Coffey sold his Thunderbirds to John Baker, partnered with Brabham to bring a fifth club to the fold in Knoxville, Tennessee, and the new league was off and running for the 1988–89 season.[1]

Greg Neish, journeyman Double-AA enforcer: "I started out playing for Johnstown in the All-American League and boy, was that something. There were only three teams with professional players, the Virginia Lancers, Carolina Thunderbirds, and us. We traveled around playing weekend beer league men's teams like the Danville Fighting Saints and the scores would be 20–1.

"Johnstown was kind of an out-of-the-way, dreary place in Pennsylvania, so I told them I wanted to play for one of the southern teams. The Virginia Lancers coach, Kevin Willison, was from the same area of Alberta as me so it worked out well.

"The All-American League was bad, but it was a crazy first year in the East Coast League, too. We opened that season in Knoxville and they had the Ice Capades in there the week before. When they put the boards up for our game they found there wasn't any ice in the corners because they had squared the ice sheet off for the figure skaters. There was no way they were going to postpone us because it was the first hockey game in Knoxville in something like 20 years and they sold out the place. So they crushed ice cubs, mixed in some water and packed the corners of the rink with the stuff hoping it would turn into ice. It didn't really work, but we played the whole game with that soup there anyway."

Brabham, Coffey, and possibly some minority investors kept the league together with duct tape at the beginning. Unable to pay a full-time salary to league commissioner Patrick Kelly, who was a former NHL coach, Brabham hired him to double-up as manager of the LancerLot, where Kelly would sometimes drive the Zamboni.[2]

From its rudimentary beginning with just five teams, the East Coast League flowered to become one of the most successful lower minor-league operations in the history of all professional sports. The league housed a whopping 31 teams for the 2003–2004 season, expanding coast to coast with teams in Idaho, Nevada, California, and even Alaska. This coverage made the East Coast moniker rather silly, so the league simply changed its name to the letters ECHL—let it stand for whatever the hell you want.

The ECHL played the 2016–17 season with 27 teams spread throughout the country, including Alaska, in four divisions, with 26 of the clubs enjoying an NHL affiliation. The league is now a well-established developmental circuit with more than 600 alumni having skated in the NHL, and is also well represented with the ever-growing names of former players and coaches etched on the Stanley Cup itself.[3]

This ECHL is a league that decided to dedicate itself to developing its players with two eyes fixed upon the upper echelon of the sport. That league wouldn't want or need any part of somebody like me.

But the original East Coast Hockey League had the gall to invite me to a training camp at the Thunderbirds' home rink, the Winston-Salem Memorial Coliseum, on Thursday, October 20, 1988—a full two weeks after the NHL and its top minor-league affiliates in the American and International Leagues had finished with their preseason schedules. Bottom of the barrel minor leagues hold their camps late so they can act as a catch basin to collect the refuse that's been flushed down the drain by NHL clubs and the higher minor leagues.

I was mailed a tryout agreement and questionnaire by the Thunderbirds, and among other things it notified me to bring all of my own equipment "including underwear, workout attire, and running shoes" because the team "did not have enough quality equipment for everyone at training camp."

In contrast, years later when I returned to attend a game of one of the American League teams I had played for, the club's trainer greeted me with a brand-new pair of skates and an unwrapped bundle of sticks.

The Thunderbirds' questionnaire sought what I figured was the usual medical history of the players, but also wanted to know the "number of packs smoked daily, number of cups of coffee per day, and number of alcoholic drinks per day." I wondered who in their right mind would be honest with their answers to any of those questions.

The five new ECHL teams planned to run three days of training camp and play at least one exhibition game before a shotgun start to the regular season. I didn't think the Thunderbirds needed much more time than that because a good number of the guys at the tryout were returning from the previous year's team that played in the All-American League. Even Brian Carroll, who had taken on the dual position of general manager and coach, had played five years for the Thunderbirds during the team's original run in the Atlantic Coast League.

All Carroll needed to look for during tryouts was if the guys he planned to have back still had their limbs intact. Any surprises found in camp would be a bonus, and the spare parts he needed to flesh out the initial roster could be culled from the rest of us.

Two days before I was to fly to Winston-Salem I received my first taste of classic lower minor-league hockey fare when I was notified that our facilities at the Memorial Coliseum weren't ready for use. The training camp site had to be moved 160 miles north to Vinton, Virginia, where we would share ice with the rival Virginia Lancers at the old but reliable LancerLot.

Vinton was a sleepy little town that may or may not have enjoyed better days. It was situated next to the slightly larger city of Roanoke, a place I faintly recalled being the hometown of Tony "Mr. USA" Atlas, who was one of the best-built men in the entire World Wrestling Federation. I met up with some of the other players who flew into Roanoke Airport and we were shuttled to our team-provided, two-star motel, a real dump.

Armed with a camcorder, Gator left a day earlier than I because he chose to take the less expensive but slower train route from Boston. This was before everybody had a cell phone, and because I was never told where I would be staying, I couldn't relay the information to Gator, so he was on his own to find me once he arrived in Roanoke. Gator was dropped off by his train some 30 miles from Vinton where he boarded a connecting bus for the balance of the trip. He was tutored on the history of the area by the bus driver, who was most proud of the Roanoke Star plugged in and ablaze in glory atop a mountain. I saw it, too. It looked like a big Christmas ornament.

The bus pulled into Roanoke at midnight and Gator hadn't a clue where I was. He started out looking for me at a Sheraton, which was wishful thinking. The girls at the front desk wanted to know if he was a hockey player, and then asked if he drove a red BMW. After apparently presenting himself as undesirable for further consideration, he was quickly tossed away with directions to my motel for a short rest and early wake-up call to watch me give it a shot at the LancerLot Arena.

Henry Brabham, a self-made businessman who owned a small oil company, had the LancerLot built in 1984 when he bought the Virginia Lancers to compete in the Atlantic Coast Hockey League. He likely named the team and the rink to remain in lock step with his "Lancer Mart" chain of convenience stores.

According to his stepdaughter, Lisa, who eventually married my old nemesis, Bill Whitfield, Brabham's clubs lost money every year. But he got lucky when he sold his original franchise, renamed the Roanoke Valley Rampage, in the summer of 1992 for a quarter of a million dollars. The unlucky new owner not only suffered through a dismal 14–49–1 first season, but during the second period of the season's last home game played during a freak blizzard the night of March 13, 1993, a supportive roof beam began to buckle, forcing all players, staff, and 63 paying customers to evacuate the arena. Four hours later the LancerLot roof collapsed under the weight of 16 inches of snow.[4]

Nevertheless, for his efforts in establishing the league and helping to nurture it into the success it has become, the ECHL rightly honors the "Godfather of the ECHL" by awarding the Brabham Cup to the team with the best regular-season record each year.

As for Patrick Kelly, who had more than 800 career wins under his belt as an NHL and minor-league coach before jumping to the ECHL, his gamble to stick it out with the league earned him the honor of Commissioner Emeritus. In 1998 he was inducted, along with Brabham, into the Roanoke Valley Hockey Hall of Fame, and the current ECHL playoff championship trophy, the Kelly Cup, is named after him.[5]

Considering the LancerLot was home to a professional sports team, I expected our locker room to be a step above those of the public rinks I skated in back home, but it wasn't. We just had long benches to sit on and a few well-placed rubber mats on the floor so as not to step on cement with our skates.

But this was my first training camp and I didn't know what to expect, so I simply listened to and copied what everybody else did. I fully intended to go along for the ride, and the one thing all the guys in camp told me was to show the coach I could skate.

I knew what that *really* meant. The coach already heard I was tough, that's why I was invited to camp in the first place. What he didn't know was if I could skate well enough to play for his team. I kept asking my friends and they kept telling me the same thing over and over, "Show the coach you can skate. Show the coach you can skate." I eventually stopped asking.

The first five minutes of our initial practice Friday morning was a casual stretching period and I easily blended into the crowd. Gator later told me that he couldn't pick me out from the 32 other players on the ice during those five minutes because most everybody else was about the same size. When the on-ice instructor blew the whistle to pick up the pace, however, Gator said he was able to pick me out right away.

I hadn't practiced skating backward much over the years and when we all spun around the three goalies in camp lapped me. Gator said later he felt embarrassed and sorry for me, and that he was a bit disappointed in himself for talking me into doing this. But I didn't need Gator to clue me in. I knew I was totally out of place, hockey talent-wise, and I was easily without question the worst player there. And that was the good part.

Puck drills were a complete disaster for me. I did all sorts of things to let others take my place in line; I continued to stretch out, retied my skates, fixed my shoulder pads and chased after wayward pucks. But there was only so much I could do to dodge the inevitable. Eventually I had to take a few turns with the drills and I screwed up every time. The pucks were like cannonballs—every one that touched my stick exploded. In fact, a couple of passes were so hard that they literally took the stick right out of my hands.

After the drills we split into two teams and scrimmaged while Coach Brian Carroll and team owner John Baker sat in the stands to watch and take notes. I skated my right wing as best I could but couldn't keep up with my linemates and was forever out of the play on every shift. Every time a group was on the ice with me they were effectively playing shorthanded, five men to four.

After the first session ended I took my skates off, winced in pain and massaged my feet as always. My skates always hurt my feet, especially along the sides. Once I took my skates off it felt as though I was standing on pins and needles, and my feet were so sore I could hardly walk. Carroll noticed this and told me I was tying my skates too tight, which was cutting off the circulation. He told me to keep the laces fairly loose from the toe to about a third of the way up, and then start tightening the laces from the middle of the boot. I felt like an idiot that he had to teach me such a basic instruction about the most important piece of hockey equipment, but it worked because my feet never hurt again.

With some time off before the next practice session I retreated into the stands with Gator and Mike Chighisola, another friend of mine from home who had played college hockey at Ferris State and then a bit with Carolina the year before in the All-American League.

Chighisola stood about 5-foot-9 and was probably 20 pounds lighter than the 175 he listed for his body weight on the questionnaire. He was a skinny kid, and I wasn't surprised because all I ever saw him put in his mouth were cigarettes and coffee. I watched Chick later when he was playing as a member of the Virginia Lancers in Johnstown. There were no partitions separating the players' benches from the stands at Johnstown's War Memorial Coliseum, and during the game I saw Chick reach back to take drags off a fan's cigarette. He was a human smokestack and probably one of the reasons for the silly training camp questionnaire we had to fill out. Even so, he didn't deserve to be in this league.

Chick toyed with the rest of the guys in camp. He pulled off moves nobody else could match, like the spin-around stunt Denis Savard used with the Chicago Black Hawks. I watched Chick perform it during the scrimmage to get around a defenseman and follow with a 20-foot wrister into the top corner. His talent was obvious, but the problem with Chick was that he drove everybody crazy with his motor mouth. He was easily the most skilled player in camp, but he was traded to Virginia before the first game of the season and ended up the Lancers' leading scorer. I think the owners wanted some parity in the league in order to hold the interest of all the league's fans throughout the season. In any case, before one game against us he told me he was going to score five goals to beat us, and he did, but Virginia ended up needing much more than Chick because they finished in last place and out of the playoffs.

Chick was also a wild storyteller prone to exaggeration with tales only loosely based on the facts as he knew them. Years later I bumped into him while walking my police beat in the Hanover Mall and he told me how well he was doing, that he was driving a Mercedes. He took me out to see it and sure enough it was a Mercedes, but 20 years old with 200,000 miles on it.

As we sat relaxing in the LancerLot stands, Chick told Gator and I stories about the toughest guys I could expect to meet in the new East Coast Hockey League. He said the Johnstown Chiefs would be the roughest crew with the likes of Brock Kelly and Rick Boyd, and Darren Servatius could kill you with one punch. Chick also warned about the War Memorial's boards, which were squared off in the corners, not round like in most rinks. "Those guys will let you go into the corner after the puck," said Chick. "But they know it's just going to get stuck in there so they'll let you go in first and then crush you."

After listening to Chick spiel on like a drunken sailor I wondered what I could be getting myself into if I somehow actually made the team. Did I really want to offer myself up as a sacrificial lamb to be slaughtered by the likes of Servatius and Boyd? These guys were killers. Maybe my buddy Bob Sylvia was right. He was the guy who let me play on his Pro-Am team in the summer to try and dissuade me from pursuing pro hockey. He sat me down one day in his basement den and tried to reason with me. He said all these guys I was going to be going up against had been fighting since they were 14 and they're all pissed off because they're stuck in the minors. He said I didn't know what I was getting myself into, that I was going to get hurt. He said I could be coming home with one eye. Holy Shit.

Later on, however, I discovered the power of rumor, of stories started with a spark of truth before spreading like wildfire into the closest thing to a lie. Eventually I was the one who ended up being known as a killer. Boyd wound up playing in the International League, so I missed out on fighting him. I fought Brock Kelly three times, and Servatius never did anything out of line to even warrant my challenging him.

I know I made a name for myself as one of the better, if not easily one of the most willing, fighters in the league, but I'd love to know what exaggerated stories were floated around about me, especially coming from Chick. Years later I had people coming up to me saying, "I heard you were a killer, you murdered people down there." I had to laugh. For sure my manipulated reputation made me out to be tougher and crazier than I was, and in some respects that situation can be of some benefit. But discerning the truth from reputation and rumor can be difficult, and that could be a bad thing as well.

After four years of skating I should have improved more than I had, but the problem was imbedded in that I only strove to become a better hockey fighter on the ice. I never practiced starts and stops, backward skating, crossovers, stick handling, or any of the other fundamentals that are drilled starting at the lowest levels of youth hockey. I was a terrible skater my first year pro, and that was a reputation I was never able to shake, even after my skills improved. When Steve Carlson brought me in to fight for Johnstown a year later, he told me that he was surprised I skated as well as I did. He told me he heard from everybody how tough I was, but that I couldn't skate a lick. Fully 10 years after my rookie season with the Thunderbirds, coaches continued to mouth the same old premise, "He can fight but can't skate." And that helped conspire to keep me from playing more games over the years.

The second training camp session later in the afternoon was going the same way as the first. I could do nothing in the way of playing hockey to bring any positive attention my way, and I still hadn't fought, so I didn't show the brass any useable talents I could offer the team. We took a short break while ice was being made again and Gator walked down to scold me like I was his little brother.

"Doug, what the hell are you doing out there? Why aren't you going after anybody?"

Gator was right, but I didn't know what else to do. I knew I was supposed to fight, but I didn't know how to go about it. It was one thing fighting with Gator in the Boys' Club or in a local summer league, but this was a professional training camp, I didn't know how to start a fight here, or if I was allowed to, or if the coaches wanted me to. I didn't want to get anybody mad at me for ruining the tryout or the ice time.

It also didn't help that all the other experienced players were telling me not to fight. One of them was a big-shot defenseman who had been sent down to the Thunderbirds by the Hershey Bears of the American League. He kept talking to me, I didn't know why, but he kept telling me, "Try to skate a bit, show them you can play."

I told this to Gator but he would have none of it.

"Doug, the guys on the team are screwing you," Gator started. "If you keep trying to show the coach you can skate you're definitely going home because you *can't* skate. These guys don't give a shit about you, they only care about themselves. They want to make the team and they don't want to have to fight you to do it. The only way you're going to make the team is to fight the biggest, baddest guy on the ice. You've already wasted too much time."

I had never really considered the viable possibility of actually making the team. My original goal was just to get invited to a pro camp and get into one fight. But Gator was right. Fighting was the only skill I could offer the team, it was the only reason I was there, and I was in danger of going home without doing what I could do best. I had walked right into a trap. Nobody there had my best interests in mind; they were worried about their own spots on the team.

Bill Whitfield: "I was an all-star my first year pro in the All-American League, and an all-star my first two years in the East Coast League, but I was still nervous about making the team. I didn't know for sure where I stood in any training camp, and in the minors nobody should feel as though they have a spot all sewn up. I wasn't going to take anything for granted."

We were going to take another short break before scrimmaging, and as the Zamboni prepared to emerge from its cave to make a fresh patch of ice, I stalked the biggest kid in camp, a lanky 6-foot-5 defenseman. Everybody else had already exited for the locker room, but he remained behind to skate a few quick laps. I challenged him to fight right then and there, while Coach Carroll and Baker were still in the stands comparing notes.

But the kid wasn't a tough guy, in fact he was quite horrified at the situation I presented to him and flatly declined my offer. He may have been big but he had a fawn-like quality about him, and even with everything I had at stake I couldn't bring myself to attack him, so I let him cower back to the locker room.

There was another big guy in camp, a 6-foot-3, 220-pound left wing who had been telling everybody from the first day he arrived at the motel that he was going to be the team's enforcer. The kid seemed so physically soft and goofy to me that I hadn't given him much thought. He also hadn't played rough during the scrimmage so he didn't paint himself as an obvious target.

Then again, what the hell was I doing? He was probably thinking the same thing about me. We were both doing nothing, the only difference being that he was better at doing nothing than I because he could actually skate and carry the puck. Now here was a kid who could show the coach he could play and maybe make the team on his size alone.

That was it; I decided he was my man.

I lined up with him on the wing and the moment our shift started I slashed, hooked, held and banged him from one end of the ice to the other. I did everything I could think of to get him mad at me but he didn't flinch, he completely ignored me. He broke from me at center ice for a pass down the left-wing boards that sailed too far ahead. He halfheartedly followed the puck in behind the net and I traced his strides with my mind made up. I was on a collision course I couldn't turn from. I didn't know if I was making the proper decision to just attack this kid and make him fight me but it didn't matter because I locked myself in like a guided missile and didn't care. The worst thing that could happen was to be sent home, and I figured on that anyway no matter what I did in camp.

I slammed into him directly behind the net, gave him a little shot in the face with a cross-check and dropped my gloves. At this point he was forced to defend himself and it was bombs away on both sides. I dropped my head again, just as I had done against Bill Whitfield in the Pro-Am, and the big goof punched my helmet off my head, sending it rocketing up five feet in the air. If he had landed that punch on my chin it may have sent me back home in a black bag and there would likely be no *GOON* book or movies. I lost my balance for a moment and scrambled. For a split second I flashed to something Commander had told me—that above all, never fall down. He said a guy could get hammered in a fight, but if he pulled his opponent down and landed on top it could look like he won.

I settled my legs and started to unload my arsenal of shorter, tighter punches like a boxer. I returned the uppercut favor and punched *his* helmet off. Then I started to land some solid shots, going over the top and underneath with left and right hands.

The kid was in over his head. He started tiring and was having trouble warding off the beating. Sensing trouble, the other players converged en masse to stop the fight. I shook myself free from the sea of arms and skated slowly to my bench, fully out of breath but damned if I'd let anybody else know it. The other kid remained behind the net putting himself back together—fixing his shoulder pads, fishing for his helmet, stick, and gloves. He was rocking woozy, maybe as much from exhaustion as the punches I landed, but his body language screamed to everybody in attendance that he was a beaten soul.

I was too hopped up with excitement, almost in a daze from the adrenaline rush to analyze or know how I had done. Hell, I figured I lost. "Shit," I thought as I skated to the bench, "there's my one fight." Of course Gator was there to film it, and was all too happy and proud to present me with a viewing of my victory after the scrimmage.

Fighting your own potential teammates during training camp was not a novel concept or isolated anecdote, at least in my day. It was simply the easiest way to deal with that kind of job competition, especially when two tough guys were going after one roster spot.

I was getting my skates sharpened recently and struck up a conversation with the owner of the pro shop who told me about a camp he attended in the early 1990s for the defunct Louisville Icehawks of the East Coast Hockey League. Richie Lovell, a self-termed "college washout," was a 21-year-old fresh out of junior hockey in New York State. Competition for a job was desperate and fierce. He said the team already had 13 guys signed, and there was also property expected to be sent down to them from the team's NHL and International League affiliates.

Lovell: "There were 65 guys for four spots. There were two guys, not goons, they could play, and they kept fighting each other. It was Fight #4, and one of the guys said, 'I can't fight you again, my hand is broken. The other one said, 'I don't care, you have to fight.' It was a bloodbath. They went at it, and then came the sticks. It was a swinging match with the sticks.

"I'm sitting on the bench thinking, 'What the fuck is going on here? What am I doing here?' You don't want to leave, but coming out of juniors, there was fighting, but it wasn't like this. In junior, I was one of the older ones, but we had 16-, 17-, 18-year-old kids. They fought, high energy, get-up-and-get-'em, 160, 170 pounds. The kids fight with emotion, they're angry. But this was the first time I saw grown men fighting. It wasn't the same. There was anger, but it was more like, this is my job.'"

Now you may ask, "Where in the world is the head coach while all this madness was going on?" Exactly where my coach was—in the stands with a clipboard taking note of everything going on in the scrimmage, scanning the sea of players for anybody who may be of some use. The 5–10, 180-pound Lovell was actually chased around and challenged by a 6–4, 240-pound monster. He didn't want to fight, but the spotlight was on him so he had to answer the bell. He hung on for dear life and caught the big lug with a lucky shot to put him down. The big guy was cut the very next day. Lovell hung around for another week, was himself eventually cut and gladly headed off to play in Europe.

This gladiatorial mayhem wasn't just relegated to the lowly minor-league coliseums. Of course the stakes are higher, at least money-wise, in the Big Leagues. One of my all-time favorite training camp stories came from former NHL referee Paul Stewart who, as a player, was invited to the expansion Quebec Nordiques' first NHL training camp in September of 1979. Joining him in camp that fall was another tough hombre, Wally Weir.

Paul Stewart: "Well, he and I never got along all the way playing against one another in the Eastern League and WHA and all. In training camp it was 'Qui est Numero Un, Who is Number One, Wally or Paul?' We're playing on the same team in training camp and we fought three times in 10 minutes, and I told the brass it was to the death. We were going to go to the death until one of us lived and one of us died. It sure woke up a lot of people.

"Wally was from Quebec so he got the job anyway. But I had a one-way contract and I was making $30,000 more than him, plus I was getting paid American money so it didn't matter to me. I went to the Central League and had a great time. Then I went and eventually got back to Quebec and we actually ended up being the best of friends."

Like Stewart, I also must have made some kind of an impression on the powers that be because the Big Goof I beat was cut before our first and only exhibition game and I was selected to play against the host Virginia Lancers on Sunday night. Years later I thought about this moment. Why was I chosen to play when I had trouble standing up on my skates? At the time I figured that was how the tryout process worked; everybody, or most everybody, got an exhibition game to showcase themselves. I had no concept of cuts, of being nervous and having a sleepless night wondering about the list that would be posted on a locker room wall the next morning. I never went through that kind of hell competing for a spot on a team in high school or college. But in short time I came to realize that the coach needed team toughness, and there were no real enforcers in camp, so he wanted to see what I could do for him, what I could offer to the team, plain and simple.

Virginia didn't have the toughest team in the world. Its best fighter from the previous year, Mitch Malloy, was away in the International League, but I figured at worst I could call upon Bill Whitfield to fight me again.

I skated only three shifts in the entire game but made each one count. Somehow I touched the puck before Curtis Brown scored to give me an assist and the team a 2–1 lead in the second period. On my second shift I fought Whitfield, and he got the better of me, again.

I didn't have a handle on anybody else playing with Virginia; I didn't know who else was a tough guy. On my final shift of the game in the third period I lined up beside, of all people, John Baker, who shared the same name as our team owner. He was a University of Maine product and friend of Whitfield's from back home whom I discovered later was just a hard-working kid trying his best to make the Lancers as a regular player. But I was panicked to wring the most out of what I figured was my final opportunity on the ice, and I also wanted to make up for my loss to Whitfield, so I forced Baker to fight me off the face-off and beat him soundly to cap my night's work.

> **Whitfield:** "I thought I got the better of him in our fight, and then he beat up my friend. After the game we talked and Doug let it be known that if he made the team he wanted to have a Jay Miller/John Kordic thing going with me, a rivalry where we could fight every time we played against each other. I was thinking, 'Jesus Christ, I've got to fight this meathead every night?' But the toughest thing about fighting Doug was that he was such a nice guy. It was hard to get mad at him. That was his personality. Smitty would shoot the shit with you even after you beat his brains in."

After pulling a training camp invitation out of my ass and getting into the one fight I wanted during tryouts, I was overwhelmed to have been chosen to play in the exhibition game. The two fights and assist in that game were more than I could have ever dreamed the night before, so when I was cut from the team the next day it was impossible for me to be *too* disappointed.

Monday's itinerary announced that the bus to Johnstown for the season-opener was "leaving tonight at 10:00 p.m. Be sure to be here by 9:15 p.m." There were nine players listed below the travel times. They were instructed to "come up to the office to see Brian Carroll at the time listed beside their name."

It was dread time. Each player had a 20-minute meeting with the coach. I was second-to-last at 2:40 p.m. I went into my meeting with Carroll and before he could say a word I told him that I knew why I was there. I told him I wasn't upset he cut me; on the contrary, I was elated he had given me the opportunity to attend camp and play in the exhibition game.

Carroll shook my hand and told me to continue to work on my skating. I had no money left to get home so he gave me a hundred-dollar bill out of his pocket for a bus ticket back to Boston.

3

A Second Life

It was a long ride home ... not because I was cut loose by the Thunder-birds, but because it was a long-ass haul on a bus from Roanoke, Virginia, all the way back to Boston's South Station.

I told Brian Carroll the truth; I wasn't upset that he let me go. In fact I felt as though I succeeded, I pulled it off. I pushed my way into a professional hockey tryout and had the fight I wanted in training camp. On top of that I played in an exhibition game and had two more fights, never mind the assist. And was I really one of the team's final cuts? Maybe I was, but it didn't matter, the important thing was that *I was there*. I set out to do something difficult, one may say improbable, and for one of the first times in my life I succeeded. Ultimately I discovered I could fight but I simply didn't have the other hockey skills necessary to stick around.

Carroll didn't exactly offer me any encouragement. He told me to go home and work on my skating, but he didn't tell me to work on my skating *because when you get better we're going to bring you back.*

During the bus ride home I tried to evaluate my next move in life. I fig-ured that at 23 years old playtime was over, and while I knew I'd continue skating because I enjoyed the exercise, it was probably time to grow up and find a real job before I ended up sleeping in a cardboard box somewhere.

Despite taking stock of my future, I wasn't on the fast track to corporate success as a weekend bouncer and part-time fitness instructor when Steve Plaskon and Mike Kuzmich, two of my Boston-area friends on the Thunder-birds, phoned me in early December, a little more than a month into their season. They told me that a couple of players the team thought would be able to handle the enforcer role had gotten the hell beat out of them, and Bill Huard, a legitimate tough guy, had quit and gone home. They asked if I was interested in coming back down to fight, I said I was, and they in turn told me they would talk to the coach. Carroll called me the next day. The team flew me down Thursday and I had my first real, regular-season professional hockey fights Friday night.

Brian Carroll: "You're always looking for toughness in hockey, and there are a lot of guys who are brought in strictly for their toughness and then learn to play pretty well. The general feeling is that at least if you have one talent you can work on the other parts of the game."

Waiting in the locker room for the start of my first official professional hockey game at our home rink, the Winston-Salem Memorial Coliseum, against the Knoxville Cherokees, was nothing like the exhibition game I played in at the end of training camp. This time I was there with the team because I was needed. I didn't have to worry about my skating, puck-handling skills, or whether I could keep up with the other players. All I had to do was know the jersey numbers of the fighters on the other team, and if possible, whether they threw punches with their right or left hand.

Still, I am not ashamed to admit that as I sat on my locker room stool contemplating my fate, which was now just minutes away, I was so nervous and fearful that my hands were literally shaking. I tried to fiddle with my hands so others wouldn't notice, but when I folded them it felt as though my

Above and following page: **An unlikely member of the Carolina Thunderbirds of the new East Coast Hockey League.**

arms were now shivering. I was a little fearful of being injured, as my thoughts brought me back to the conversation with my friend, Bob Sylvia, and coming home missing an eye. But the main concern I had was whether or not I could do the job. I didn't want to embarrass myself in front of the coach, my teammates, and the three or four thousand fans in the stadium.

At this point I gathered strength from what I had read about heavyweight boxing champ Mike Tyson. He said he was always afraid; that he was afraid when he trained, when he warmed up in his locker room, and especially when he was making his way to the ring, where his fear inched toward the boiling point on each step. Tyson used his fear of being hurt and losing as motivation during his training. He turned the fear into a positive. Knowing that his opponent wanted to hurt him, Tyson had to make sure he hurt *him* instead. Fear made Tyson so angry that when he finally stood face-to-face with his mark, he had aroused himself into a caged animal ready to rip his face off. Likewise, by the time my game started, I couldn't wait to get out on the ice and kick some ass.

But there was more preparation ahead of me. My teammates told me that the Knoxville Cherokees had two main guys who did the bulk of their fighting. A French-Canadian from Quebec, Alex Daviault, jackhammered short, quick rights. Some said he was the tougher of the two, but I worried more about his roommate, a kid out of British Columbia with the apt name of Greg Batters, because he threw with both hands. Batters wore jersey Number 9, while Daviault was Number 27.

Steve Plaskon took me aside while I was getting dressed and taught me how to tie down my jersey, as I couldn't afford to have my shirt lifted over my head and blind me during a fight. Most professional hockey jerseys come equipped with a "fight strap" sewn by the manufacturer into the lower inside rear of the shirt. There are quite a few different types. Mine was of the older fashion "ribbon" variety and consisted of a pair of nine-inch strips of cloth that could be tied around the garter belt I wore to keep my socks up, or knotted around a little loop attached to the top of the back of my hockey pants. No matter the particular style, the idea behind the fight strap was to literally keep a jersey in place during a scuffle.

Plaskon went a few steps further with me. He cut out the factory-installed ribbons, placed a nickel on the lower outside of the shirt, grabbed it from the inside and secured the circular lump of cloth by wrapping a skate lace around it. He did the same to the front so that I had four long lengths of skate lace hanging from inside the front and back of my jersey. I tied the laces around my waste to create a double harness that made it virtually impossible for anyone to pull my jersey up and over from the back or front.

When I skated out for the warm-ups and looked around, I didn't know how many people were in the stands but it appeared as though there were a couple of thousand more fans in attendance than there were at the exhibition game. While the Guns 'N' Roses song "Welcome to the Jungle" rocked from the sound system, fans were taking photos of the players and pounding on the glass for so much as a smile from us. My entire body was quaking with anticipation and excitement. As my teammates warmed up the goalies, I wandered by the boards to center ice and plopped myself down to stretch out and stare at Daviault and Batters. They had no idea who I was or why I was there. I stared into their faces and thought they looked like rough, tough kids. The fear flooded back to me.

As I stood on the bench for the national anthem, I was so excited I began to hyperventilate. I had never been as pumped up for anything in my entire life. Again I felt like a guided missile unable to veer from a prescribed path. I was outside of my body with no control, being dragged along toward the inevitable. There was nowhere to run or hide; I had to fight these two guys, and there was nothing I could do to change that jarring fact.

Earlier in the locker room I noticed I wasn't included on any of the three set lines written out on the lineup card taped to the wall. My name was added on the side, alone and painfully apart from all the other players. I was the extra guy. I wasn't going to skate a regular shift, but that was fine by me. I recalled the stories about goons plying their trade in the minors, how they sat alone at the end of the bench waiting to get tapped on the shoulder by their coach to go out and do their thing. My role was clear. There was no question, fuzziness, or room for interpretation of what I had to do.

Paul Stewart: "A reporter once asked me what my role was on the team and I told him I got the roll that was left over because everybody else got the English muffin. When all the good people of the town headed for the hills, I was left alone to fight the bad guy, whoever he was."

Now I was the hired gun, the tough guy, just like Paul Stewart. I was Gary Cooper standing alone against the bad guys in the movie *High Noon* and I loved it.

The game didn't start out rough, but near the middle of the first period a Knoxville player whacked one of my teammates deep in our end and put him down, face-first on the ice. Seconds later Carroll barked, "Smith, take the right wing!"

I hopped over the boards during a change on the fly with two numbers flashing like beacons in my brain: 27 and 9 ... 27 and 9. I lost sight of the guy who slammed my teammate, but there was Number 9 in front of me in Knoxville's left corner.

Greg Batters lifted his head and saw me for a fraction of a second before I plowed into him at full speed. He didn't even have the puck. The impact was so violent that my stick snapped in half and our gloves flung high into the air as we both crashed to the ice. It was as I imagined being in a car accident would be like—an explosion sending debris flying, followed by a few seconds of unearthly silence, then consciousness slowly returns the senses—in this case my senses were awoken by the crowd's roar as we arose up on our skates. I was surprised Batters was able to get up at all after the hit I laid on him. He might have been knocked for a loop but he was on automatic pilot when we squared off.

All play stopped and everybody in the arena tuned in to us. It was prime time for me. We had our fists up and glided in a slow, tight circle measuring each other's distance. At least that's what I gathered from watching the game tape later because in all honesty, I can't recall doing any of it. All I remember from that moment was that I felt as though I didn't know what I was doing. Maybe it was a combination of being so excited and nervous that in fact I was on auto pilot as well. Batters reached out and grabbed my right sleeve with his right hand and I reached in and grabbed his left sleeve, which made it nearly impossible, at first, for either of us to throw any quality punches.

I do recall, however, that after a few seconds of grappling for position I sensed I was either stronger or he was dazed from the body check, so I was able to wrestle my right hand free from his grasp and fire off three short uppercuts in quick succession that landed under his chin and rocked his head back, bang … bang … bang.

The uppercut has always been my favorite punch because it's very difficult to defend against and devastating when it connects. It is also somewhat safer on the hand because you're not coming over the top and hitting a helmet, although the trajectory of the knuckles with an uppercut can sometimes lead straight into the cutting shears of the upper teeth, which can do obvious damage to both fighters.

I wrestled Batters hard to the ice. The long square-off afforded the officials ample time to arrive on the scene and they quickly untangled us. I immediately headed for our penalty box without any commotion. I felt a fighter appeared more professional and business-like when he left for the box without causing more of a disturbance once everything was over. I didn't much care for guys who continued to wrestle, punch, or argue once the officials had their hands into the fray. Besides, I held no animosity and held too much respect for Batters to show him up after my victory. This was just like any other job, and once I finished the current assignment I simply left the worksite.

The home crowd was cheering for me as I skated toward and entered the penalty box. Here I was, the least-talented player on the ice and they were giving me a standing ovation. One fan charged down from his seat to the top of the glass separating us and told me that Batters had been coming into our rink for a month kicking the shit out of us, and this was the first time anybody stood up to him.

My head was swimming, I was in heaven. "It can't be this easy," I thought. "This is the first time anybody stood up to this kid and it was me and I just beat him?" Right then I knew it didn't matter how well I could skate; as long as I was willing to fight there was a place for me on this team.

I had broken myself in against Batters, so I was a little calmer as I sat in the penalty box and prepared to take on Alex Daviault. My teammates told me he was a fast puncher, that he'd grab hold of me and jackhammer shots like a machine gun. Be that as it may, I was preoccupied with how scary-looking his face was.

I studied Daviault whenever he skated close enough to me while sitting on the bench. He had dark, raccoon-circled eyes set deep into his skull. His skin was heavily scarred and appeared as though it was shrink-wrapped over his face. I found out later that it didn't take much more than a backhand slap to slit his skin open, like an over-ripe tomato that burst under the beating summer sun. His eyes were framed in scar tissue swollen and red. His face reminded me a bit of the mask worn by former Boston Bruins goalie Gerry Cheevers, who had black-stitched scars painted on his mask wherever it was hit with a puck to illustrate the damage that would have been done to his face if he hadn't been wearing protection.

A badly scarred face on a fighter can be deceiving, however. In some situations it can present a guy who has fought so often that he has caught his full share of shots. For others it merely represents a poor fighter. That is why great boxers such as Muhammad Ali, Sugar Ray Robinson, and Sugar Ray Leonard were called pretty; they fought so often but were so talented that their faces escaped *relatively* unscathed.

> **Brock Kelly:** "[Alex Daviault] showed up every fucking time. I remember one fight where I got him real good, exploded his nose. It was so bad I stopped punching because I felt sorry for him. We played them the next day and the first chance he gets he wants to fight me again. I couldn't believe it. Either this was the toughest kid in the world or the dumbest, I didn't know which."

I don't know if Alex Daviault was dumb, but he was one tough bastard. We scored a goal and I was told to take the right wing, beside Daviault. As I hopped over the boards for this, my second shift, I thought about how easy it would be to skip out of this assignment. I could come back to the bench later and tell everybody that Daviault refused to fight. That would have gotten me off the hook. But I pumped myself back up and glided into position as our goal was being announced and barked to myself, "You're down here now, this is what you dreamed about. Don't be a phony, do your job."

While we waited for the other players to line up, I asked Daviault if he wanted to go. He mumbled something in broken English and nodded. A moment after the ref dropped the puck we stood up out of our crouch, squared ourselves off, and backed up a few feet before flinging our gloves and sticks far away, far enough not to trip over.

We grabbed each other quickly and Daviault began to fire away with his patented barrage of short right hands at my head. Luckily I had a good grab of his right sleeve or he may have destroyed me. He landed about 10 punches all about my head but my hold on his jersey stunted his power. I just kept telling myself to stay in control, stay calm, and rip his helmet off.

We were both about the same height, but Daviault lowered his head, which made him shorter. I stood straight up, and while he was coming over the top with straight rights I stopped throwing my right-hand counters and let him continue to punch away unimpeded while I concentrated on grabbing his helmet. I forgot to do this against Batters, but it was something I practiced countless times with Gator in the Boys' Club and on the ponds to keep from breaking my hands.

After I finally managed tear Daviault's helmet off, I took up pounding at his squash with my right. After a few seconds of that I decided to try out another move I had studied on video and practiced with Gator—switching hands. I let go of my hold on him with my left hand, grabbed his jersey with my right and popped him square in the nose with an overhand left that buckled and dropped him to the ice. While he was still down I retreated to the penalty box to the wild delight of the crowd.

Two up, two down. I could hardly believe it. While in the box trying to catch my breath, I watched the ensuing face-off at center ice in total shock as Steve Plaskon disregarded the dropped puck and pitch-forked the opposing Knoxville center in the stomach with such force that his stick blade snapped off. To this day I don't know whether he did it in retaliation for a previous act or if my fight elevated him into a wild frenzy.

I figured Plaskon would be kicked out of the game for attempted injury (or murder), but he was merely given a penalty for spearing. Once he got into the box with me, Daviault began yelling at him, and in a matter of seconds Daviault climbed over the PA announcer's station that separated each penalty box, reached in at Plaskon, and began to trade punches. Despite the opinion I had of Plaskon's stick work, He was my friend and teammate, so I helped him pull Daviault into our box and we both went to work pounding on him.

I couldn't have dreamed up a better first game for myself. I fought and beat the two toughest Knoxville players and felt as though I contributed to the Thunderbirds' win. I was really part of the team.

After the game I didn't throw my jersey into the laundry pile. I didn't like the fact both Batters and Daviault were able to grab hold of my sleeves so easily, so I took the shirt home for more alterations. Just like football players, the less fabric there is for an opponent to grab the better, so I hemmed the jersey two inches up from the bottom, just enough so it wouldn't look too ridiculous. I also cuffed the sleeves, rolling them up three inches so they would just hang down to meet the top of my long-style gloves, which I slit down the sides so they'd slip off my hands without much effort.

My uniform wasn't the only thing that needed an adjustment.

I was nervous and unsure of myself, and even a bit afraid. It was something I had not experienced before, to be that uncomfortable in my own skin.

My homemade coin-and-skate lace fight strap.

I didn't like the way my mind was not in sync with my body. I was in a daze sitting in the penalty box after my first two fights. I couldn't really recall what I had just done. It sure wasn't like a street fight. I was calm in those, relaxed, thinking about what I was doing and what I planned to do next. These hockey fights were so quick, rapid fire and over, it was if I didn't believe I had the benefit of time to think and strategize. I was truly on automatic pilot, just unconsciously going through all the motions I had practiced for years with Gator. Hell, the only reason I was able to recount my fights with Batters and Daviault so completely is because I've watched the video a hundred times since. Watching those videos was like watching a movie with actors I didn't know.

I was acquainted with some of the guys on my team, but I didn't have any real friends with me to hang out with and talk to, to bounce things off and get their opinions and thoughts on what or how I was doing. I certainly doubted my ability to fight these opposing tough guys who had been dropping the gloves since their early teenage years. Even though I had beaten Batters and Daviault, I knew all it would have taken was a solid, well-placed punch to knock me out in front of everybody. Was I just kidding myself? Worse, was I fooling everybody else? Was I just sliding along the edge of a razor, one fight away from falling down and being sliced in half? I was so afraid of letting everybody down and embarrassing myself.

We had a week off before our next game and that made things even worse. I felt like I was tied down on railroad tracks with a locomotive roaring toward me. My entire body struggled with this blind panic fueled by the doubts I had about confronting all the tough guys coming at me. I couldn't eat much because my stomach felt queasy. I had trouble falling asleep, and then when I did I'd have dreams about failing—flunking a test in school, getting caught stealing in a store, my girlfriend breaking up with me. A person who studied dreams would have had an easy time with me. I know more than a few times I thought about quitting and going home—where I'd be safe.

While driving back and forth for practice, I took note of a sign for a hypnotist. I was a little familiar with this because I knew a guy back home, a former boxer who was a licensed hypnotist. He wasn't like the guys I'd seen in the movies swinging a pocket watch back-and-forth to put somebody into a trance, or the fruitcake from *The Three Stooges* who had eyeballs painted on the palms of his hands. This boxer just *talked* to his clients. He used the power of positive thought and persuasion to help people believe in themselves. I could take boxing lessons to make me a better fighter and inject steroids to make me stronger, but there was no pill I could take to give me confidence. I decided to see the hypnotist.

I was as honest as possible with the man. I told him about my life, what I was doing with the Thunderbirds, and my fears and concerns. He in turn reinforced what I already knew to be my strengths—I was a decent boxer, I could take a punch, and I was physically strong. He had me visualize myself on the ice, with strong legs beneath me like oak trees; my base was too strong and sturdy to fall down. He had me think about all the punches I had taken in my life as a boxer. I had never been down, never been knocked out. *I* was the tough guy; *I* was the guy the other players should fear. It was all positive reinforcement. He made me think about all the skills I possessed, all my strengths. No negative words came out of his mouth. He reminded me a bit of Anthony Robbins, a motivational speaker who I had watched a few times on late-night television. I wasn't brainwashed to think I was invincible, but I left the therapist feeling upbeat and confident about the abilities I had. In the immediate games after my session I was still a bit apprehensive, but I thought more on the lines of what I could bring to the table toward my success, rather than all the ways I could fail.

My uniform was all customized and my psyche recharged in time for the best fight of my life against Rock Derganc, another French-Canadian from Quebec City. He had spent a little time with the Virginia Lancers before being reunited with his hometown pal Alex Daviault in Knoxville during his own struggle to hold on to an enforcer's job.

I caught up with Rock in Knoxville, where he had designs on bulking up his resume against big Bill Huard, who had returned to the Thunderbirds after an abbreviated two-week retirement. Huard quit because he became disenchanted with the slumming life of the East Coast League. I understood where he was coming from in as much that I knew he had played juniors in Canada, where the kids are treated like gods, and then he spent the fall in an NHL camp with the Los Angeles Kings. Living the high life in sunny Southern California fresh out of junior hockey may have spoiled him and tainted his view toward a future life in pro hockey.

The Utica Devils, the top farm club of the NHL's New Jersey Devils, convinced Huard to come back. They asked him to play out the season with the Thunderbirds and if he performed well they'd reward him with an American League contract the following year. With a new lease on his game, Huard came back and became one of the rising stars of the league not only as a decent fighter, but a talented forward on his way to a 27-goal season, an AHL contract, and eventually the NHL.

After being chased around, hacked and harassed by Rock for most of the first period, Huard skated toward our bench in the middle of a developing play yelling, "Smitty, Smitty," before jumping over the boards. Up until that time only the coach had sent me out to do my thing during a game—otherwise I took up my usual spot at the end of the bench talking to the back-up goalie or fetching water and taping sticks for the regular players. But I had been monitoring Rock's antics against Huard and this time I jumped over the boards on my own. My stick and gloves were literally off before my skates hit the ice. Rock and I met face-to-face, grabbed each other about the neck and started throwing punches. Rock threw lefts, I threw rights, and most every punch landed. It must have lasted about 20 seconds, and when you're throwing unimpeded punches one after another, 20 seconds accounts for a lot of punches.

As luck would have it, the Thunderbirds' video crew didn't film this road game. I wanted a copy of the fight so desperately that I took out a small advertisement in the Knoxville newspaper asking anybody who may have filmed it to please get in touch with me. Nobody ever did.

While Rock and I put on a bang-up show, Huard would have done just as well or better if he were willing to fight. With me on the team, however, it was more beneficial for the Thunderbirds to have the talented Huard playing on the ice and not sitting it out in the penalty box, or worse, watching television for a couple months with a broken hand. This is also part-and-parcel of what an enforcer is supposed to do for his team.

I thought it strange when I watched my collection of old hockey fight tapes just how much the great Bobby Orr fought during his time with the Bruins. Orr was tough and he won most of his fights, but wouldn't arguably the best player in the history of the game be more valuable to his team playing rather than sitting in the penalty box? If I am a team owner or coach I don't want Bobby Orr fighting. I don't want Ray Bourque or Wayne Gretzky or Sydney Crosby dropping their gloves, either. Teams bring in guys like me for that job.

The Virginia Lancers came through for me with another tough kid who made sure Bill Whitfield didn't have to do all of their fighting. Greg Neish was a big boy out of High River, Alberta, a left wing who broke in the year before with a handful of penalty-minute riddled games for both the Johnstown Chiefs in the All-American League and Baltimore Skipjacks of the higher AHL.

Greg Neish: "The first time I fought Doug was in Winston-Salem. He was a big guy from Boston, real big. I remember that. He punched me so hard he cracked my helmet. His balance wasn't too good and I remember thinking that if he could stand up he would've been a mess to handle. The only thing that saved me was I was able to get him off balance and pull him down."

The Lancers were killing us and it was something like 9–1 when I took a shift late in the third period. I lined up beside Neish and asked him if he wanted to go and he declined. That was okay, the game was out of hand and Neish wasn't a dirty player running around taking advantage of us, so I told him fine, we wouldn't fight. But there is an unwritten rule of etiquette in all of sport that once a team has the outcome of a contest firmly in the bag it should apply a degree of mercy so as not to show up an opponent. I told Neish not to touch the puck or even think about trying to score another goal or I was going to come after him. I figured that if he didn't want to fight he'd better not feel as though he had a free pass to do as he pleased with the rest of his game.

A few moments later, Neish effortlessly broke free of me down the left wing and took a pass from his center for a partial breakaway over our blue line. Maybe heeding to the lopsided scoreboard as much as my warning, instead of moving in closer on my goalie he let a low slap shot go from the face-off circle that somehow found its way into the far corner of the net.

It didn't matter to me if Neish's heart was not in scoring the goal. While his teammates were congratulating him by the opposite boards, I cruised over and attacked him like a rabid dog, as I said I would. I fired a barrage of straight rights toward his head and didn't stop throwing punches even as I lost my balance and fell to the ice.

Five minutes later, just as my penalty expired and with time winding down in the game, a scrum developed behind our net after a whistle. While one fight raged, three of my teammates locked up with individual Lancers and looked on. The Lancers were down a player due to a minor penalty, so I had nobody to dance with after I left the penalty box and meandered down to see if I could get involved. Much to the credit of the Lancers' coach, he kept the rest of his team on the bench despite the fact his team on the ice was now outmanned.

Everybody was paired up; there were no extra bodies, so I was lost on the ice with nothing to do in front of the net. Joel Burridge, the younger brother of former Boston Bruins forward Randy, was trying to goad one of my less-physical teammates into a fight while the officials were preoccupied with two other combatants, so I wandered over and told him I would sucker him if he threw a punch. He behaved.

When everything was finally broken up and me still wandering around with nothing to do, I flashed to a memory of Boston Bruin John Wensink challenging the Minnesota North Stars' bench in the Boston Garden back in the late 1970s. He just wandered over to the Stars bench after beating up a guy during a mini brawl and lifted up his arms, offering to take on any and all interested comers. Nobody budged. What the hell. I skated over to the Virginia bench and did the same thing. Nobody budged.

*   *   *

Coach Carroll had originally signed me to a standard seven-day tryout contract for $150. It was obvious I was brought in on a look-see and very much day-to-day basis, so Brian didn't want to risk signing me through the end of the season and waste $150 a week if I wasn't going to be needed.

Brian Carroll: "Doug knew the score. It was a no-guarantees type of thing."

With me presented to the team as a totally expendable commodity, I can't imagine that the Thunderbirds ever expected what eventually unfolded. I was told about the guys who were brought in to fight before me. I suppose they were tough kids, but there is a big difference between a person who gets into drunken fights at a party or bar and a legitimate tough guy.

Most of the tough guys I've been around are quiet and reserved. If not a calmness, real tough guys own a sense of confidence that doesn't require a strut or loud voice. It is kind of like the Teddy Roosevelt saying, "Speak softly but carry a big stick." I was never much for talking. I didn't fancy myself an intellectual and wasn't much of a debater. I did my talking with my fists. In any case, kids who thought they were tough guys were brought in. Most of them were friends of other players; high school or college chums with reputations born from various antisocial encounters of assorted value. They all got mopped up on the ice and earned less ferocious reputations when they were sent scurrying back home with their tails between their legs.

I am not the toughest guy in the world, and I own the valuable knowledge that there's probably somebody right around many corners capable of kicking my ass. But I'm pretty confident of what I can do with my fists, without being drunk, and I don't think the Thunderbirds fully understood the glory I found in dropping my gloves to fight. Maybe there was a measure of luck involved, as I could have just as easily been destroyed by Greg Batters and Alex Daviault in my first game, but I wasn't, and it didn't take long for me to become a fan favorite. The hockey fans in Winston-Salem appreciated me, and the fans on the road could have hated me enough to buy a ticket when the Thunderbirds came to town. Maybe more than anything else I may have been kept around with the Thunderbirds because of my popularity with the fans.

During my first week in Winston-Salem I was taken care of by a member of the team's booster club, which was made up of a group of enthusiastic hockey fans who would do anything to help out and be associated with the team. Donna Fowler housed and fed me, and made sure I got to the rink on time. When it became clear I was going to stick with the team for a while, I was passed off to three of my teammates, Scott Allen and Gary Garland who I knew from home, and Frank Lattucca. They had a two-bedroom apartment in a small complex and I slept on the couch in the living room. I was immediately tabbed with the nickname "Fresh," which was probably a play on the name of rap singer Doug E. Fresh and not the fact I was a rookie.

We had to pay for our rent and utilities, which wasn't bad split four ways. Food was a different story, however, and the bill for that depended on individual taste. I was the pizza king. I could get two for $8.99 at a local joint and by the end of the season I had multiple columns of empty pizza boxes stacked from the floor to the ceiling.

I read Bobby Orr's book, *Orr on Ice*, which had a photo of him preparing his favorite pre-game meal—a big, juicy steak. Ideally I would have liked to concoct a diet of lean red meat and boneless chicken breasts, a nice piece of fish thrown into the mix once a week and a selection of fresh fruit every day. That would have been a menu fit for a champ. But budget constraints dictated peanut butter-and-jelly sandwiches. I also ate a lot of macaroni-and-cheese, and for a little variety I'd cut up a hot dog to mix into the pot. Scotty Allen gorged himself on whatever breakfast cereal was on sale. Sometimes he'd go on a health-food kick and devour Total for a while. Other times he'd feel as though he needed more of a kick to stay awake during practice and he'd switch to Fruit Loops for the sugar boost. He also ate a lot of salad, which forced us to pay a premium for toilet paper.

Once a week or so I'd go out to eat with some of my teammates and splurge on a $5.99 plate of steak tips with a pitcher of water. Sometimes I'd go crazy and shoot the works by adding a salad for an extra two bucks. But what I really looked forward to was the spread of sandwiches and soda the club set up for us after home games. I made a point to grab extra subs. I would specifically target the high-ticket turkey sandwiches and put a few in the fridge to enjoy the next day.

Some of the guys, like Bill Huard and Michel Lanouette, had naturally lean, muscular builds. Others remained in a semblance of decent condition with all the skating we did, but there were many who weren't in very good shape, and that's probably one of the few reasons why they didn't get out of the East Coast League. They didn't eat well, they partied all night, drank, smoked weed and chased girls. I think the only thing that saved me was that I drank a lot of water instead of alcohol.

The $150 a week was subsistence pay even by 1989 standards. There was a salary cap in the league, a total of $3,600 a week each team could spend on its players, but I don't know how closely it was followed. The better players received more, but it would have been tough for me to survive on a weekly check of $150. Management figured as much and slipped an extra hundred-dollar bill into my pay envelope. I suspect that some of the better players got more.

Regardless of the amount, I got a very large kick out of being paid to play hockey. I also received a big charge out of the simple things many of the other players seemed to take for granted, like the free undergarments the team supplied and laundered for us after each practice and game. Before my first game the Thunderbirds' trainer asked me whether I preferred long or short-cut thermals to wear under my equipment, and from then on there was a clean pair hung in my locker stall every day.

Then there were the free sticks and tape.

Everything has to be taken into perspective, and my only frame of reference prior to joining the Thunderbirds midway through the season was that I paid for everything hockey-related including ice time, skate sharpening, and all of my equipment. Here the team was sharpening my skates for free whenever I wanted, and there was a storage room packed with hundreds of sticks for the taking—and I took.

Even though I barely had cause to use a hockey stick, I made sure to take a few new sticks every time I was in that storage room whether I needed them or not. Even in later years, when I knew I was only going to be with a particular team for a single game or weekend series, I'd be sure to grab five sticks and immediately cut and tape them to my personal specifications so nobody else would want to use them. At the end of my stint with the team I'd take the sticks home with the rest of my equipment. One of my biggest thrills came when the Thunderbirds started to stamp my name and number on a particular brand and style of stick I had picked out. It made me feel like a big shot, a real pro.

In the Thunderbirds' training room there was a table set up with three different cases of tape—plain white cloth tape, black sticky tape, and a plastic opaque variety. Before every practice and game I'd scoff at least a six-roll row of the white tape. The equipment manager would sometimes see me do this and look at me with a puzzled expression.

It was like the Eddie Murphy movie, *Trading Places*, where Murphy plays a down-and-out black man suddenly handed the life of a wealthy, white, Wall Street type. There is a scene in which Murphy is given a tour of his splendidly furnished brownstone home, and while the rooms are being presented to him he shoves trinkets and cigars into his pockets—only to be told to relax, that everything in the house belonged to him.

My consumption was fed by not having a handle on how long I was going to be with the team, and like Eddie Murphy's character, part of me didn't really believe my good fortune and I was intent on taking advantage of the golden goose before it got cooked. I stockpiled my daily take of merchandise into the small apartment, turning it into a mini-warehouse of sticks and tape. More than a decade after I played my last game with the T-Birds I was still using those sticks and rolls of tape.

There were times when the Thunderbirds likely weren't drawing enough fans to support payroll and the players would have to be paid with checks made out from the owner's personal business checking account. But for me, any money was a bonus because I would've played for space on the couch and pizza. I certainly never needed a financial incentive to fight, but hell, if the owner wanted to throw a couple extra bucks my way I wasn't going to complain.

The team's owner, John Baker, approached me in our locker room after the first period of a home game against Knoxville. He took exception to a defenseman out of the University of North Dakota, Tom Benson, running around, banging and sticking everyone on our club, and offered me $50 if I would "get that bastard next period."

Little did Mr. Baker know that I would've paid *him* $50 for the opportunity to get Benson because I didn't like college kids.

Nick Vitucci, ECHL Hall of Fame goaltender: "The guys on the team used to go to a sports bar across the street from the arena called The Locker Room. One night there was a bunch of Wake Forest College kids there, and before long I heard a bunch of screaming and yelling. I look over and see Doug dragging a college kid by the collar of his shirt out the front door. I ran out to the street and it was like a scene from a movie; there's about 15 fights going on. I looked at Doug, our eyes met, and he was smiling and winking at me while whaling on this guy."

I don't know, maybe I was jealous that I didn't go to college, but I did know that the college kids I had played against in amateur hockey leagues were all weaned on face-mask hockey since they were children. They knew they couldn't get hurt wearing a mask so they'd do odd things like dive headfirst to block shots. I particularly didn't care for the manner in which they body-checked, as they took the lazy man's approach, and the method that took the least amount of effort was to hit somebody while skating straight up, leading mask-first with the arms and stick raised into an opponent's face.

It was all bullshit. The face protection they wore made these 5-foot-8 kids play seven feet tall and overly aggressive, running around like chickens with their heads cut off banging into everything and everybody in sight. On top of that the rules didn't allow them to fight in youth, high school or college hockey—especially the American kids—so they naturally played far tougher than they would have if there had been a piper to pay. In a lot of ways they felt invincible—that is, until they came across a jerk like me who would force them to ante up for their misdeeds.

I am certainly not the only person who felt this way about face-mask hockey, and I have pretty good company in those who share my opinion. A big smile crossed my face after reading a piece that the great Bobby Orr wrote in his book, *Orr My Story*:

Bobby Orr, NHL Hall of Fame defenseman: "Often, in the current game, I see little pests with face shields or visors acting like tough guys and not having to account for their actions. Those pests take away from the honor of the game and actually help create more opportunities for injuries. Their job is to provoke retaliation, and they are almost never the guy paying the price."

The score remained close for the rest of the game so I didn't get a shift during the second or third periods. In fact, it wasn't until we scored an empty-net goal with seconds left to play that the outcome was sure to go our way.

While it wasn't my fault that I couldn't get at Benson, I still felt as though I was letting the owner of our team, my boss, down.

When the buzzer sounded to end the game I was the last one off our bench. Most of my teammates skated over to congratulate our goalie but I drifted toward Knoxville's college hero. I knew there was an opportunity there for me to do something, but I didn't know exactly what Mr. Baker expected of me at this point with the game over.

I gave Benson a little shove and swore at him. If he was Daviault or Batters he would've dropped his gloves immediately, but this kid had no spine, he wasn't that kind of player, and he was likely relieved that the officials came over and separated us. One of my veteran teammates knew I was a powder keg and wanted to watch me explode. He got into my ear and needled me, he said I had to do something "and do it now." That was all the prodding I needed to reassure the validity of my actions and push me over the edge.

Benson drifted back toward me and actually started to offer an apology, but I didn't hear a word he said because I was in a state of panic, the kind when a book report is due the next day and I haven't started it yet. The teams were edging toward their respective exits and time was running out for me to act so I attacked him.

I unloaded a barrage of punches that hammered him to the ice. He scrambled to his feet but I whipped him down again behind our net and continued to bang away, much to the screaming delight of our fans, who were not only able to witness their Thunderbirds win, but also enjoy a post-game melee as a parting gift.

While I was tangled up and writhing on the ice with Benson and the officials, Batters leaned over into the mess and gently tugged at my jersey to get my attention. He knew he had his own job to do. His coach certainly expected something from him, and if Knoxville owner Bill Coffey were in attendance he would also expect Batters to get involved.

Batters kept poking me and tugging on my shirt saying, "Smitty, give me a chance. Save some for me." I thought it was funny, Batters wasn't even angry; in fact he seemed to be whining. It was as if he were begging me for a turn on my new bike. This was the business side of being a team's enforcer. Batters held no animosity toward me; he just knew he had a responsibility to fight me at this moment. The refs didn't seem to be bothered much either because once I was free of Benson they allowed me to square off with Batters behind our net. I was exhausted but I was in heaven. This was the kind of wild scene I'd dreamed of being part of and something the fans had come to expect from a goon of my caliber.

One official skated in and asked me if I wanted to continue. I waved him off and away we went, but it wasn't much of a fight. I was too tired to do much more than grab Batters' well-rested arms and hold on for dear life. I think it bothered him that I wouldn't let go and exchange punches, so he

Trying to ward off a Greg Batters head butt during an end-of-game brawl I started against Knoxville...

initiated a trio of head butts, which luckily connected only lightly with my forehead and not my nose or mouth.

Through it all the crowd never stopped cheering for me. When we were finally broken up I was the first of the players off the ice, and as I walked along the runway, just before disappearing under the

...and a note from management thanking me for it.

stands, Mr. Baker hustled over, slapped me on the back and said, "Great job Doug, thank you."

Thank goodness. I needed a little something like that to reassure me that I didn't do anything wrong.

Additionally, I thought my antics were money in the bank for Mr. Baker. I figured everybody in the rink would go home, to a bar, or to work the next day and tell somebody else what had happened in the game. It was the best damn advertising the owner could ever hope to get. All it cost him was an extra $50 in my pay envelope the next week with a handwritten note on a small Post-it that read, "Doug, we appreciate your great job, a little extra for you!—Mgmt."

Management encouraged fighting because it was like honey to bees as far as paying customers were concerned. And while I received my little taste of the nectar, others made out far better than I did, as I found out later.

> **Greg Batters:** "I was in the Los Angeles Kings' training camp with Bill Huard, so we were friends. When we were playing against each other for the first time in the East Coast League he told me he got $75 every time he fought, so he asked me to fight him. Well, I told him I wouldn't unless he gave me half the money. He agreed and we fought. We both got kicked out of the game and I went to his dressing room to get my money. But the owner of the team was in there and, well, it wasn't a smooth transaction. I think Billy got into some hot water."

Being paid a bonus to fight wasn't a quirk found just in the minor leagues, because I learned there were similar agreements among players and management in the NHL as well. One veteran enforcer of five different NHL teams whom I became casually acquainted with during his playing days told me of a bonus paid to the player who led the club in penalty minutes at season's end. The players involved kept track of each other's minutes and knew what they needed to accumulate for a lead. During one narrow race for the "black-and-blue" bonus in St. Louis, one player came from behind to take the lead at the end of the final game of the regular season when he engaged in a meaningless fight, and then smartly put himself handily over the top with a 10-minute misconduct penalty.

In the less-lucrative East Coast League, players found still more ways around the money crunch. Some worked part-time jobs, and there were a few established veterans who played only home games because they had regular full-time jobs around town as electricians or carpenters and simply couldn't afford to be away on extended road trips.

Greg Neish: "I didn't get a bonus for fighting, I wish I did. I didn't make much money, $300 a week, and with that you had to pay for a place to live, furnish it and pay the utilities. When the season ended I went back home and worked for a guy who put fences in."

We had two characters on the Thunderbirds who bucked all of the trends. They were skilled players but weren't tearing up the league in scoring, and they didn't fight a hell of a lot so they didn't receive bonuses toward those ends. They also didn't have regular jobs on the side. Yet while I shared a small apartment with three teammates, these two guys furnished a lavish spread in an upscale suburb of Winston-Salem. While their teammates inhaled breakfast cereal and chunk-light tuna at three-for-a-dollar, they dined out every night, ignoring the house specials while still managing to secure a bankroll hefty enough to support daily tee-times and a round-the-clock squiring of ladies. Of course their lifestyle fueled jealous rumors of drug dealing and the like. I never knew for sure how they pulled it all off, but I would have loved to have known what their angle was.

The East Coast Hockey League wasn't like I had envisioned professional sports, but I was quickly learning that this was a team and a league being run by the skin of its teeth. It almost seemed like an experiment, as if we were testing the waters with rules that could be bent for the sake of the fledgling league's survival. I remember Greg Batters being thrown out of a game for starting a brawl during warm-ups, and when it was discovered that his team wouldn't have enough bodies to play two full lines, the officials allowed him to come back and play.

In any case, I was game to be in on the experiment, and I felt the same way even after my first road trip.

4

Road Trip

My first road trip with the Thunderbirds was to Pennsylvania for a game against the Erie Panthers. Erie. I remembered learning about the Erie Canal in elementary school. I recalled a drawing of a mule plodding along the river bank, pulling an old boat up the canal with a rope. Education aside, for this mule of a hockey player, Erie now was just a grueling, 500-mile drive from Winston-Salem that may have been easier to endure if not for the stinking sardine can of a bus we used for the excursion.

I was told that the bus was in its eighth year of service with the Thunderbirds, having likely opened for the team during its 1981–82 inaugural season as a member of the ill-fated Atlantic Coast Hockey League. Back then the longest drive was much worse—800 miles all the way to Cape Cod to play the Buccaneers, a franchise owned by World Wrestling Federation guru Vince McMahon, which folded midway through its first season. My guess was that the bus had been a random, second-hand Greyhound job picked up at a liquidation sale by the original Thunderbirds' owner and converted for the team's use on the quick, and more likely on the cheap.

The front half of the bus had its original seats intact, but the back half had the seats removed so that sleeping bunks could be installed for use on overnight trips. It reminded me of the arrangement they had on *The Partridge Family.*

There wasn't much that could compete with the long grind home to Winston-Salem from Johnstown or Erie through a cold winter night after a loss or two. There was little to no heat, and the shocks were so worn that after the trip I'd walk off the bus feeling as though I'd been riding a pogo stick for eight hours.

During those times I had the odd feeling that our management would rather take the risk we crash and burn on an icy mountain road than pay for an extra night's lodging in a cheap motel so we could begin the last leg of our trip in daylight.

Painted along each side of the bus was "Carolina Thunderbirds Pro

The Thunderbirds' tin-can bus.

Hockey." It was as if we needed to have that announcement on the bus for a degree of self-esteem and keep people from laughing at the wreck as they passed us on the highway. The bus also frequently broke down, forcing us to call the nearest transport service to come out and rescue us from the side of the road.

At least we never hit a deer. I never realized how plentiful the stockpile of deer was in this country until I started taking those long trips on the mountain highways. I lost count of how many dead deer I saw wasting away on the roadside, usually in pairs and mangled from a confrontation with the endless parade of 18-wheelers that drove the nation's economy. Some of them were dusted white with lime from highway workers. It wasn't a sight for nature lovers.

Because I was new to the team I was given the sleeping bunk at the rear of the bus. I first thought it was an act of kindness traditionally bestowed upon a rookie to be placed nearest the bathroom, but I quickly found out that I was directed to the last bunk for quite a different reason. Between the smell of exhaust pouring in through the rear panel and the stench reeking from the shit bin beside me, getting off that bus to get my face punched inside some obscure rink would be a gift. And despite having the bathroom so close, I would have rather sat on fire than on that toilet seat. It smelled so bad in there that most chose to urinate out the windows.

The bathroom's hinged door slammed open and shut as the bus drove along. The action worked like a fan and offered up a foul stink on every bump and turn until somebody tied it shut again to keep the smell to a minimum.

The bus constantly reeked of the acrid combination of shit, beer, and the fermenting sweat that seeped up like poison gas from the equipment bags stored in the compartments below. It was no wonder many of the guys just got drunk on road trips.

If my nose didn't keep me awake throughout the night, my ears were constantly being singed by my pal Mike Kuzmich, who refused to stop talking to me. Kuzzy was like Jerry Seinfeld—he could talk for hours about absolutely nothing.

The bus was equipped with a TV/VCR combo for our entertainment and that made things a little more bearable. There wasn't much variety in our viewing pleasure, however, as we usually only had a choice of two films, including the latest porno flick from somebody's home stash, or the classic movie *Slap Shot*, which was about a hockey team playing in a league like ours. I was able to memorize every line of that film my first two weeks with the club. In fact, some of my teammates told me that our bus was the same one used in the movie, though that may have been some wistful, nostalgic thinking.

We were given $12 a day for meal money while on the road, and I did my best to budget the meager sum by purchasing most of my food at the various multi-service gas stations along the route. I was the pizza king on the road, too. I bought pizza and pre-wrapped things advertised as being made from meat that I'd warm in the gas station's microwave. It was either that or 20 Snickers bars, which were often more appealing than a soggy tuna sub prepared a week earlier by some redneck cashier with a pistol strapped to the side of his leg.

As bad as the road trips were, I enjoyed the new experience. It was pure minor league hockey to me and I soaked up the whole scene including the short meal money, crowded bunks, breaking down on the side of the road, playing cards with the guys, and sharing stories about our hometowns. It may have been a little dysfunctional, but it was something like a family nonetheless.

There were others on the club who weren't as enthusiastic. They had been on these long tours for a number of years and had their fill of 16-hour roundtrips to Erie. I could understand why few of those guys looked forward to hitting the road, and the choice made by some to stay home and bang nails.

There was also the strange outbreak of something we called the "Johnstown Flu," which would mysteriously strike down some of the veterans and render them unable to accompany the rest of us on the long trips north. Sometimes the flu struck because of the long distance involved, other times because a guy didn't want to face a physical beat-down—especially that far away from home. There were times when we were forced to go into Erie and Johnstown with only 12 players and we'd get the hell beat out of us.

Road trips were so costly for the fledgling teams that the league scheduled Friday and Saturday, or Saturday and Sunday games at the same site to cut down on expenses. After the first night game it was customary for the host club to direct the opposing players to the favored local night spots, and many times both teams would hang out together drinking and doing their best to get laid.

Before I could think about the Erie nightlife, however, I had to get through my job at hand, and that concerned Panthers goon Ron Aubrey. At 6-foot-4 and 230 pounds, Aubrey easily matched Brock Kelly as one of the biggest guys in the league.

Not much was known about Aubrey back then. There was a rumor he came from a wealthy logging family in Maine and that his daddy was going to bankroll his efforts through the minor leagues. He began those efforts the year before with one game for his home state Maine Mariners, the top affiliate of the Boston Bruins in the American League. Now he was working as Erie's enforcer. One thing was for sure, nobody on my team liked him.

While it would seem as though tough guys would be the scourge of every opposing team, that isn't what it was like at all. There was a lot of respect for guys like Brock Kelly and Greg Batters. Hell, I went to a bar with Darren Miciak after we fought and sparked a bench-clearing brawl in Erie and we watched our fight together on the local news howling with laughter and patting each other on the back.

But nobody, not even Aubrey's teammates had much of anything good to say about him.

Grant Ottenbreit, Erie Panthers enforcer and roommate of Darren Miciak: "Aubrey was a clown, honest to God. I drove to training camp with three friends, 1,600 miles from Yorkton, Saskatchewan. Aubrey was there and nobody knew anything about him. I think he was like Doug; he got a late start in the game. He was talking to one of the top players, Daryl Harpe, telling him he was going to kick all our asses. But he didn't fight anybody. Miciak and I ended up fighting each other and we were best friends. We were going off the ice at the end of the first practice and Darren said, 'Hey fat ass, where are you going?' So we went at it and we both made the team."

Brock Kelly: "Nobody sat down and wrote the book, but there's a code, an unwritten rule among guys who fight. There were things you didn't do, a right way to act. Aubrey didn't play it straight up. If you turned your back you had a chance to be sucker-punched. He'd come off the bench and go after a tired guy at the end of his shift and blindside him. There was just something about him."

Chris Hampton, ECHL fan from Nashville: "I used to hang around the rink and listen to the players mention some of the tough guys in the league. I was curious who were the other fighters and I remember several names being mentioned—Grant Ottenbreit, Darren Miciak, Alex Daviault, Greg Batters, Michel Lanouette, Gary Garland, Mike Marcinkiewicz, and Ron Servatius. As far as the feeling I got about Doug Smith, he was a tough gamer who would take on anybody. The only one I ever really remember hearing the guys dog talk was Ron Aubrey. You didn't see Brock Kelly or Bill Huard jumping people from behind. He didn't have a very good reputation among the tough guys. I didn't much like him myself because I didn't think he was a very honorable fighter."

Jacques Mailhot, legendary minor-league enforcer: "I don't understand why everybody talks about Ron Aubrey. I have no respect for Ron Aubrey; he was the most arrogant player I ever met, absolutely retarded. He's the black sheep of them all, an out-of-shape clown, a speed bag in a suitcase."

Greg Neish: "I played with Ron on the Roanoke Valley Rebels during the 1990–91 season. He was a strange guy but I didn't have a problem with him. But the strange thing was, we had a guy named John Valo, he was a big kid from Michigan who was scared of his own shadow, but he'd fight Aubrey during practice. We couldn't understand why because they were roommates. I guess he just didn't like him.

"I retired after three years with the Wichita Thunder in the Central Hockey League. I was 28 and we had won the league two years in a row. The next year there was a Tough Man Competition in Oklahoma City and the guy putting it on was getting a bunch of players from the CHL to compete. I was manager of a shop that rebuilds John Deere tractor engines and my boss gave me the day off so I could go down there. I lost a decision in my first fight but I got $500 for three, one-minute rounds, so it wasn't too bad. Aubrey was in it—the Dancing Bear, he was so big. The ring is a lot different than the rink, he could just smother you. I think he won the whole thing."

Today, when I think about the guys I played against and fought, it's a little sad we all live so far away from each other. I know I would have enjoyed hanging out with guys like Darren Miciak, Greg Batters, Rock Derganc, Darwin McCutcheon, and Grant Ottenbreit. They were genuinely likeable people. Ron Aubrey is the only one who, if I had run into him on the street after my playing days, I would have probably fought. The funny thing is, we could probably get a match put together today.

It turns out that Aubrey went a step further after the Tough Man Competition and began a professional boxing career at the age of 40. Capitalizing on his hockey fighting past, he started out with the nickname "The Enforcer" before settling with the apt moniker "The Iceman."

Aubrey's initial plan was to box five or so years and parlay his first six or seven fights into six-figure payday against a ranked contender.[1] I actually wished Aubrey's dream would have come true, as it would have made a great story, but I think his time has come and gone. Usually tipping the scales in the neighborhood of 300 pounds, Aubrey fought in the ring for seven years, going 12–4–1, all in Oklahoma City.

Most of the guys Aubrey fought were fairly new to the game, with many of his 50-inch-wasted opponents enjoying their boxing debuts. One such notorious newbie was 6-foot-3, 357-pound former offensive lineman Denshio Cook, who lost his scholarship at Oklahoma State University after a first-degree rape conviction of a 13-year-old babysitter. He was then kicked off the team after being convicted of being in possession of three pounds of marijuana. His second conviction of pot possession got him five years, with three served, in the Oklahoma State Penitentiary. In any case, the two behemoths boxed to a draw, despite Aubrey being knocked down three times in four rounds. Cook, who has had his share of judicial decisions go against him, thought in this case there was some "home cooking" going on with the local judges.[2]

After a two-year hiatus, the 48-year-old Aubrey made somewhat of a comeback in September 2014 to fight former world heavyweight champion Samuel Peter, who'd been out of the fight game for more than three years. In Oklahoma City's "Rumble on the River," a 34-year-old Peter, looking fat at 291 pounds, knocked out a Macy's Parade float-like, 301-pound Aubrey 2:34 into the first round with a quick right to the head.[3]

According to the website BoxRec, after the Peter fight, Aubrey was ranked 625th out of 1,144 registered heavyweight boxers in the world, and 227th out of 338 in the USA.

Before I put Aubrey to bed, with respect to the fact that he will have been roundly beaten up on these pages by me and others, I must at least attempt to present some balance. First off, despite my own feelings toward Aubrey when I played, I have to give him due credit because everywhere he went to play hockey he piled up penalty minutes. For that fact alone I remain envious of him. I also know firsthand that anybody who steps into a boxing ring, by definition, has a huge set of balls. Anybody who questions that fact can easily find out for themselves—if they have the nerve.

After talking to various people, I found out that Aubrey was in fact a heralded hockey player from the area of Portland, Maine who helped his Cape Elizabeth High School hockey team to its first state championship in 1985. He had the desire and tenacity to trudge through 12 years of minor-league hockey, earning the distinction of tying the record of playing for the most pro hockey teams (23) in a career. He played a total of 296 games in six different leagues, including 9 playoff contests, and amassed an astounding 2,278 penalty minutes—nearly 38 hours in the penalty box. When given the chance he fought the toughest guys available, and some of his dancing partners included such notable big-time NHL brawlers as John Kordic, Craig Coxe, Link Gaetz, and Darren Langdon. He went on to establish a large drywall business in Oklahoma City, and is also married with three daughters. I was sincerely rooting for him and a big payoff in Europe, but at the very least I hope that he and his family live out a long and wonderful life.

All that being noted, my teammates had seen enough of Aubrey during the first month or so of the season to give me their lowdown on him. They said he wasn't much of a puncher but he was intimidating because he was so big, burly, and strong. One of the reasons he didn't intimidate me, however, was that I didn't plan on battling against his size in a wrestling match. I was never a good wrestler, on the ice or off, which is the main reason why all of my opponents could expect knuckle sandwiches from me in lieu of a bear hug.

The game didn't start out rough and I didn't take a shift early on, so I just watched Aubrey skate around during the first period. He was a big guy but I could tell he was a big dope. I knew guys like him my whole life—a big dog with a big bark but little bite. All somebody had to have were the balls to challenge him, and I did.

I was sent out on the right wing for a face-off at the Panthers' blue line in the second period at Erie's Tullio Convention Center. Aubrey was across from me on the opposite side so I skated over in a very obvious and deliberate manner to change positions with my teammate and take my place beside the big guy.

I didn't know if Aubrey knew about me right then because I was a newcomer to the league, so maybe I took him by surprise when the puck was dropped and I challenged him. He ignored my shove and skated into the play, but I chased after him and offered a two-handed slash across his arms, which grabbed more of his attention. When the whistle blew for an offside we came together at center ice for a quick skirmish that was quickly extinguished by the officials, who jumped in between us. While we were tied up, Aubrey started yapping at me, making faces and sticking his tongue out, so I wiggled my left arm free and fired a shot over an official's shoulder that cold-cocked Aubrey square in the jaw and knocked him on his back. The big guy knew who I was after that.

The next day I ran into Grant Ottenbreit at the rink before the start of our second game. He told me that Aubrey had gone back to the bar earlier in the day to start drinking. He said Aubrey told him he knew he was going to have to fight me again and he wanted to get drunk so he wouldn't feel it. That gave me a good chuckle, but Ron Aubrey ended up getting the last laugh on me.

After the season was over I met up with Aubrey again during a summer free agent camp run by Boston Bruins scout Joe Lyons on Cape Cod. Lyons had made a name for himself, and a few bucks, by charging minor-leaguers and college players $300 for a three-day session of drills and scrimmages. Pro scouts and coaches from various North American and European leagues flooded the sun-baked extravaganza looking to grab any driftwood they could use to shore up their rosters for the upcoming season.

Lyons knew me and my game, but for some reason he paired Aubrey with me on the same team. We were even put on the same line. Hell, Brock Kelly was the only other known fighter attending the camp. I approached Lyons and asked what he was doing and why he couldn't put Aubrey on one of the other teams so I'd at least get a chance to fight somebody. But Lyons blew me off saying, "Don't worry Dougie, don't worry, just wait until the scrimmages, wait until the scrimmages."

I thought about what would happen if I scrimmaged the team without Brock Kelly, how the whole thing would be a waste of time with all of those scouts in the stands watching how bad I skate. Nick Fotiu, a former NHL tough guy who was coaching with the New Haven Nighthawks in the American League, had even given me a phone call to ask if I would be attending the camp.

Bullshit, I wasn't going to wait until the scrimmages, I couldn't take the chance. My only selling point was my fists. Lyons told all of us not to fight during the practices, but it was the same crap I listened to at the Thunderbirds' camp. I learned my lesson there.

After 10 minutes of free skating and shooting drills our team got together at center ice for a talk from one of the instructors. I stood next to Aubrey and didn't listen to a word being said; I was thinking of a way to start a fight.

When the players split into four smaller groups and headed into each corner to start another round of drills I challenged Aubrey to a fight right then and there and he flatly declined. He gave me a look as if I were crazy and repeated what Lyons had said, "No fighting during the practice session."

Aubrey turned away from me and started slowly skating off into the left corner. I followed behind and cross-checked him in the back. With that he spun around mad as hell and dropped his gloves. He started swinging wildly and immediately knocked me off balance with a left. I fell down to one knee and Aubrey dropped on top of me with both fists pounding as if he were trying to hammer drywall nails through the top of my head. I managed to get back on my skates and began to trade punches, but made the mistake of not getting in tight with a good hold on the big monster. He held me out with his long arms, pulled me forward and then dropped all his weight to the ice, using his brute strength and momentum to whip me into the boards. We got up again and I squared off to continue, but the other players converged and held us off to end the fight.

Lyons walked onto the ice and sent both of us to the locker room where Aubrey asked me what the hell I was doing. I told him it was nothing personal but that he knew as well as I did the only way either one of us was going to get out of camp and to a better place was to fight. I think he understood what I meant.

Catching a left from big Ron Aubrey (left) during a free agent camp on Cape Cod.

I separated my shoulder when Aubrey flung me into the boards. I was in a panic to play in the exhibition game later that night so I went to a chiropractor friend to have it adjusted, but I wasn't fit to play. My shoulder was so sore I couldn't tie my sneakers, never mind my skates. Aubrey ended up fighting Brock Kelly in the scrimmage and got tuned-up, but two years later Fotiu had him playing with the Nighthawks. I thought it could have been me.

> **Jacques Mailhot:** "I was at one of Joe Lyons' camps, too, playing on a line with Brian Horan and Ralph Barahona. We were doing real well, flying, scoring goals. Before the second game Aubrey changed teams so he could play against me. During warm-ups he skated over and said, 'How are you doing, Jacques?' I thought, 'Okay, I'm ready for this guy.' I beat the shit out of him that game."

I certainly took my share of beatings in hockey, but I'm glad most of the guys I played with or fought against at least held some respect, and even a measure of liking for me.

Aubrey didn't finish out that first year with the Erie Panthers, as he was part of a five-player deal that landed him in Knoxville. It was a move that foreshadowed the vagabond lifestyle in store for him over the next 10 years. He even had two stints playing with my old Thunderbirds club, and one year he actually wore my old number 19!

In any case, even without Aubrey in Erie, I managed to engage in my most comical fight there. When I returned to Erie with the Aubrey knock-down on my resume, everybody present at the Tullio Center was fully aware of my act.

Everybody knew what Gary Garland was all about as well.

Garland was a pal of mine from Boston who was splitting time between the Thunderbirds and whatever higher-level team his friendship with veteran NHL enforcer Chris Nilan could cook up for him. He was a good player but too small to stick in the International or American Leagues. That didn't stop him from trying though, and he was kicking some serious ass here in the East Coast League.

Before the puck was dropped on a face-off, an Erie player was so terrified at the prospect of having to fight Garland that he decided to get an advantage and sucker-punched him square in an eye. I watched Garland drop like a stone from the bench and was incensed. Later in the game I was sent out for my first shift and it was of course no coincidence that the Erie player who had given Garland a killer black eye was out there as well. Now he really had cause to be afraid.

"Guess what, tough guy…," I began with a stone-cold, straight face, "we're going to find out just how tough you really are. As soon as this puck is dropped I'm going to kill you."

You can tell most everything you need to know about a person during a confrontation by the expression on their face. The eyes give you away, and this kid's eyes told me he wanted to curl up in a corner and suck his thumb.

As soon as the puck was dropped the kid turned and skated as fast as he could away from me. I dropped my stick and gloves and chased after him, somehow managing to grab the tail of his jersey. He kept pumping his legs trying to escape for dear life and there I was, riding him like a water skier. I got some shots in on the back of his head before the scene sparked yet another bench-clearing brawl.

I didn't receive a bonus for that melee—it was on the house. And while there were some trying times in store for me during the balance of the season, in time I'd have a chance to orchestrate a few more wild scenes on the ice.

5

Popular Loyalty?

The Thunderbirds were jockeying for last place with the Virginia Lancers before I arrived in December, but only a handful of points separated the club from the second-place Johnstown Chiefs. We were near the middle of the pack in scoring but were giving up more goals a game than any other team. It wasn't long before Brian Carroll was let go as coach.

Brian Carroll: "It was a game before the Christmas break. The league was so close at the time that if we won we'd be in first place and if we lost we'd be in last. Well, we only had 12 players and two of them were guys filling in who lived in the area and were doing me a favor. We lost and the owners didn't like that, so they made a change. Both of the team's owners were fans, but they didn't really know the game. I remember them telling me that I should have gone crazy that night, throw sticks onto the ice and stuff, but that's crazy."

I liked Carroll because he treated me with respect, even though as an ultra-novice hockey player sometimes I didn't think I deserved to be treated like all the other guys. Carroll never returned to hockey. He went on to operate a heating and air-conditioning business in the Winston-Salem area where he lived with his wife and two children.

Remaining true to the characteristics of an unstable franchise scratching out an existence in an unstable league, the Thunderbirds ate through two other coaches in the span of a month before a more permanent replacement was found in-house, so to speak.

The choice of Brandon Watson to lead the team was interesting. Watson had been a referee in the old Atlantic Coast Hockey League, and Referee-in-Chief for the new ECHL. He had been on the ice officiating during some of my fights for crying out loud, and now he was going to slap on a suit and tie to stand back of our bench.

Having a new boss come in is a nerve-wracking situation for any worker bee, never mind somebody like me holding on to a job by the skin of his ass.

The good thing was that Watson not only knew all about my game, but he was also from the Boston area—for whatever good will that was worth. Watson knew I was a poor hockey player, but he still sent me out there. He would even put me out to start a game, especially if a team like Knoxville was starting a physical line with Daviault and Batters. He would also tell me to skate a bit, to make my presence felt before committing to a fight.

Looking back, I wish I had been more comfortable as a player to have been able to absorb and apply the lesson Watson was trying to teach me. Hindsight is futile, but if I had been a better skater and able to prowl around terrorizing people without always having to resort to a fight, maybe I could have proven a more valuable commodity and played longer at a higher level.

Despite my familiarity with Watson, I worried about whether I'd be needed for much longer, especially with Bill Huard back on the team scoring and fighting so well. I also figured I'd be the easiest guy in the world to let go while the team was going through turbulent times. I didn't skate a regular shift and I wasn't part of the X's and O's game plan. I knew my role was necessary, but didn't feel as though I was much more than an insurance policy to cash-in during signs of trouble.

With a new coach, practices returned to being real danger zones for me because they exposed so many of my weaknesses. I still couldn't handle passes and my shots rung off the masks of our goalies or missed the net completely.

I was useless as a linemate during games because I had no hockey sense. I never watched the puck or where the play was going because my head was always swiveling around either stalking the other team's tough guy, or making sure he wasn't going to jump me. I would watch myself on the game films and it was comical; a pass would come my way, scoot past and bang on the boards with me totally oblivious and uninterested. Playing with me was still like skating four men against five.

Scott Allen, roommate: "A bunch of my buddies from New Bedford drove down to visit me and take in a game. Doug somehow got the puck free and clear in the neutral zone and had himself a breakaway from center ice. Now most guys would move in on the goaltender for a better chance to score, but the moment Doug reached the blue line he wound up and took a slap shot. He didn't want anything to do with carrying the puck any further than that. My friends thought it was the funniest thing and they still talk about it."

I was credited with my only point during the season, an assist, after blindly getting rid of a loose puck that found its way onto the blade of my stick. A couple of my teammates then ended up touching the puck before it went into the net. For me, handling the puck was like playing hot potato—the moment I received it I got rid of it so as not to get burned. I stayed out for the face off at center ice and while I was waiting on the wing for the puck to be dropped I heard my name announced over the loud speakers: "…assisted by Number 19, Doug Smith…." I never even realized I had an assist coming.

At that moment I flashed back to an old story I remembered about Boston Bruins rookie enforcer Stan Jonathan, who was sent down to the minors for three games by his coach, Don Cherry, because he was scoring too much and not fighting enough. Cherry made it clear to Jonathan that there were other guys on the team whose job it was to score, and his job was to play tough and fight. I thought it was a funny and interesting story when I read it, but it wasn't funny at that moment because there were no lower minor leagues to send me down to, only home. My goal was to have a stats line that read all "0's" across it, except for in the games played and penalty minutes columns. When the puck dropped I likewise dropped my stick and gloves and pummeled the poor bastard beside me. I didn't need anybody to remind me what *my* job was.

> **Scott Allen:** "With Doug it was black and white, there was no gray area, he just wanted to be a hockey fighter and he would be disappointed if he got an opportunity to be on the ice and the other guy wouldn't fight him.
>
> "But Doug was very smart about it as well. He analyzed his fights and he took into account his opponents' strong points and weaknesses. He asked for information from anybody who had fought his opponent before, or even if the person had just seen or heard about how somebody else fought him. He also thought about what he did well himself, and the things he could do to improve. The bottom line is, anybody who played the game has nothing but respect for somebody like Doug who wants to do it. It's not an easy job."

And I never stopped trying to do my job. Through my first 11 games with the Thunderbirds I racked up 130 penalty minutes to lead the team, and you can bet those minutes were earned the hard way. I got my share of minor penalties, too, but those roughings, cross-checks, elbows, and slashes were all done in the honest pursuit of starting a fight.

The next-closest guy to me on the penalty list for the T-Birds was Michel Lanouette, who had 128 minutes in 13 games. But Lanouette was our best part-time player who played a regular shift in home games. In fact, I was there in part to keep Lanouette from fighting because he was likely permanently disabled by a serious eye injury suffered earlier in his career.

Bill Whitfield had played against Lanouette for a couple of years and he hated him for some reason, so there was always a chance they would lock horns whenever we played Virginia. In one game at home there was a stoppage in play by the boards and a little pushing and shoving ensued before Whitfield and Lanouette separated from the officials and prepared to do battle. The moment Whitfield dropped his gloves I skated in front of Lanouette, as if preparing to take a bullet meant for him. I dropped my gloves and took on Whitfield before either of them fully grasped what was happening.

My motivation was two-fold. On the one hand my job was to protect my teammates, and because Lanouette was one of our better defensemen we couldn't afford to have him sitting in the penalty box. On the more self-serving side, I felt that any penalty minutes up for grabs belonged to me, and whenever I could I was going to grab them.

Bill Whitfield: "I heard that after every game Doug would call home to his mother and tell her he got into one or two fights. He'd be angry and tell her that he should have had another one."

Actually, I would call Gator or he would call me at my apartment after every home date to get the blow-by-blow account of what I did in the game. I would also mail him newspaper clippings and videotapes of my fights, which were then broadcast throughout the Boys' Club.

I was receiving one or two shifts a game and getting into one or two fights. The reason I was usually disappointed with my performance was because the game's rules allowed a player three fights before being sent to the showers. If I were still sitting on the bench at game's end it meant I still had at least one fight left in me. Not that I could do anything about it, because if I didn't get the ice time I couldn't get the fight. It was just the *idea* of not fighting as often as I possibly could that bugged me.

I was forever plagued with the fear that I would be let go by the Thunderbirds on any given day, but the team kept renewing my seven-day contract because, I think in part, I was everything they expected. Not only did the fans enjoy watching me fight, but rarely does anybody turn out to be exactly as advertised, and I certainly was.

Management knew all along that I was a brutal skater who couldn't play a regular shift, but they heard I loved to fight and witnessed it during training camp. Now they saw that I never wavered from that promise during the regular season. I was certainly a far cry from some of the guys who had been brought in to do the fighting and either got dusted or fled the scene.

There are also guys who play tough in camp or early in the year but peter out as the season wears on. Sometimes it's just the nature of certain players. There are guys who don't particularly want to fight but feel as though they must in order to showcase all of what they can offer a team. Sometimes it's all about what you *have* to do in order to sign a contract. It is like all those flowers I bought for my girlfriend when we were dating, and now that we're married she wonders why the flowers disappeared. After fighting a bit early on, some tough guys stop dropping their gloves because they believe they've made their point. Others fight only in front of the home crowd or when management is in attendance but they won't fight on the road. Those guys are called "Homers."

There was one kid in Johnstown, Mike Marcinkiewicz, who was a real lunatic in his home rink. His reputation was broadcast to all points via the rumor mill when he supposedly handed Brock Kelly his ass during training camp. But when Marcinkiewicz came down to Winston-Salem to play us he'd wear a face mask and disappear.

I suppose I didn't know any better. Marcinkiewicz had been playing hockey since he was a small boy, and he had come to the East Coast League off four years in the reputable Quebec Major Junior circuit. He knew how to play the game, and I don't mean just with his stick and puck. His paycheck

Attacking a member of the Knoxville Cherokees.

was coming out of Johnstown, and if he were able to make himself a fan favorite there he'd be a hard guy for the team to gas.

That is why I looked forward to playing in road games. I was aware of the homer act and knew that not many guys would be able to ignore my advances to fight in their home rink.

There were also a lot of guys I played with who bitched and moaned about their lack of ice time. Most everybody playing on a sports team thinks they should be playing more than they are, but not me. I knew I sucked, I knew I couldn't play, so I was content, even honored to simply be a member of the team wearing a jersey and sitting on the far end of the bench while waiting for my opportunity to fight the other team's toughest players. In that sense I didn't rock the boat or create animosity with my teammates or coach.

I wasn't part of a regular line for most games so in some ways my role wasn't much different than that of a boxer sitting alone on his stool waiting for the bell to ring. But a goon should watch the game like any other player. I always took notice of how the guys on the other team played. If somebody was taking liberties with my teammates he became the object of my desires. When I was told to get on the ice by the coach he never had to say, "Doug, get that guy," because I already knew who my target was, as I had been watching him act like a jerk for the last 40 minutes. There was never any surprise on my end; I always knew what my assignment was because I had been monitoring the flow of the game. My role was situational and no different than the coach putting out his power play or shorthanded lines. When the appropriate time came during a game I would be unleashed to do my thing.

If I was sent out for a face-off, the first thing I'd do is line up beside my mark and challenge him right then and there. Usually we'd wait until the puck was dropped before we went at it in order to avoid—and this was funny because it doesn't make any logical sense—a "delay of game penalty." If I was sent out on the fly I'd track my target down like a guided missile and explode upon him. In either case, if I challenged a guy and he didn't want to fight I'd usually get off the ice so a real player could take my place and try to score a goal. In many of those situations, just the knowledge I was ready and willing to fight went a long way toward keeping the other team's tough guys in line. That is the beauty of intimidation in hockey; sometimes you don't even have to drop your gloves to keep order. I remember reading in Don Cherry's book, *Grapes*, that when his favorite enforcer, John Wensink, was injured, he would want to dress him just so he could be on the bench to growl at the opposition. They wouldn't know Wensink was hurt, just that he was there and apparently ready, willing, and able to hop over the boards if anybody got out of line.

I was the least-skilled player on the team, but I was one of the few players

fans made posters for, and three of them hung from the second balcony of the Winston-Salem Coliseum near the "Go T-BIRDS" sign.

One of the posters was an Uncle Sam knock-off with the words "I WANT DOUG SMITH" printed underneath. Another was a rendering of Michel Lanouette and I dubbed "The Bruise Brothers." My favorite was a full-color cartoon caricature of me standing over an opponent I had knocked out. Printed underneath was "THE TER- MINATOR," a spoof of the Arnold Schwarzenegger movie.

The team also handed out a "VISITORS CHECK LIST" at games. It had the team logo, address, and phone number at the top, and 10 directives for an opposing team to fol- low so that "YOU MAY LEAVE HERE IN ONE PIECE..." The first order was, "STEER CLEAR OF DOUG SMITH." I got a kick out of that and grabbed one for myself.

Then there was "Win a Date with the Thunderbirds" night at the Coli-

Top, above and opposite page: **Fan-made posters that hung around the Winston-Salem Coliseum.**

seum, which was sponsored by the team's booster club. After warm-ups before the start of a home game, an emcee dressed in a tuxedo came out to center ice and pulled one of the ticket stubs that college-aged girls dropped in a bucket at the turnstiles. When the chosen girl came down to the ice she was asked which T-Bird she wanted to go with on an all-expense-paid date and she said, "Doug Smith." I was mortified.

The booster club rented a limousine for us, they supplied me with a corsage to give the girl, and we were set up with a fancy dinner at a nice local restaurant. When we arrived a bunch of my teammates were already there at the bar waiting to bust my balls. The girl was nice enough; I don't even recall what we talked about, I just rambled. I didn't know what she expected. Who the hell was I? I felt like Mike Tyson with Robin Givens.

There were tons of girls. Teammates would drag me into a bar after a game, I'd be dressed in the best clothes I owned, sporting a black eye, and everybody knew who I was. It was so easy. I would stand still and attract girls like a hanging strip of flypaper. On the road the girls didn't even care who you were in particular, just that you were a member of the hockey team. But if they knew you were the tough guy, well, a busted nose, shiner or some fresh stitches appeared to be far sexier to them than 50 goals. Hey, what can I say other than girls love the tough guys.

On top of that, if you were with the visiting club hunkered down for a weekend series, the girls knew you had a motel room to go back to. There were many nights on the road when five or six guys ended up sharing one room so a teammate could entertain a guest in private.

Despite all the popularity and attention, I still felt as though every day could be my last with the team. I had the uncomfortable feeling I was hanging on to my spot with the Thunderbirds by the skin of my ass, even as folks wanted to know everything about me—where I was from and how I came to be on the team. I was being treated like somebody special, a local celebrity, but I didn't feel like a celebrity. Maybe the hypnosis had done everything it could, because I still felt like a big dumbbell from Boston still managing to walk deftly on that razor blade, blindly going about my strange business as a rookie goon and faking everybody out.

After my fast start with the T-Birds I calculated a goal for myself. I figured I could rack up 100 penalty minutes for every 10 games played, and if I got into 20 of the final 25 regular-season games I could easily reach the vaunted 300-minute mark.

But I didn't count on my fights drying up.

Guys who fought during my first spin around the league stopped obliging me. It was as if they got sick and tired of seeing me around. I was the panhandler the other tough guys gave a dollar to once, maybe even twice, but after a while when they crossed my path and I tugged at their coats they just

Corralled by an official—away from the play, of course.

passed me by. I am sure it was also the case that the opposing coaches realized all I could do was fight, so they had their players ignore my antics. I played in 17 of the final 25 games, which was okay, but I wound up with only 48 more penalty minutes—a huge disappointment.

Four of the five teams were going to make the league's Riley Cup playoffs and we battled down the stretch against Virginia for the fourth and final spot. There were many player moves made by teams during this desperate drive toward the playoffs. A big one that interested me was Erie shipping Ron Aubrey to Knoxville in a multi-player deal. There had actually been some talk that he was coming to the Thunderbirds, which would have surely signaled the end for me because he was a much better hockey player than I.

The end for me came anyway, but in a roundabout way. We were on the road in late February—our playoff hopes hanging by a loose thread with only a couple of weeks left in the season—and the team owner, John Baker, called me into his hotel room in Erie. The T-Birds had acquired a new player, and Mr. Baker said he wanted to play him. This meant they needed to free up a spot on the roster, so he wanted to place me on the injured reserve list for 14 days with full pay, and if we made the playoffs I'd come back.

I got a short reprieve before the decision was made. One of our players who lived a few hours from Erie went home to visit the day before and didn't arrive back at the rink until after the roster had to be submitted, so I was inserted into the lineup. It ended up being my last game for the Thunderbirds and a real great send-off because we had a nice bench-clearing brawl at the end of the second period.

We were fighting for our playoff lives, but the Erie Panthers came into the game seven points shy of clinching first place in the league, so they weren't too interested in laying down for us. The game was hard-hitting and heated from the get-go. Some cheap shots went unpunished by the officials, and the crowd of more than 2,000 raucous fans added to an environment that was reaching a boil.

I was on the ice when the siren blasted to end the second period, and immediately drifted to center ice for a clear visual of everybody unloading from their respective benches. Sure enough, Darren Miciak, bless his soul, came right after me. I landed three lefts, he missed with a big right, and then I switched hands to unload a right uppercut that dropped him to his knees before I landed on top. The refs took us off the ice, but a few more fights erupted and I snuck back out. I floated around the periphery pushing guys and challenging them to fight, but anybody who wanted to battle was already going at it. Soon I was concentrating on taking care of one of our leading scorers, John Torchetti. I helped pull him away from his slugfest and escorted him off the ice.

Erie Morning News sportswriter Bob Jarzomski was there to witness it all and handed me my favorite nickname when he wrote in his game story the next day that, "First off, Carolina's Doug (as in Thug) Smith was dispatched for his usual duty and went at it with Erie tough guy Darren Miciak...."

Doug the Thug. Boy, I really loved the ring of that. You still can't rub the smile off my face when I re-read that little blurb. The screenwriters of the movie, GOON, obviously liked it as well, as they used for it for the nickname of their title tough guy, Doug Glatt.

I don't know if that fight sparked us, because we ended up losing 4–2, but we really stuck together in that game and we were fired up going forward. We ended up going 7–2 over our last nine games while Virginia went 1–7–1. We made it into the post season with an unimpressive 27–32–1 record, three points ahead of Virginia.

Unfortunately, Mr. Baker didn't make good on his quasi-promise of bringing me back if we made the playoffs. I was to remain on injured reserve. When Knoxville found out about this they inquired if they could "borrow" me for what they knew would be a physical first-round war against the tough Johnstown Chiefs. Furthermore, Knoxville agreed to return me if the T-Birds made it past their first-round series against the regular-season champion Erie Panthers.

The league approved the move and some of my teammates encouraged me to leave for the extra money I would make. They also said I could help them out in the long run by beating the shit out of Johnstown's star players, either injuring them for the championship series or by helping third-place Knoxville win the series outright, as the Thunderbirds figured they'd have better luck in a final series against Knoxville than Johnstown.

I thought about it. I would be playing, and Knoxville certainly had a better chance to advance to the championship round than the Thunderbirds. But these were my Thunderbirds, my teammates and now my friends. I felt a part of the team even if I wasn't dressing, and I didn't want to play for a group of strangers, so I decided to stay put whether I was needed to play or not.

Johnstown ended up beating Knoxville, as expected, but we staged a major upset over Erie to reach the championship final. After being hammered by Johnstown in the first two games and losing a handful of players to suspension, we somehow rallied to win the series 4–3 and claim the first East Coast Hockey League championship title. I didn't skate one shift in the playoffs and my name isn't included on the official championship roster. I didn't even travel to Johnstown for the seventh and deciding game.

When I look back now, I realize I made a mistake. I should have gone to Knoxville and played. The penalty-minute totals in those playoff games were absurd, and I could have gone crazy and had a hell of a good time. Maybe that kind of showing would have helped me in my future pursuits. The fact is, players play. Watching from the stands or waiting by the curb for the team bus to return home should have only been my last resort.

Before the playoffs began we were told the team was to be sold, but that we were all set because a buyer was in line and we'd all be back for next season. The day before we won the championship we were told the team was in fact going bankrupt and would fold.

The day after we won the championship the captains held a team meeting to determine who would receive championship rings and a share of playoff money. Guys who didn't play much during the regular season because of injuries were singled out and debated over. There were also players in question who were traded or released late in the year.

There were some hard feelings at that meeting. My name was brought up because I didn't play during the post season. I felt dejected but had nothing to say because I understood the reasoning. But all three captains, Jay Fraser, John Torchetti, and Michel Lanouette, argued on my behalf. They reminded everyone I was with the team for most of the season and that I did all the dirty work. They pointed out that I had a chance to make more money playing for Knoxville during the playoffs but declined in order to stay with the Thunderbirds. My name was quickly put back into the ring hat, but I wasn't awarded a share of playoff money.

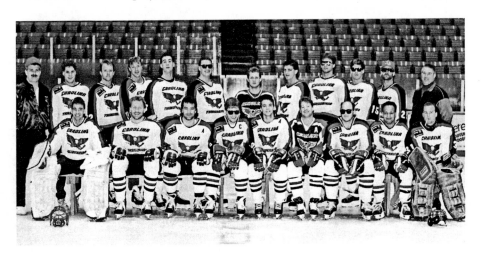

The laid-back Riley Cup Champion Thunderbirds (I am fifth from left in the top row).

Before I left for home the team announced to the public that it would sell off our home and away game jerseys. The team's equipment manager told me that of the 100 or so applicants for the shirts, 60 wanted mine. I decided to buy my own, $200 for the pair. I kept my home jersey with my last name on the back and gave Gator the road shirt.

I received my championship ring in the mail during the summer. It was a thick gold band with a large black onyx stone embossed with our Thunderbirds team logo. On one side of the band is my number, 19, and on the other is my printed last name. I wore that ring to bed for a month, and to this day it's my most prized possession. I say that with absolutely no hesitation. When I think of where I had been the year before—the dream, the fantasy, and then to wear a championship ring—it's ridiculous. Many years later, when my story was being adapted and filmed as a movie, GOON screenwriter, producer, and co-star Jay Baruchel was quoted as saying that while my story was true, it was too Hollywood and nobody would believe it. I suppose that stands as a compliment.

The Thunderbirds ended up staving off bankruptcy and came back for a second season, with new jerseys. Chris McSorley, a high-level minor-league toughie and brother of two-time Stanley Cup-winner Marty, was brought in for his first coaching job. He would have been a fun guy for me to play for, but I never received a letter instructing me when to report to camp or a questionnaire asking how many cups of coffee I drank.

I wasn't invited back, the team changed its name to the Winston-Salem Thunderbirds, and old pal Ron Aubrey joined the club and took my old Number 19 halfway through the season. So much for loyalty, but deep inside I knew what it was all about. I simply couldn't skate well enough, and the availability of an extra spot for me was further constrained when the league decided to trim the number of roster spots from 18 to 17 players per team—a move designed to eliminate cavemen like me from the league.

McSorley went out and grabbed a bunch of guys with AHL and IHL experience to upgrade the club. Steve Shaunessy was a tough defenseman who could play and fight. Trent Kaese, Len Soccio, and Joe Ferras came in and scored 56, 51, and 45 goals, respectively. They helped cut the team's regular-season losses in half from 32 to 16, tying Erie for first place overall in the new eight-team league, which added the Greensboro Monarchs, Hampton Roads Admirals, and Nashville Knights to the schedule.

But the re-tooled Thunderbirds didn't win the championship. McSorley was replaced mid-season by my former captain Jay Fraser, who went on to lose in the finals to Greensboro, which was owned by former T-Birds boss Bill Coffey.

What the hell, I had my 15 minutes of fame. I played in 28 games and got a ring. It was impossible to be that disappointed as I never convinced myself I actually had a career in hockey anyway. I just looked at it as a challenge, as something I could do while biding my time putting off an adult life. The Hanover Police Department wanted me to think about entering the police academy, and in the meantime I went back to work the desk at the Boys' Club, take the odd police detail, and continue to press my luck as a weekend bouncer at a local nightclub. I figured my days dropping the gloves were over, but little did I ever imagine my best hockey experiences were yet to come.

6

A Third Chance
with Johnstown

I thought I had an even chance of coming back to the Thunderbirds. I figured at least I could get another invitation to training camp. I mean, a lot had changed since I wandered onto the minor-league hockey scene the year before. I proved I could fight, and my skating had improved—if only because I had been on the ice so much with the team. The most important thing I had going for me, I had thought, was that I was no longer a complete unknown. My name was out there. Somebody would give me a shot.

I figured my hockey career was going to resume again so I continued to skate and play in games anywhere I could during the summer to improve my skills. The shoulder separation I suffered fighting Ron Aubrey at the Joe Lyons Camp in June sat me down for only a week. With a season of minor-league fighting under my belt I went back to the Pro-Am Summer League, but this time around I wasn't so interested in fighting. While I played very aggressive and was still viewed by the other players as a jerk and definitely a guy to steer clear of, for the first time in my life I played hockey looking to improve upon other aspects of the game.

I also skated every morning with Commander, and one of the regulars who joined us during the open-ice practice sessions was Link Gaetz, who was coming off a stint with the Minnesota North Stars and spending the summer on Cape Cod as a guest of a Boston Bruins player.

Gaetz was a well-known and successful, if not notorious, goon in juniors and the minor leagues before he laced them up with the North Stars. The "Missing Link" Gaetz stories are many, and most come from reliable if not impressive sources, including a great little tale written by Bryant Urstadt for *ESPN The Magazine*, where Nick Fotiu, who logged 914 games in the NHL and WHA over 14 years, said Gaetz had the talent to have been one of the top-10 defensemen in the NHL. In another interview, Fotiu was also quoted as saying that Gaetz was "the scariest hockey player there ever was."[1] When somebody with the fistic reputation of Nick Fotiu says something of this magnitude, it's difficult to ignore.

My favorite quip came from former Minnesota North Stars General Manager Lou Nanne, who was instrumental in drafting Gaetz in the second round of the NHL draft back in 1988. Gaetz was in attendance for the draft sporting two black eyes, supposedly from a bar fight the night before. Nanne said, "In the first round we drafted Mike Modano to protect the franchise. In the second round we drafted Link to protect Mike. In the third round we should've drafted a lawyer to protect Link."[2]

Assaults, drunk-driving arrests, and destruction of private property aside, it may have been his role as a passenger in an April 1992 car accident that finally did in Gaetz. He was thrown from a car driven by a drunk friend and suffered an injury to his brain stem, which left him semi-comatose for a week and partially paralyzed for a time. He recovered enough to attempt an NHL comeback, but his motor skills were hindered and his substance abuse issues were still alive and well. A later DUI arrest basically sent him packing and he became a Ron Aubrey–like figure, wandering around the minors and anywhere else he could to make a buck fighting on skates for the better part of two decades.

Hopping from sunny Mexico City to West Palm Beach, through wintry Cape Breton and Anchorage, Alaska, he roamed the hemisphere until the end was ushered in during the 2005 season in the Quebec Senior League, when he changed out of uniform during a game to get a hamburger at a concession stand. How beautiful an ending is that? There was a bit more, however, as a little later he put on skates once again for the pay-per-view "Battle of the Hockey Enforcers." In this sad epilogue, the once feared NHL heavyweight title contender was knocked down twice during a first-round defeat.

Before becoming fully engulfed in his well-chronicled troubles, Gaetz was a big, muscular, bear of a kid who showed me just how far removed I was from the NHL. He would give me a head start for a race from end to end with him skating backward. Even with that setup I didn't find him beating me by a mile any big accomplishment, but he raced Commander in the same manner and beat him, too. Gaetz eventually left us for training camp, short-lived NHL stardom, and as many would agree, a real-life nightmare.

During this time I was also introduced to player-agent Brian Cook. He was a rink rat like me and hung around any sheet of ice where potential clients could be found to fill his player stable. While I was enthused at the prospect of coming back to the Thunderbirds, I wasn't 100 percent sold on a return so I asked Cook that if he heard of any club in need of a fighter to get in touch with me. He said he would.

Near the end of August, Cook invited me to participate in a one-day hockey fight clinic he set up at a nearby rink for his clients who were getting ready to leave for various training camps. The guest instructor was Boston native and former NHL referee Paul Stewart, a local hockey hero of mine.

As a player, Stewart went from playing hockey at a prestigious prep school and then in the Ivy League, to literally fist-fighting his way up from the lowest rung of minor-league hockey all the way to the WHA and then the NHL, where he played 21 games for the Quebec Nordiques during the 1979–80 season. I tried to emulate the attitude of Stewart, who accepted and proudly embraced his role as an enforcer by regarding his protection of teammates as a noble responsibility.

With Stewart as our teacher, we took over the small rink in the middle of Hingham's Pilgrim Arena that was used for curling, and in front of passing groups of startled hockey moms, we worked on such professional ice hockey skills as the most effective grips on a jersey, skate leverage, and punching and blocking technique. We practiced various stick and glove dropping options, as well as the fine art of wrestling for position in order to switch punching hands. After receiving my championship ring, this preposterous fight camp stood as the highlight of my summer.

Of course I never received an invitation back to the Thunderbirds. The East Coast League was growing in size and stature. Three new teams joined the ranks and the league was gaining more attention from the NHL, which had a growing interest in using the circuit as a second-tier feeder system behind the American and International Leagues.

In the past, the old Eastern League and all of its incarnations attempted to attract fans by offering wild entertainment in a carnival-like atmosphere complete with bench-clearing brawls and the cultivation of legendary wild men. But the young ECHL decided it was going to divert from that path of destruction during its sophomore year and instead try to become more of a developmental league for rising talent. The last thing the Thunderbirds or the league as a whole needed was a raw-skilled knucklehead like me further tarnishing their image.

As I contemplated my next move as an adult in the real world, I managed the Boys' Club while training to become a cop. However, near the end of that second ECHL season, the Johnstown Chiefs, who had grabbed an affiliation with the Boston Bruins, found themselves hovering around last place and lacking in the tough-guy department. Big Brock Kelly had been traded and Rick Boyd, whom I missed out fighting the previous year when he left the Chiefs for work in the International League, had returned to the team only to be called away to the Maine Mariners, the Bruins' top farm club in the American League.

Word got around to the agents that Johnstown was looking for somebody to come in and help out on short notice. True to his word, Brian Cook called and said the Chiefs wanted me for a home game on Wednesday and a three-game road trip over the weekend. Nothing was promised after that, but I didn't care and jumped at the chance.

The opportunity came out of the blue and worked like a pair of electric paddles on my hockey heart, which had been pretty much left for dead. Not only was my improbable hockey experiment shocked back to life, but Steve Carlson was the Chiefs' coach, and the anticipation of meeting that legendary figure made the 550-mile drive in my car to Johnstown much more bearable.

Carlson had been a well-traveled minor-leaguer who logged some time in the WHA before playing one season in the NHL with the Los Angeles Kings. But his big claim to fame was a featured role in the movie *Slap Shot*, where he played one of the Hanson Brothers. The child-like, fun-loving, psychopathic Hanson characters were based on Steve and his two brothers, Jeff and Jack, who teamed up for a number of years playing together as a terrifying trio throughout North America.

I met Steve in his office at the Chiefs' rink, the aptly named War Memorial. His walls were decked out with photos of him and his brothers from their playing days and the movie. He must have thought I needed a chiropractor the way my head was swiveling from side to side, checking everything out. After he had talked for a while I interrupted him and said, "You'll have to repeat everything you said over the last 10 minutes because I've been staring at all your pictures and didn't hear a word."

Carlson laughed. He told me he knew what I was all about, that I wasn't a very good skater but liked to fight. He basically told me it was the fighting he wanted from me, nothing else. His words were music to my ears.

I hadn't fought since the Aubrey battle during the summer, and while Paul Stewart's fight camp was fun, I didn't really learn anything there that I hadn't already adopted as standard practice. So to prepare for Johnstown I developed a ritual with Gator that I would continue to use every time I was called up to fight for a club.

At the Boys' Club I fit Gator with a pair of 12-ounce boxing gloves and had him punch me in the face. He didn't sock me hard enough to do any damage—at worst I suffered a bloody nose or lip—but I felt as though the exercise toughened my facial skin and bone structure. If nothing else I always felt prepared to fight and confident in my ability to absorb a solid punch without being rocked to La-La Land.

This kind of conditioning really had its foundation for me at a young age, sparring with my dad. When most people are clocked with a shot to the nose their eyes tend to well up with tears, which can blur vision. After being hit a hundred or so times by my dad I got used to it and my eyes stopped tearing.

I also prepped my hands for battle over the years because there is no more useless injury for a fighter than a broken hand. The old-timers taught me early on during my amateur boxing days how to strengthen my hands and wrists, and for years I pounded a bucket of sand hours at a time while watching television to thicken my tissue and bones. The karate instructors at the Boys' Club had me punch a block of wood they secured to a wall—100 shots with each hand every day. Over time the little strings of muscle and connective tissue intertwined about the hand bones grew thick, and the skin over the knuckles turned leathery. I swear that even the bones become larger and stronger. With all the shots I've connected with over years on the ice and off, I've only busted a few knuckles and never sustained a boxer's fracture. I never had to wear a cast, and that's a testament to my varied hand training.

Hand injuries are also avoided by knowing the proper way to throw a punch, which I did. Most people throw roundhouse shots during the heat of battle, and that makes sense because it's the easiest, laziest, most unconscious way for an untrained person to throw a punch during the frenzy of a real fight. But the most effective and safest punches for a fighter to throw come from a tight body, with the fist starting out about six inches from the shoulder and snapped out straight with as much of the back, hips, and legs utilized for ultimate speed and power. The entire body literally stands behind as a supportive superstructure for the relatively small hand.

My first game for the Chiefs was against the Virginia Lancers, and I intended to give my hands a workout halfway through the first period when I challenged my old friend Greg Neish before a face-off. Neish didn't want to go, and I chased him around a little until a line change brought Mike Black out near me. I challenged him and he wouldn't fight, either.

Bill Whitfield: "Some coaches would say, 'Stay away from Smith, he's not hurting us.' Other coaches would send somebody out for him. It depended on the flow of the game. But in general, unless it was necessary, you didn't want to fight him. The Number One thing was you didn't want to get hit by him."

Throughout the first period another old dancing partner of mine, Darren Miciak, was causing mayhem. He was running around banging guys, sticking them, creating havoc and generally disrupting the flow of the game. I liked Miciak. He was rough around the edges and personable. He was a lot like me in that he wasn't a particularly skilled player and was also struggling to find a place for himself in pro hockey. When Miciak had been let go by the Erie Panthers, coach Ron Hansis told him, only half kidding, that he could keep him around to drive the team bus.

Grant Ottenbreit, Miciak's roommate in Erie: "Darren thought about it. He thought about turning it into a Hollywood story. He'd be driving the bus and all of a sudden the team would need him to play and he'd become the hero."

Miciak had already stumbled through 30 penalty-riddled games with the Knoxville Cherokees and Hampton Roads Admirals before I caught up with him during his two-game stint with Virginia. We shared some small talk in the rink before the game. We didn't talk much about hockey, but we both knew why we were there and it was left unspoken that we'd probably end up fighting each other.

On my second shift I challenged Miciak off a face-off. I tapped him with my stick behind his legs, backed off and squared myself with him, but he just skated away. I chased after him a bit and cross-checked him lightly but he didn't pay me any mind.

Miciak ignored me, so I was a little perturbed when he goaded one of our better defensemen, Chicago Black Hawks draft pick Dan Williams, into a fight late in the first period. I challenged Miciak again in the second period and was ignored again. I chased him all over the ice and eventually tripped him, receiving a minor penalty that Virginia capitalized on with a power play goal for a 2–1 lead.

After the goal was scored I figured that Carlson hated me and was thinking, "Boy, just what we needed, and what a mistake I made bringing this bonehead to Johnstown." But when Miciak continued hacking away at my teammates on his next shift, Carlson told me to jump over the boards. This time it didn't matter what Miciak wanted to do, he was going to have himself a fight.

Miciak: "Doug came after me every fucking game. He nailed me with probably the hardest punch I've ever been hit with. We were going at it pretty good in Erie, both of us were throwing punches when he caught me flush.

"He hadn't played in a while when he was brought in to Johnstown, but everybody knew about Doug, how he was. My coach told me not to fight him—'Don't fight him because he can't play,' he said. Plus, I had gotten into some trouble with misconducts while I was with Hampton Roads, and I had to be careful or I'd be suspended. Doug came up to me at center ice and said, 'Hey Meesh, want to go?' I told him I couldn't and skated away, but he kept bugging me down the ice."

When Miciak said he didn't want to fight for the second time I floated to my position high on the right wing in our end. One of my defensemen fired the puck around the boards to me, and out of the corner of my eye I noticed Miciak bearing in. Later on while watching the videotape of the game it appeared as though Miciak was merely skating in to check me, but I dropped my gloves and stick and immediately began to pound on him.

Miciak's helmet came off during our initial contact and he had obviously been taken by surprise because he still had his gloves on. He bent over and covered his face while I whaled on him with uppercuts and overhand noggin' knockers.

The beating looked worse than it really was. I didn't hurt Miciak, and I didn't feel bad about getting the jump on him—at the time. I figured we were both on the ice for the same purpose, he knew it and I knew it. When I looked up and saw him coming at me it wasn't for a pat on the ass; it was as good an invitation to fight as I needed.

> **Miciak:** "It was embarrassing, I couldn't fight. But I wasn't angry with Doug. I respected him. He had a job to do. He did what I did."

When I came to my senses and realized Miciak wasn't fighting back I stopped punching and simply held him down. Then, moments after an official pulled me away from Miciak, his teammate, Toronto Maple Leaf's draft pick Scott Taylor, came in after me. Taylor charged in with his stick raised high into my face, but he would've done better to drop his gloves and fire punches. Instead I grabbed him and rifled off three straight rights to his face before a pair of refs moved in to save him, too.

I received five minutes for fighting, a 10-minute misconduct, and a game misconduct for my efforts. Taylor, a good hockey player, was also lost for the balance of the game so it was a solid win all-around for the Chiefs. Coupled with my earlier tripping penalty, I was off to a great start with 17 penalty minutes in my first game. I hardly noticed we lost, 3–2.

I bumped into Miciak at the rink after the game. Of all the fights I had or would later get into, to this day it remains the one that bothers me the most, as I did come to feel, pretty quickly, that I jumped him a bit, and that was just not my way of doing things. I explained to Miciak that I thought he was coming after me and apologized for not giving him more of a fair shake. He was such a great guy, and I had a lot of respect for him, and I told him that.

While in Johnstown I shared a room for a couple nights with Shawn Byram, a 6-foot-3, 220-pound specimen out of the Western Hockey League where he played juniors before being drafted pretty high by the New York

Islanders. He actually ended up playing four games for the Islanders late the next year after tearing it up in the American League. But he didn't care about being down in this league. He was making good money working off an American League contract, and in the short time I was with him all he wanted to do was look for women.

It seemed that getting laid was the top priority for many of the kids I played with or against, and I suppose if I was in their shoes I would've been a whore myself. Not that I was looking for a medal of virtue, as I certainly enjoyed the comforts of a pretty girl as much as the next guy, it's just that I wasn't secure enough in my hockey role to drift off socially.

During my longer stint with the Thunderbirds, after early practices I did what many of my teammates did, which was kill the rest of the day shooting pool, playing golf, and chasing around the various skirts we had designs on. But because hockey was such a new experience for me, and I was never fully cemented with a job, I couldn't afford to concentrate only part-time on my game and go too girl crazy.

Unlike me, most of the other guys knew were they stood with the team. They had either already taken their shots at higher leagues or come to the realization that the East Coast was the end of the hockey road for them. They were content being good enough players for where they landed and were going to experience everything the minor-pro game had to offer—and that certainly included attractive, agreeable woman.

I am certainly not the first one to notice that young, good-looking male athletes in great shape have a relatively easy time getting girls. Those guys were usually the most popular kids in high school, and I'm sure in college as well. I can only imagine what the addition of hundreds of thousands or millions of dollars does to improve upon the situation.

The social scene at the higher levels of pro sports is something I can only imagine. If I can believe the stories some of my NHL acquaintances have told me, off nights in the NHL can mimic the best and worst of what Sodom and Gomorra had to offer, with episodes of such wanton excess unimaginable except maybe to devout readers of the *Penthouse Forum*. Said one veteran NHLer, "You're in a Chicago bar wearing an Armani suit and the women are lined up, pointing you out. They don't even know who you are in particular, they don't care, just that you're a hockey player."

The experience I had in the low minors certainly lacked the money part of the female equation, but I recognized that a hockey player could have an easier time of it than a lot of ordinary Joes working the pick-up scene. There are many wide-eyed kids out there playing professional sports and experiencing all that comes with running wild and free. Some are looking for it, some just find themselves out with the other boys and all of a sudden "stuff" happens. Some of the stuff in Winston-Salem included threesomes, a kid's first dalliance with a married women, a lily white kid bouncing off the walls because he had sex with a black girl for the first time, and a 22-year-old's wild encounter with an uninhibited 45-year-old cougar. None of it added anything new or special to the annals of human experience, it was just that the sporting lifestyle, maybe the *irresponsibility* of it all, magnified the sexual interactions and awakenings for some of us.

While I'm sure some of the female groupies at the NHL level are 10's, a pretty girl is a pretty girl and the ECHL had its full share. I admit that I am certainly not a cosmopolitan man, but my God, those Southern girls in Winston-Salem were the prettiest pack of women I have ever seen in any one place in all my life.

I shook my head witnessing too many ugly hockey players on the road to nowhere have meaningless relations with good-looking women. There remains no secret behind their conquests. I mean, look at rocker Mick Jagger. He was never a physically attractive guy but he was always getting beautiful women in his day—and probably still today. Is it because he is witty, has great pick-up lines, irresistible charm? I doubt it. He capitalizes on his celebrity, and so did we, albeit on a much smaller stage.

I don't want to totally knock women, either, because many men are guilty of playing the hero-worship game as well. And I don't just refer to the guy making a fool of himself fawning over players from behind the fence of the players' parking lot, or a 50-year-old battling in a crowded sea of children alternately begging and profusely thanking a 19-year-old Alex Rodriguez for his autograph—"Thank you *Mr.* Rodriguez, thank you *Mr.* Rodriguez." Hell, just take those full-of-themselves ESPN guys who play it cool on their telecasts giving shit to athletes, demeaning them and poking fun while showcasing them screwing up in a highlight film. But when they get one-on-one with an athlete everything changes—their tone, demeanor, and attitude. They turn into soft, sweet, ass-kissing butter.

A very few times a media type will grow some balls and challenge an athlete. What usually happens next is beautiful, and a couple of instances stick out in my mind. One was when John Stossell of the television show *20/20* aggravated pro wrestler Dave Schultz by asking him on national television if his livelihood was fake. This is akin to asking a guy if his daughter is a whore. What followed was an embarrassing moment fit for a pencil-neck like Stossell, who was merely slapped on either ear by Schultz and collapsed to the floor for an eight-count both times.[3] He went down as if he were shot with a gun. What a pussy.

Then there was tough-talking Jim Rome, who on his ESPN show delighted in calling NFL quarterback Jim Everett "Chris" in clear reference to the female tennis player, Chris Everett. After being called "Chris" twice, Everett warned Rome not to do it a third time. Rome pushed the envelope a third time and Everett manhandled the girlish Rome like a lion on a baby wildebeest.[4] It is so heartwarming to see people get what they deserve.

*   *   *

We traveled to Knoxville for a Friday night game and I was told they had a big black kid from Canada on the team. His name was Darren Banks, a sturdy 6-foot-2, 230-pounder who was putting together a pretty impressive season scoring goals and fighting. He was definitely my man. I challenged him the first moment we met on the ice but he wouldn't fight. I didn't know what his problem was, but I had become used to his act from the second part of my season with the Thunderbirds when a lot of tough guys stopped fighting me.

Banksy had a big mop of Brillo Pad hair and the first thing that came across my mind when I saw him was that he looked like the character Buckwheat from the *Little Rascals* movie shorts. When he wouldn't fight me I pushed him and said, "Come on Buckwheat, let's go!" I didn't mean anything racial, and if he looked like Shemp Howard of the *Three Stooges* I would have called him "Shemp" instead. The way the politically correct crowd operates, if I said that in a game today the liberal thought police might want me in jail for a hate crime.

Even so, Banks did have a tough time playing hockey in a league primarily situated south of the Mason-Dixon Line.

> **Brock Kelly:** "I can't believe some of the things guys are getting in trouble for saying in the game today. I think back to the things that were said when I was playing. I felt sorry for Banksy, he took a lot of crap. When he came to Nashville to play against us some fans would hang a basketball net up behind the goal and they'd yell, 'Shoot it up here, Nigger.' The Canadian boys weren't too cool about it. We didn't grow up with that. But that's the South, I guess. Maybe it will never change."

Banks and I ended up pushing and shoving, and we didn't stop when the referees came in to separate us. Our efforts were rewarded with unsportsmanlike conduct and misconduct penalties, which pushed my two-game tally up to 29 minutes. Oh yes, we lost that game, too, 10–6.

All in all I've got to give Banks credit. While I wasn't impressed with his act in Knoxville, a few years later he managed to fight his way to the NHL with the Boston Bruins. Great for him—I'm just glad he didn't get there using me as one of his whipping boys.

Our next game on Saturday night was only a hop, skip, and jump away against one of the three new teams in the league, the Nashville Knights. None of the games made me more excited than this one. Troy Crowder, one of the NHL's premier fighters with the New Jersey Devils, had been sent to Nashville on a rehabilitation assignment and was actually dropping the gloves down here. Unfortunately, Crowder had been brought back up to the Devils earlier in the afternoon and went on to fight Toronto's John Kordic in a game later that evening. I was crushed.

> **Grant Ottenbreit:** "I'll never forget the kid. I heard he was close to tears in his locker room because he missed out on a chance to fight Troy Crowder. I guess he was one of his heroes. I don't blame him. Crowder was one of the biggest fighters in the NHL at the time."

In place of Crowder I was left with Brock Kelly, the 6-foot-4, 205-pound block of granite whom I fought three times the year before. Kelly had been traded to Nashville after becoming a fighting fixture for the Johnstown Chiefs.

Nashville was coached by Archie Henderson, one of the giants of the minor-league world of hooliganism. My pal Commander had long since told me stories about his on-ice battles with the legendary Archie Henderson, who was rewarded for his many years of fighting in the minors with 23 games in the NHL.

When I stepped onto the ice for warm-ups I made a beeline for Nashville's bench to meet Henderson. He looked as I expected—tall and gangly with long arms and a big head. He had wide, crazy eyes and a face broken and scarred by a thousand or so punches. I bet he didn't have nearly the same damage on his face that he had inflicted on others during the 11 years he terrorized the minor leagues. I introduced myself and mentioned my kinship with Commander. In a low, bear-like voice that sounded as if it were bellowing from a cave, Henderson said with a smile, "Ahhh, the Commander. What brings you here, son?"

"I'm here to fight your boy, Brock Kelly," I answered.

Archie smiled again and offered a friendly warning. "Son, you don't want to do that. You'd do best to leave him be."

I smiled back. "Oh, me and Brock are old friends, you ask him. Don't worry about me."

With that I said my goodbye and waited for my chance to fight the big guy.

I didn't know much about Brock the first time I fought him. He went crazy the year before with Johnstown in the All-American League, and everybody I knew who had played against him tried to give me a critique of his fighting style. But a lot of times, especially against a legitimate monster like Brock, unless you've actually fought the guy yourself you don't *really* know what to expect.

Brock was a weird-looking guy with thin, slithery eyes. He looked like he was always squinting—that is, until he fought. When Brock Kelly dropped his gloves, for some reason those thin eyes popped open big and wide and he never blinked. I have punched him flush in the face and his eyes always remained wide open. When the fight was over his eyes went back to squinting, as if he needed glasses. I also wasn't aware just how strong Brock was the first time we fought my rookie year, so he was able to straighten me out with his long left arm and pummel me with rights.

> **Brock Kelly:** "Doug wasn't very good on his skates. You could get him by pulling him off balance. I was 6-foot-4, I could hold guys out and go toe-to-toe. But I didn't like the 5-foot-10 guys who were three-feet wide. They would put their head into my chest to start out and hit above their head. They wouldn't even look up, just keep switching hands, and unless I could get them out there it wouldn't be much of a fight for me."

I wasn't bothered too much that Brock got the better of me the first time we fought. For one thing, he was no slouch, and for another thing, I'd been beaten up before and I knew I would probably lose again somewhere along the line. One of my strong points as a fighter was that I actually enjoyed fighting. That may read strange, but it was a characteristic that set me apart from many other hockey enforcers at all levels.

Most kids who start out playing hockey don't set as their goal to become the next Dave Schultz; they want to be the next Wayne Gretzky or Sydney Crosby. In my day every kid aspired to be Bobby Orr, whistling past opponents and pirouetting around a defender before firing a laser beam into the far low corner. When I put on my first pair of skates at 19, I wanted to be Dave Schultz.

I also loved rematches. If I lost a fight you'd be sure I'd be back for a second try—10 rematches if need be. That may be why a lot of my opponents got sick of me. I could never get enough, I was never satisfied, and I'd never go away. Then again, a scorer wouldn't be totally satisfied with one goal because two were better, and as far as I was concerned, two fights were better than one.

The second time I fought Brock I pulled him close and didn't allow him the opportunity to string me out and lock his arm. I clocked him good with a couple of overhand shots and wrestled him to the ice. Our third fight was more of a dead-even wrestling match. I figured we were 1–1–1 against each other and I looked at this fourth opportunity in Nashville as the rubber match.

He was playing defense and I cross-checked him in front of his net. The whistle blew and we stared at each other. I dangled my gloves by my side, feigning to drop them and said, "Let's go."

Brock backed off a bit and mimed our first fight together. He lazily reached out with his left glove as if he were grabbing hold of my sweater, and in slow motion he made a long, buggy-whipping motion with his right.

He had certainly talked with Archie Henderson, but Brock didn't need a heads-up from his coach to know why I was on the ice with him. I knew he wasn't afraid of me; he just wasn't interested in fighting because there was no particular need at that point in the game, so he was trying to embarrass me in front of the home-town crowd.

"Yah, you forget what happened in the second fight don't you, you piece of shit," I barked.

But he had me. He had it all planned out and he showed me up in his home rink. That was all right, though, because all Brock did was pass on to me a lesson that was taught to him.

> **Brock Kelly:** "When I was in camp with the Philadelphia Flyers, Dave Brown was their big guy and I chased him from one end of the ice to the other. I dropped my gloves and he just flicked his hand at me as if to say, 'Get out of here kid.' For the first time I didn't know what to do or how to act. I thought, 'Should I just attack him?' But I didn't do anything."

That was my final game for the Johnstown Chiefs. I didn't dress for the Sunday game in Knoxville, didn't get another chance to challenge Darren Banks. The Chiefs were out of the playoff picture and they didn't need to finish out the remaining eight games with me drawing out any more money. Steve Carlson told me I did a good job, that I did everything he expected and that I wasn't as bad a skater as people had told him. He shook my hand and wished me luck.

I had to get through a court date first, and then the disappointment of being cut from a team I thought I made out of training camp, but lady luck was still very much on my side.

7

My Second
Training Camp

My three-game taste with the Johnstown Chiefs gave me a hint that I could continue playing, even if it meant traveling around as a vagabond to pick up odd games here or there, whenever or wherever a team needed a fighter to help out on short notice.

I patched together a video clip of my fights and typed a brief resume to send out to all of the minor-league hockey clubs in operation. I figured, what the hell, I wasn't looking for a contract and I wouldn't cost much money. I could be used as a stopgap for a week or weekend's worth of games. It seemed I had nothing to lose in that scenario, but I found out I had a lot to lose on the local rinks.

I continued to play in the summer Pro-Am League on Thursday nights and skated shinny hockey every morning in Quincy. Summer shinny was packed with friends of mine from the East Coast League and other guys I became acquainted with from the higher minor leagues who skated to stay in shape. A few NHLers were regulars, as were a number of local boys who had played high school or college hockey.

While I continued to play my rough-and-tumble game in the Pro-Am, there were no officials present to monitor shinny hockey, and even a guy like me who was always looking for a rumble didn't fight during shinny. It was basically indoor pond hockey made up of a group of fellows who paid $5 a head for an easy-going skate.

During one particular session a local firefighter showed up on his off day. He was a good-sized guy about my age who was playing as if scouts, reporters, and a television crew filled the empty stands. It is important to reiterate that nobody body checked anyone during shinny hockey; the roughest scene would be a push—not even a shove, but a push. This idiot was running around chopping at guys, shoving, knocking people down, and he was doing it to me as well.

It was obvious to me that this guy had heard through the grapevine that I was some kind of half-assed minor-league tough guy and he wanted to try me out. The situation clued me into what Lyndon Byers must have been thinking when I challenged him to fight during the warm-up before a Pro-Am game a few years before. It is an old scenario that was played out 150 years ago in the Old West, when the young bucks came out of the woodwork to challenge the fastest gun in town.

The fireman slashed me one too many times and I dropped my gloves. He was game and immediately followed my lead because this was exactly what he wanted. The fight didn't last long. He may have been a tough guy in high school, he may have been a tough guy in the barroom, and he may have been the toughest guy on his hook 'n' ladder, but I turned him into just another chip of ice in short time. In fact, I did such a good job that he finished the rest of shinny time in the local hospital emergency room.

I thought that was the end of it; I mean, two guys agree to fight and may the best man win, right? That was the way I was used to doing it on the ice, but this piece of shit fireman lost the fight he started, embarrassed himself, and then decided to sue me. In my younger days I would've tracked him down and given him another beating; maybe lynch him up on the flagpole in front of his station. But I was a special police officer in Hanover now, working details and lining myself up for a full-time position, so I had to behave myself.

The mess dragged through the courts for a few months. In the end I was hit with his hospital bills, a few hundred bucks for some bridge work. At least I never saw him again at shinny hockey.

But there was some good news. Trusty player agent Brian Cook set up a tryout for me in the fall with a new team in the East Coast League, the Cincinnati Cyclones. Cook was certainly a man of his word. I asked him to keep his eyes and ears open for any work for me, and not only did he come through time and again, but he never took one cent from me. I would also be among some friendly faces in the Cincinnati camp as Mike Chighisola, some of my old Thunderbirds teammates, a few guys from Johnstown, and even some skaters from shinny hockey were going to be there as well.

Again, the ECHL held its tryouts after all the higher leagues were finished with theirs in order to have an opportunity to grab the cut players. I drove my car to Cincinnati, Ohio, in time for the first day of tryouts, Saturday, October 13. The Cyclones' home arena didn't have its ice ready, so we had to use the nearby Xavier University's Northland Ice Arena for our first skate. We were also told that we'd have to venture over the border into Kentucky to use the Alpine Ice Arena on Sunday for our double-session. "Here we go again," I thought. This was shaping up to be like my first training camp with the Thunderbirds—another cheap, start-up operation. But I was dead wrong.

In the Xavier University rink we all had our own stalls in a carpeted locker room. The Cyclones even supplied us all with matching equipment so everyone would be wearing the same style and color pants, socks, and gloves. We were also given sharp training camp jerseys emblazoned with the Cyclones' logo—a far cry from the pullovers we wore at the Thunderbirds' camp, which looked as though they were scoffed from a high school gym class.

Things were definitely looking up in this, the third year of the ECHL. The Thunderbirds' camp encompassed just three days—two days of tryouts and one exhibition game. In Cincinnati, our first of two preseason games was scheduled for the sixth day of camp. Yes, things were looking more professional here, and I was looking better, too. People in camp were telling me that I skated well for a big guy. Two years ago nobody could have gotten away with saying that to me because it would have been such an obvious lie I would've taken it as a personal insult and would want to fight the wise guy.

My skating was greatly improved—for me—as it should've been because I'd been skating hard for at least five days a week for two straight years. Now I felt I could show a coach I could play. I still didn't have a clue what to do with the puck during the heat of a game, but at least I could somewhat keep up and not look, too much, like a fish out of water.

I also knew what I had to do in camp to win a spot on the team, and I didn't need Gator around to prod me into doing it this time around. I had a fight the first day of camp, and afterward the Cyclones' coach and director of hockey operations, Dennis Desrosiers, took me aside and said, "Smitty, you don't have to fight, I know why you're here, I know what you can do, save it for the exhibition games."

Holy shit, I could hardly believe it. Desrosiers basically told me I wasn't going to be an early cut because I was already slotted to play in the exhibition games. He lifted a world of pressure off my shoulders.

In any case, the biggest threat to my position on the team seemed to be Steve Shaunessy, a 6-foot-4, 220-pound monster from the Boston area who was drafted by the Pittsburgh Penguins out of Boston University. Shaunessy had played in the higher International League before slipping down to the East Coast, where he went nuts with my old Thunderbirds team in an attempt to reestablish himself as a solid defenseman and enforcer. He was in Cincinnati to give his career another jump-start and continue his quest to follow in the footsteps of his brother, Scott, who fought his way to an NHL cup of coffee with the Quebec Nordiques.

While Shaunessy stood as the man to beat, he was also probably the best defenseman in camp and a crown jewel for the club, which created less tension between us. In any other situation he would be the guy I'd have to target and challenge to win a job, but his wasn't mine to take. He kept telling me I was going to make the team; that it was going to be him on defense and me out at forward, the two tough guys kicking ass.

It all made sense. Shaunessy was another one of those players who probably didn't belong in this league. I figured that Desrosiers would want to keep Shaunessy playing on the ice, and if he needed to throw somebody to the wolves it might as well be me because I wasn't any more valuable than a chunk of raw meat.

Desrosiers' instructions and Shaunessy's assurances made me feel as though I was getting a free pass through training camp, and I felt confident enough to chart my place on the team. I was feeling so comfortable about my chances that I struck up a side deal with another guy trying to make the team as an enforcer, Rock Derganc, the tough winger whom I had my best fight against during my first year with the Thunderbirds.

Rock and I agreed not to fight each other during camp unless we absolutely had to. Of course Rock didn't know what the coach had told me earlier after my fight the first day. We made a stipulation that if the enforcer job came down to just one of us making the team we'd both fight Shaunessy because he was the headliner.

> **Rock Derganc:** "I knew Dougie, he did the same thing I did and we had respect for each other. I had two fights in camp and I fought the big guy, Shaunessy, because I didn't know him too well."

Derganc was cut loose before the exhibition games. He certainly had more hockey skill than I did, and I can't really say I was that much better a fighter than he was, but I think I may have had a better reputation as an enforcer. I was also about three inches taller and 20 pounds heavier, and in a choice between two guys with equal attributes, size does matter in this game.

Even so I felt bad for Rock because we were in the same boat. We both knew the only chance we had of playing pro hockey was to fight. He was going to keep plugging away, drifting from rink to rink, punch some faces, get his face punched, and see what happened. I shook his hand and said my goodbyes. Never in a million years would I have imagined where I'd end up fighting him the next time we met.

The Cyclones opened camp with 38 players and six were gone before the exhibition games. While I counted on the promise from Desrosiers that

I would play in at least one of the preseason games, I didn't think I would dress for both. I also couldn't believe some of the guys I was dressing in front of. There was one kid, Joe Burton, a little 23-year-old American-born center out of the University of Michigan–Dearborn. He had talent and finesse, and he wasn't playing. I tried to convince myself that maybe he already had plans to play somewhere else, or that he was so good that the coaches didn't need to see him anymore and that the training camp games were for guys the coaches weren't sure of, like me.

I don't know, maybe it was his decision, but Burton ended up leaving to play the year in Europe. He came back to the States later to skate in the new Central Hockey League, which wasn't that much different in the talent department than the ECHL. He went on to become a legend there, scoring 35, 32, 59, 66, 53, 74, 73, and 40 goals, respectively, during a ridiculously productive minor-league career.

While I never played high school or college sports, my little taste of professional hockey taught me that not all of the most-talented players in a tryout fill all of the available roster spots. Later on, after coaching high school hockey, I became somewhat adept at picking out the top players; it was no problem pinpointing the best skaters, puck handlers, and shooters. Those were the kids we stockpiled for the high school team. But the pro game is different in that a coach must sift through the player pool and tab guys who can fill particular roles. The team couldn't simply be made up of all the best skaters and stick handlers because there would also be a need for penalty killers, a stay-at-home defenseman, a set-up guy, a defensive forward, and most important from my end, a team needed a mucker or a grinder, somebody to do the dirty work, a fighter or two.

I can imagine that quite a few talented players cut from the Cyclones left camp shaking their heads trying to figure out what was going on in the coach's mind to keep a particular guy over them. Usually it was because their nicely-shaped square peg didn't fit into the available round hole. But there was another, innocently sinister component to the tryout process that was likely rearing its head. Because the league was smartly marketing itself as a second-tier NHL breeding ground, affiliation agreements required players with NHL contracts, or contracts from their American League affiliates, to have first dibs on roster spots. In those cases it didn't matter if one guy was better than another, the guy with the NHL contract was going to stay.

I didn't worry about NHL deals; that was another world apart from me. I just knew I could fight on skates and not a lot of other guys wanted to do that sort of thing, so I was in my glory when we traveled to play a very tough Johnstown Chiefs team for our first preseason game. During warm-ups I skated over to my old coach from the previous year, Steve Carlson, to renew acquaintances. Hell, I figured maybe there would be some day down the line he may need me to come in and fight for him again.

It was a classic, minor-league preseason game with the penalties piling up early as desperate players were doing anything they could to garner some attention. I noticed right away that many of the Johnstown guys were targeting Shaunessy; it was as if he were wearing a bull's-eye, and one guy after another took a run at our big guy to try and shine a favorable light on themselves.

Bobby Goulet was the first to drop his gloves with Shaunessy, but he was outsized and outslugged. Shaunessy ended up getting five minutes for fighting, two for instigating, and another two for roughing. This gave me my first stroll on the ice since pre-game warm-ups as I was sent over to the box to serve the extra penalty.

After the Shaunessy fight, a Johnstown player quickly received a game misconduct for a vicious high stick. A few minutes later, Johnstown enforcer Rick Boyd took a heavy hit from our big defenseman, Jay Rose. Boyd, whom I filled in for the year before with the Chiefs when he was called up to the AHL, dropped his gloves and hammered Rose.

Rose was another kid from the Boston area, a wiry, six-plus-footer who was drafted by the Detroit Red Wings out of high school but smartly chose to attend Clarkson University. He played a few games in the AHL and was looking to get back into the pro ranks when he joined the Cyclones. He was game to mix it up, but he wasn't a threat to me because he was a quality player. The only thing that bothered me was that he got to fight Boyd, who should've been my man.

Halfway through the period I finally got to take my first shift—unfortunately there was absolutely nobody on the ice worthwhile to fight. But damn did I almost score a goal.

I was meandering around mid-ice when our defenseman, Boyd Lomow, rushed the puck out of our end and fired a clearing shot over our blue line that sailed a bit wide of Johnstown goalie Chris Harvey, who turned to watch it hit the backboards. Harvey, a Boston Bruins draft pick out of Brown University, was caught a bit out of position when the puck took a funny bounce off the boards and careened into the slot. I had snuck in past the brain-dead defense to find myself charging at the stationary puck and staring at the open net. At just the same time as I whipped my stick at the puck, Harvey had regrouped to poke it away as I slipped down in a heap.

I got my second shift a few minutes later with us up by a 2–1 score. There weren't any particular tough guys on the ice, but I couldn't stand my inactivity any longer so off a right-corner faceoff in Johnstown's end I socked Tony

Bobbitt in the face with a straight right. We stared at each other for a moment, we kind of squared off, but the play continued and Bobbitt skated off toward a scrum of players on the far side.

Bobbitt was probably pissed off at this point, so he rammed one of my smaller linemates into the boards during a tie-up and whistle. The hit was from behind and though not overly hard, it was definitely a message from Bobbitt and as good an invitation as I needed to attack. I came from the side and surprised him with a crosscheck to the head before quickly dropping my gloves and grabbing his jersey. Unfortunately, the officials were already on the scene and separated us before a proper fight could get underway. I was given two minutes for the cross-check and a double-minor for roughing, a nice six-minute tally in all. Bobbitt, the not-so-innocent victim, received two minutes for roughing.

Luckily Johnstown didn't score a power-play goal while I was in the box so I didn't hurt my team too much with the extra cross-checking penalty. But while I was sitting there for the balance of the first period there were four more fights, including second helpings for both Shaunessy and Rose. I was born for a game like this but everybody else was getting their hands into my cookie jar. I should have been the one taking control, taking on all comers. I knew I had to get into this action. I had to get into a fight with somebody who was game to go.

My third shift of the game was a joke. I just couldn't play. I had a few opportunities to handle the puck and I flubbed them. It was my worst nightmare. I really just showcased my ability to be of no use to the team.

But I was still in the lineup. It was 2–2 when Desrosiers sent me over the boards for a shift early in the second period to stir things up. This time 5-foot-11, 210-pound blockhead Darren Schwartz was there to greet me. I met Schwartz the year before during my three-game stint with Johnstown. At that time he was also grinding out a niche as a fighter with the Chiefs and he knew exactly why I was called in to help out. I was impressed that he didn't feel threatened and pull into a protective shell and ignore me. In fact he was the first person on the team to approach me and introduce himself.

During my experience as a player I found an amazing camaraderie among most of the tough guys. While any particular team might have 15 highly skilled and trained hockey players, there were only one or two designated fighters on each team, so we made up a small and unique club. We prepared ourselves to battle each other, but I appreciated my opponents' job because it was the same as mine. That was why I had no problem getting splattered by a guy during a game, and then hanging out with him in a bar a few hours later. Many times it's the same way during training camp between two or three guys literally fighting for the same job. We understand the challenges of the job and motivation of the other guy, and we know that nothing is personal, it's just business.

Schwartz was the type of player I would have wished to become if I'd only started skating earlier. He scored 26 goals and checked in with 270 penalty minutes during his rookie season. He ended up scoring a whopping 62 goals a few years later with my old Thunderbirds team while still logging more than 200 minutes in the penalty box. I don't care what league you're playing in, 62 goals is impressive, and Schwartz represented my definition of a complete and valuable hockey tough guy—one who could fight *and* play.

Now we found ourselves sharing the same wing, and while I don't know for sure if he knew he *had* to fight, I knew I did. I followed him for a bit and when he chased a puck along the boards I jumped him. It wasn't much of a go, but I thought I had the advantage in punches. I felt pretty strong on my skates as well, considering he was much more experienced and likely had better balance on blades. I slipped and fell to a knee near the end of the fight but got up quickly before the linesmen swarmed in to break things up. At least I got to log a fighting major against a decent opponent toward an 11-minute penalty total for the game.

The next contest was against Erie, and while Ron Aubrey was no longer there, the Panthers did have Greg Spenrath, an interesting 6-foot-3, 225-pound draft pick of the New York Rangers whom I had not tangled with before. My old pal Grant Ottenbreit was still there as well, but the flow of the game didn't allow for any of us to line up on the ice at the same time to do our thing. On top of that, I didn't receive many shifts, but I did manage to, somehow, log an assist.

Up to that point I had never played better hockey in my life than in those two exhibition games. For the first time I didn't feel totally out of place on the ice. While I was still likely the worst player on the roster, I could skate my role as an acknowledged heavyweight goon. For the first time I felt as though I belonged, or at least wasn't an eyesore, and I believed Shaunessy and another Boston-area friend, Tom Mutch, when they told me I was going to make the team. Mutch was a pretty good player and I thought he had some pull. Shaunessy had calves the size of my thighs—he was a horse and he'd fight anybody—but he wanted to play; he didn't want to waste his time on the ice fighting and he knew that I could take that burden off him.

I had practically convinced myself I was going to become a Cyclone before Desrosiers made me one of the final cuts, again. The bottom line was that with the bare-bones 17-man roster they simply couldn't afford to keep an extra guy around who couldn't be relied upon to skate a useful, regular shift.

At least when I left the Thunderbirds I knew I had little business being on the team, but I was deeply disappointed when I packed up to leave Cincinnati. It was another long-ass ride to Boston, with the only positive note being that I didn't have to bum $100 off the coach to get back home this time.

8

Delivering
with the Mailman

For a few weeks with the Cincinnati Cyclones I thought once again that my luck had turned and my time had come. I thought there actually could be a place for me in the game of pro hockey despite starting so far behind the eight ball. Instead my hopes were dashed and I was headed back home to little more than two loving parents, my sister, and one neglected girlfriend.

I made plans to enter the police academy in the spring and continued to skate out of habit as much as the necessity to stay in shape just in case my phone rang, which it did a month after returning home. It was Commander who came to my rescue.

During one of his scouting trips to New Brunswick, where the Winnipeg Jets' AHL affiliate Moncton Hawks played, Commander stumbled upon a team in a local senior league that was in need of a fighter. He said the job was mine if I wanted it. Wanted it? I didn't care if the team was based in the Amazon rain forest if it meant getting me out of Hanover with a paycheck to play hockey.

I had never heard of the Miramichi Gagnon Packers before, or the New Brunswick Senior Hockey League for that matter. I needed an education.

First, I came to learn that the term "Senior Hockey" was a misnomer, as it wasn't a collection of old-timers getting together to play glorified pickup games of shinny as the name initially led me to believe. If nothing else, my senior league experience afforded me an education to the popular scope of hockey in Canada, which seemed to sweep across every populated crevice of the country as baseball or football does in the United States.

Junior hockey in Canada takes the place of the high school hockey game that is more prevalent for that age group in the United States. Junior leagues also serve as a showcase for kids looking to attract college attention, as well as a professional hockey career primer as many players selected in the NHL's amateur draft each spring come from these circuits.

Senior hockey begins where juniors end. The Seniors are generally made up of players older than 21 who didn't go to college, weren't good enough to be drafted, or didn't want to sign a modest free-agent contract and play for a lower minor-league team a couple thousand miles away from home. The senior leagues are also stocked with retired players from all levels of the professional ranks, including dried-up minor leaguers and guys who logged a little time in the NHL. It is a place where the dinosaurs of the game can come to die with some dignity and make a few extra bucks at the same time.

National Hockey League Hall of Famer Guy Lafleur kept himself in shape with senior hockey before coming out of retirement to play three more years with the New York Rangers and Quebec Nordiques. Still other players, who find themselves at a crossroads in their careers, use the senior leagues as a holding pen between contracts.

All of the senior league teams operating throughout Canada are held together by the common goal of winning the championship of their league in order to qualify for the Allan Cup Playoffs, which aims to crown the senior amateur hockey champ of Canada. Sir H. Montague Allan donated the senior leagues' ultimate prize, the Allan Cup, shortly after the Stanley Cup became the recognized championship trophy of the professional hockey clubs. The first winner was the Ottawa Cliffsides in 1908, and except for 1945, the Allan Cup has been awarded to the best senior league team in Canada every year since.[1]

The senior league I was headed to was based about New Brunswick, which is beautiful Atlantic Canada country a good 12-hour drive north of Boston. The New Brunswick Senior Hockey League was made up of four teams that played out a 30-game regular-season schedule from late October through mid–February. A three-team, quadruple-semifinal round-robin playoff, and then best-of-seven championship final series could add another 15 games to the tally and prolong the season into March.

The teams were sponsored by local businessmen who reminded me of grown-up boys with the disposable cash to fulfill fantasies of running their own sports franchise. With the closest NHL club too far away in Montreal to service the locals, the league developed a close-knit rivalry between teams that were strategically set up in neighboring cities and towns. It was a home-brewed fix for the hard-working, middle-class and hockey-rabid residents of New Brunswick, and represented a viable, more affordable and very local entertainment option to the American Hockey League teams that also dotted the general area.

Senior hockey in Canada hinted of what baseball must have been like in the United States during the early part of the 20th century. In parts of the

U.S. too remote to be served by the Big Leagues or the minors, factories and small towns sponsored semi-pro teams and paid the best area players to stage weekend tilts that helped quench the baseball thirst of the local population.

The New Brunswick Senior League scheduled its games on or right after pay day, as we'd play two or three games a week from Thursday night through Sunday evening. I am sure the league also realized that most of its players had regular jobs, and it would be easier for them to play on the weekend than weekday, especially when it came to traveling for away games.

Each team was allowed two non–Canadian players, or "imports" as I was called. The Gagnon Packers, sponsored by local amateur sports philanthropist and crab processing company founder Edmund Gagnon, was a team that had developed the reputation of being a highly skilled but timid bunch over the years. Packers team president Dale Hicks took drastic action after the club had been slapped around a bit while starting the season a ho-hum 2–2, and his inquiries for tough guys led to Commander's phone call to me.

I drove up to the City of Miramichi in the Newcastle area of New Brunswick, which was truly God's country. The hell with hockey, if I lived there year-round I'd be fishing, hunting, and camping because it was a recreational paradise. The Miramichi River was famous for its salmon fishing, and I was told that former Red Sox great Ted Williams used to go there to fish on a regular basis. Hollywood celebrities such as Marilyn Monroe, and even United States presidents would escape to the locale for private retreats.

I spent my first night in Miramichi as the guest of Mr. Gagnon, whose immediate job was to pawn me off on one of my new teammates. Gagnon took me to the leather shop owned by the club's goalie, Dennis Roy. While we were there, Gagnon made a phone call and announced, "We got Jacques Mailhot coming in tomorrow."

"Holy shit, Jacques Mailhot!" I don't remember if I said that to myself or out loud, but it didn't matter because right then I knew senior hockey was going to be an un-fucking-believable experience.

Jacques Mailhot was one of the stars of my hockey fight video collection. I had watched him go toe-to-toe with a guy for a minute—I'm talking full-out punches flush to the face—and then abruptly stop, shake hands with his opponent, and skate to the penalty box. When the penalty was over they came out and did it all over again. I had film of him fighting Steve Shaunessy's brother in the Quebec Nordiques' training camp, and when he was called up to the Nordiques I watched him on television fight Cam Neely and Lyndon Byers in the Quebec Coliseum. Now he was going to be my teammate.

Now, everything here must be put into perspective. In general, fighters who make it to the NHL and stay long enough to make a large stain, like the

Nick Fotius, Dave Browns, and Georges Laraques of the world, do so because they are, in general, the toughest bastards around on skates. Those who go on to become "minor-league legends" generally have a deficiency that keep them from either making it to or sticking in the Big Leagues. Sometimes it may be that they lacked size or strength, had weak skating ability, poor balance, or a lack of discipline and tendency to take bad penalties. Sometimes it could be something out of a player's control, like being stuck in an organization that doesn't care to utilize him, or a coach that screws him over. But I think just as often it's that these borderline NHL enforcers were more than tough enough for the minors, but not quite so fearsome when they got their shot in the NHL, or they simply choked when given the opportunity on center stage. Jacques Mailhot built himself into one such character, and I was more in awe of him than an NHL veteran because I could more easily relate to him.

Mailhot lived the life of a journeyman enforcer I could only dream about. Born an hour outside of Quebec City in the town of Shawinigan, his favorite team while growing up was the Montreal Canadiens. When the New York Islanders began to establish their dominance in the NHL during the early 1980s, Mailhot became a fan of John Tonelli, a hard-working, talented, checking forward who could also score. As a player himself, Mailhot learned early on that his limited ability, combined with his formidable physical stature, dictated a particular role if he chose to pursue a career in hockey.

Jacques Mailhot: "I realized that I would never be the fastest or most-skilled player, so I knew I would have to be a grinder, a guy who wasn't afraid to go into a corner for a loose puck or dig it out along the boards. Then I got into my first hockey fight. I kicked butt and it grew from there. I loved the game so much that I was willing to do anything to be part of it."

Mailhot was not drafted out of juniors so he entered the world of senior hockey and started to forge his reputation in the now defunct Republican League, where he racked up 760 penalty minutes in 140 games during the mid-1980s. He was such an intimidating force that one of his teammates, Serge Bernier, who had retired from a lengthy pro career in the WHA and NHL, encouraged him to send resumes out to NHL teams. He received many responses, but because he couldn't speak English very well he chose to pursue a spot on the hometown Quebec Nordiques.

Mailhot: "At my first day of rookie camp the newspaper guys are looking at my skating ability, seeing me as a local kid looking for a dream shot, that sort of thing. Even my dad told me to just have fun. Nobody gave me a chance. I was the only one who believed I could make it.

"I fought Richard Zemlack that first day and did pretty good. I was all excited. I was playing with Joe Sakic, he was 18 years old, I was skating right next to him. It didn't register at the time, but now when I think about it, Wow!

"I destroyed Scott Shaunessy in my next fight. He was a big kid they drafted and made a big deal about. The next day I fought him two more times. On my way off the ice Ron Lapointe put his hand on my back and said, 'Good job kid, you've got a contract.' I got cut at the big camp and was on my way to Fredericton to play for Lapointe."

Mailhot went berserk with the Fredericton Express in the American League and when Quebec fired head coach Andre Savard part way through the season, Lapointe was promoted to the big club. That summer, Quebec rewarded Mailhot with a two-year contract. It was a two-way deal that paid him $40,000 if he played in the AHL and $175,000 if he played in the NHL. They also gave him a $20,000 signing bonus, more money than he'd ever seen before.

On December 15, 1988, two days before I made my pro debut in North Carolina with the Thunderbirds, Lapointe brought Mailhot to Quebec City for a game against the hallowed rival Montreal Canadiens. However, Lapointe was in turn fired and replaced by Jean Perrone, a move that pretty much signaled the end for Mailhot as well. He remained with the Nordiques for a little more than a month but only dressed for 5 of 13 games. He got into his first NHL fight and did just fine against one of the best, Calgary's Tim Hunter, during a long West Coast road trip. When he returned to Quebec he was inserted into the lineup against the Bruins, the game I watched on television, the game that ended his dream of an NHL career.

Mailhot: "Everybody thought [Tim] Hunter would kick my ass but I held my own, and at that point I figured they were saying, 'We're not going to let this guy go.' But the end came with Boston. I held my own in a fight against Lyndon Byers, but Cam Neely was kicking our ass. He had two goals and two assists and we were down 4–1 with a minute left. All of a sudden Perrone grabbed my shoulder and said, 'Go get that guy and kick his ass right now, don't let him leave the ice.' That was the first and only time I was ever told to get somebody by a coach. I went out and lined up next to Neely and we had to wait for the face-off because of a television commercial. I said to Neely, 'Coach told me to fight you, but I don't think it's right.' He said, 'Fuck off,' and pushed me. I dropped my gloves before the puck was dropped and the tall ref, Mike Cvik, grabbed me and pulled me down to a knee. By the time I got up Neely had his left arm cocked and he unscrewed my head with two lefts. It was the hardest I've ever been hit, and I've been hit by a lot of people. Skating to the bench afterward all I wanted to do was get into the locker room and look in the mirror because I knew my nose was broken. It felt like it was in my left ear."

After the game reporters asked Perrone why he sent Mailhot on the ice with the game already decided. They asked him if he ordered Mailhot to fight Neely and Perrone denied it. Perrone came under heavy criticism for the incident and, according to Mailhot, sent him back down to the minors as some sort of self-serving punishment.

Mailhot: "I went back down to Halifax thinking this was just the start of more good things to come, that I have my whole career in front of me. But I'm young and dumb. We're headed for the playoffs and during a skate before a game [Coach] Doug Carpenter tells me that I'm not dressing. I went crazy. I broke my stick on the ice, I told him he was a jerk, an asshole, and some other words, and I left the ice. After that nobody wanted to touch me. They said Mailhot was a hothead, cocky, arrogant. It was my own fault and I have no problem admitting it."

And so started Mailhot on his hobo-like existence throughout the minor leagues, starting in 1989 with the Hampton-Roads Admirals in the East Coast League and ending 14 teams later in 2000 with the Central Texas Stampede of the Western Pro League. He ended up playing 509 professional minor-league games and racked up 3,043 penalty minutes.

Brock Kelly: "I knew the owner of the West Texas Stampede and he tried to get me to play down there after I retired. He said he'd pay me more than I was making up here in British Columbia for the mining company. He said he already had Jacques Mailhot. He said the little Mexicans were terrified of him. They'd spit and yell at him, but when he'd turn around they'd scamper away like cockroaches."

When I ran into Mailhot he had a pretty good thing going for himself. He was on a 25-game tryout contract with the Moncton Hawks of the AHL making $3,500 every two weeks, and because there wasn't enough room on the roster for him to play in every game, they let him double-dip with the nearby Miramichi Packers in order to stay in "game shape" at the tune of $600 per game.

The Packers' acquisition of Mailhot and I were received by the other teams in the league the same way Israel would respond to Iran prepping a lineup of scud missiles—they dug in and prepared for war. Of course I was in Disneyland. Not only was I going to be playing with Mailhot, but the league's rules for fighting were tailor-made for me. I guess it could be interpreted that fighting was not allowed in the league because after one fight the combatants were thrown out of the game. If they *really* wanted to outlaw fighting they would, well, simply outlaw it. But they didn't.

Very simply, fighting was *tolerated* because the league fathers knew it helped attract a thousand paying customers to a weekend tilt. If they could get a story fabricated that Doug "The Thug" Smith was coming to a neighborhood arena to fight the local hero, maybe the paid attendance would soar to 1,500.

The one-fight rule was actually a thing of genius. Teams without a willing enforcer were simply body-checked or otherwise intimidated into submission by the other team's tough guys. My job was to act as a neutralizing agent. There would be no surprise because everyone knew who I was and why I was there. I would stride onto the ice and fight the tough guy lined up beside me. We would then leave the game together, effectively canceling each other out while allowing the other players to carry on with a contest of may-the-more-talented-team-win. There is a profound sense of purity with that concept and it worked like fertilizer on a guy like me who wasn't interested in actually playing the game, anyway.

Mailhot and I were signed on a Friday night, and the local Saturday morning newspaper made it a special point to announce in a bold headline, **"Toughies join Packers; will be playing tonight."**

"Two is just the right number, it could be a tag-team combination," Packers president Dale Hicks was quoted as saying. "Guys like Roch Bois and Kevin Gaudet just don't get the opportunity to play like they can on the road because other teams just beat them around and we don't do anything about it. If a lack of physical presence has been our problem in the past we've rectified it quickly."

The publicity worked as the Packers drew 1,750 fans to the Miramichi Civic Center for Saturday night's home game against the Saint John Vito's, which I believe were sponsored by the Vito's Family Restaurant chain. Mailhot refused to play over a disagreement over money, but I didn't disappoint. It was impossible for me not to notice the name "Max Daviault" on the Vito's roster. He was in fact the brother of Alex Daviault, whom I had fought numerous times while I was with the Thunderbirds in the East Coast League a few years back. Max was bigger than Alex but he skated just like him as they both seemed to run on the ice.

Daviault was clearly a worthy target for me, but first I had a little bit of playing to do. Nobody knew too much about me other than the fact I was supposed to be some sort of tough guy from the East Coast League. Certainly Packers coach Bev Bawn must have thought I could be a good-sized power forward for him to utilize because he slapped me at wing on the second line to play with a couple of pretty good forwards, Peter Pinder and Shawn Wood.

Bawn probably further thought he hit gold when, on my first shift 1:29 into the game, I played hot potato with the puck before Pinder scored for a 1–0 lead. But just 12 seconds later, as my name was being announced for the assist, I was whistled off for an elbowing infraction. While I was in the box serving my penalty the Vito's scored a power-play goal to tie things up.

My assist and penalty washed each other out, but 30 seconds after we went ahead 2–1 my ass was back in the box for an interference penalty. At that point I felt as though I answered most of the questions anybody had of me. I skated enough shifts for everybody to figure I wasn't going to be chosen as the league's "Captain Morgan Player of the Month" anytime soon. And while my two minor penalties, which I used as attempts to entice various Saint John players into fights, produced more than a few groans from the stands and my bench, it wasn't long before I'd endear myself to the hometown fans and my teammates.

The Vito's decided to try a different tactic to get back into the game and the strategy worked. They started banging us around and after instigating matching roughing penalties on consecutive shifts, the Vito's scored to tie things up at 2–2.

I hadn't played for nearly 10 minutes, not since being called for interference midway through the period. But if there was a time to utilize my talents it was now, especially with Max Daviault prowling around like a big cat growling and pawing at my teammates. Bawn figured as much and had me go out for the last shift of the first period.

It was the first time in the game I had been out on the ice with Daviault and it was a foregone conclusion we were going to fight. I cross-checked him lightly from behind the Vito's end to get his attention as the puck was moving out of the zone. He turned, cross-checked me back, and we dropped the gloves in close—so close that we quickly came together in a bear hug and jostled long enough for the officials to come along and separate us.

Maybe on another night Daviault and I would have gone along peacefully with the refs and taken our double-minor penalties for cross-checking and roughing quietly to the penalty box for a lazy sit down. Not this time. The game had already been heated up and primed for a fight. There was no turning away for us now.

I pulled free from the official holding me and Daviault followed my lead. We squared off and grabbed each other by the front of our shirts but I was able to hit Daviault first with a quick flurry of shots, my last one hitting him square on the forehead to help send him down to his knees. That was it; that was my job. We scored two goals during the first three minutes of the second period and went on to win 8–6.

> **Jacques Mailhot:** "I sat out the first game against the Vito's but Doug played and he beat the shit out of Max Daviault. He beat the shit out of that guy and I just sat there in the stands and said, 'Holy Christ.' He couldn't skate much, and that must have been hard on him, but he sure liked to fight."

My second game the following afternoon was against the Prince Edward Island Armour Fence Islanders out of Charlottetown. The Islanders had an interesting situation in that they had one of the best goaltenders in the league, Wayne Bernard, who also happened to be a Maritimes Golden Gloves Heavyweight Champion with 36 amateur boxing matches under his belt.

A few years earlier Bernard became an emergency alternate for the 1988 Canadian Olympic Boxing Team when the in-house heavyweight suffered a broken nose. Bernard traveled with the team to South Carolina and went two rounds with eventual heavyweight gold medalist and future WBO World Champion Ray Mercer in a bout that was televised on *Wide World of Sports*. He also sparred with former Undisputed World Champ Lennox Lewis, who was in camp with Team Canada and eventually won a gold medal as a super-heavyweight in the Seoul, South Korea Games.

Despite Bernard's formidable reputation, I found the notion of picking a fight with a goaltender uncomfortable, if only from a logistics point of view. I didn't know how to go about challenging a goalie. He wasn't out there checking or roughing up our talented forwards, or talking shit with me lining up for a face-off, so I didn't really know how to engage him.

I had a lot of time to think about this because I sat on the bench for most of the game. Mailhot took over the bulk of the ice time I was given during the Saint John Vito's game the night before and made it count by leading us to a 5–2 advantage in an otherwise tame and boring game. I came to the conclusion that Bernard's fistic prowess was rested on the team's back counter as an active insurance policy. He was an excellent goalie and everybody knew about his boxing ability, so it seemed as though the Islanders hoped that Bernard could stay planted in the net with his reputation alone helping to keep games clean because opponents knew if they screwed around, Big Bad Bernard would step out of his crease and into the ring.

In this particular game, however, with the outcome firmly in hand and probably for no other reason than to appease our home fans, Coach Bawn gave me the last shift of the game. My teammates had told me that Bernard would in fact come out of his net to fight if he had to, and that if I couldn't get anybody else to go with me I could challenge him. With 43 seconds left to play and nobody on the ice worthy to challenge, I skated down right in the middle of play toward Bernard.

My trip to meet him was an adventure in itself, as the puck was moving out of the Islanders' end and I had to sift through the players skating the other way like a salmon swimming upstream. I stopped right in front of Bernard and said, "I heard you're a tough guy, wanna go?"

I could see his eyes through his mask—an expression of disbelief that somebody actually had the nerve to come out of their way for no apparent reason to challenge him. He just stood there in shock so I shook my head, turned and began to skate away. It probably took a moment for everything to sink in and register for Bernard, because a moment later I heard him yell, "Hey, wait a minute!" I turned around and he was in a rage. He tossed off his blocker, catching glove, and mask and we went at it to the wild delight of the home crowd. I nailed him with three fast right hands before he burrowed into my chest and stream-rolled me into the corner where we ended up wrestling a bit until the referees separated us.

Wayne Bernard: "I knew about Doug, I heard he was a fighter, not there to play hockey, just to duke it out. The boys had talked about him, that he had come up from the States to fight, so he was known. He was a lot smaller man than I thought. Because of his reputation I was expecting somebody much bigger.

"Miramichi never had a rugged team and we usually had a very tough team and gave it to them pretty good over the years. The first time I met up with Doug was in Miramichi. He didn't play a shift, and then with a minute left he came down the ice to challenge me. When he came down I said, 'No problem.' We squared off over near the glass. I had all my gear on and he hit me with a couple of shots, split me over the eye. Then I grabbed the top of the glass to get some leverage and hit him with a couple of rights. I whacked his head against the glass and split him, so we were both cut up and bleeding pretty well. We were in the hospital together getting stitched up, me in one room and him in another with the bus waiting outside."

If the Daviault fight introduced me to the Packers' fans, the Bernard fight announced my intentions to the entire league and created an atmosphere of mayhem for me to enjoy. I took advantage of my self-anointed role as team enforcer during our third consecutive home game when I was first off the bench to spark a brawl against the Campbellton Labatt's Tigers.

How does a bench-clearing brawl start? Well, we had our scoring line on the ice during a stoppage of play and a couple of the Tigers' toughies began pawing at our guys. One of the Tigers was Marc Roy, who I watched on one of my hockey fight videos knock out Jacques Mailhot in a Republican League game. We had the game firmly in hand and I wasn't playing, so I figured the time was right to jump the boards and go after Roy. The problem was that I never reached him because my departure off the bench triggered everybody else to hop over and Roy became lost in what became a very crowded pushing and shoving match.

I was rewarded with a two-game suspension for my part in the brawl as well as a $200 fine, which the Packers paid. The club also had to post a $500 performance bond upon my return, which supposedly would insure against a repeat performance. But I was just warming up, and so was my bandwagon.

Like back in my Thunderbirds' days, my willingness, in fact the flat-out joy I held in the act of dropping my gloves and fighting, endeared me to the fans and our cable television play-by-play man, Patrick "Hoppy" Dunn, whose love of broadcasting local sporting events tabbed him as "The Voice of the Miramichi." Hoppy was a union laborer who'd bust his ass 40 hours a week, go to the Hi-Lo Tavern for a couple of cocktails, and then do a great job as a crystal-clear homer calling our games. He lived with his dad, Cecil, and they offered me an extra room in the house for the rest of the season.

Hoppy was a one-man booster club for the team. He called me "Yankee Doodle," and I started the wheels of promotion spinning in his head.

Hoppy Dunn: "We were lacking toughness, and the first time Doug was on the ice he beat Daviault bad and the fans fell in love with him. They really took to him, it was incredible.

"I have to give him credit for being the first guy to come up here knowing what his role was and doing it. He always said, 'I know what I'm here for.' He made no bones about it and he enjoyed it. His teammates loved him, too. They knew his hockey skill wasn't the same caliber as them but they appreciated his willingness to stand up for them."

Hoppy was a gold mine not only for the Packers, but also the entire league. His shear unbridled enthusiasm toward propping up the local hockey scene was unselfishly directed at getting as many people into the league's rinks as possible. I realized and appreciated this, and when Hoppy jumped on the opportunity to drum up some excitement through me I gladly went along for the ride.

There was a lot of down time during the week between games and he would take me anywhere for publicity—the supermarket, barber shop, all the local gin mills. Hoppy was like Don King and he created a lot of buzz for Doug "The Hammer" Smith. That was the nickname he coined for me, "The Hammer." The name kind of embarrassed me because it belonged to NHL legend Dave Schultz. I preferred to be called "The Thug" from my East Coast League days, but Hoppy's nickname for me stuck and in every home game when the crowd wanted to see a fight they would chant, "Haaaamer, Haaaamer," until they got their wish with Coach Bawn relenting and unleashing me over the boards.

But even when I wasn't available to cart around and drum up business, Hoppy took it upon himself to plant storylines in the papers and even talk face-to-face with the tough guys from other teams trying to set up fights for me. I didn't mind, that's why I was there. The way I understood it from Hoppy was that most of the better fighters who had been around the block weren't as interested in doing battle with the same guys they had either been battling for years or actually been teammates with, as many of the players jumped from team to team throughout the circuit over the years. Nobody really knew me, so Hoppy would tell them about this new, tough kid from Boston who was looking to kick their asses. I told Hoppy I didn't care what he said—tell them I thought they were pieces of shit, queer, that I was banging their girls, whatever, just so long as they'd fight me, and not just on their home ice but in our barn, too.

In any event, Hoppy's first really big advertising job was to work on my rematch with the Islanders' fighting goalie, Wayne Bernard. My suspension would be up by the time we were scheduled to travel to the Island, and Hoppy built it up as the heavyweight championship fight of the New Brunswick Senior Hockey League that would pit reigning Prince Edward Island champ Bernard against Miramichi's invading Hammer.

Sides were easily chosen. The general feeling on the Island was, "Who is this Hammer guy and how dare he start a fight with our goalie!"

I bumped into a Packers fan on a Miramichi street, a knucklehead who followed the team everywhere, who claimed to be a friend of Bernard. He told me that Bernard was dying to pound on me in *his* home rink. I thought, "Oh my God, what the hell is this stuff all about? All I wanted to do was have my one lousy fight a game and take a shower, and now I'm Public Enemy Number One."

We had to take a boat to reach Charlottetown on Prince Edward Island. The water was choppy in the late fall weather and the boat tossed and rolled. I became seasick and threw up in the bathroom. I was still feeling like hell and must have been white as a ghost when we got to the Charlottetown Civic Center. Mailhot came to me and asked if I was nervous. I told him I wasn't, but I don't think he bought it because I was still nauseous, my face was pasty, and I could feel the sweat beading on my brow.

"It's okay," said Mailhot. "I've gone through it before, when you think the other team is in their locker room drawing straws for you and you think you're all alone. But don't worry, the Mailman is here for you."

That was pure Jacques Mailhot, absolutely one guy I'd want in my fox-hole.

Hoppy had already started a war of words in the newspapers. His gasoline to the fire helped draw an overflowing crowd of 2,380 fans to the Civic Center for our game. During warm-ups I thought it was strange that the Islanders had their back-up goalie in net for the shooting drills, but then I spotted Bernard at the blue line by his bench. He had his leg pads on but no chest protector or shoulder pads under his jersey. It was obvious to me that the Islanders were going along with Hoppy's storyline hook, line, and sinker. They were going to sacrifice their best goaltender to satisfy their end of this odd bargain.

> **Bernard:** "It was all written up in the paper, everybody knew about it and I was expecting to fight Doug in the warm-up. Before the game my coach came into the locker room and said I wasn't going to be playing, so that was his way of giving me the go-ahead to go at it. I went into the bathroom with Bob Doiran, we looked at each other and he said, 'It's either you or me.' I said, 'Well, I guess it'll be me.' I had no pads on because I wanted to get right at it. There were a lot of people there who wanted to see it, the building was packed."

> **Hoppy Dunn:** "I said to Bernard in the warm-up, 'Smitty the Hammer wants to go in the warm-up,' and he says, 'I'll go.' So I run down the bleachers and said to Smitty, 'You're not going to believe this, Bernard wants to go in the warm-up,' and Smitty says, 'Tell him it's a date.' Then Packers coach Bev Bawn asks me, 'Who's coaching this team?' I said, 'Sorry Bev, but I got a fight to broadcast.'"

You've got to love Hoppy. After warm-ups I waited for my entire team to leave the ice. I always did that just to make sure I was around if any nonsense was going to start—kind of like being the last line of defense. The Zamboni was about to come onto the ice when I noticed Bernard all alone at his end. We made eye contact, nodded to each other and skated toward center ice. The Zamboni stayed put.

Bernard peeled off his shirt and hit center ice bare-chested and burly at 6-feet and 220 pounds. I stripped down to my T-shirt. There were no officials

With my pal Hoppy Dunn as a member of the Miramichi Gagnon Packers.

on the ice and the fans were going absolutely berserk. They could not believe what they were witnessing—even though this was precisely the reason why so many of them had bought a ticket.

We squared off for 20 seconds feigning jabs, bobbing and weaving, just like we were dancing in a boxing ring. I looked off toward the end of the rink

I was facing and noticed both teams had come out of their respective dressing rooms and formed a horseshoe behind the boards and glass to watch.

Unfortunately, as many times happens amidst so much hype, the fight didn't amount to much. When we began to grapple and Bernard tore my shirt off we were both left with nothing to grab hold of for leverage. We threw a number of harmless punches and it ended up as a big wrestling match between a pair of worn-out ex-boxers.

> **Bernard:** "There weren't any officials on the ice and you never knew if a fight like this could go on for 10 minutes without anybody breaking it up, so we just held on to each other and wrestled. When they yelled to us that the refs were coming, that's when we went at it pretty good. At the end of it I got Doug down and ripped his pants right off. That was funny."

I showered and dressed while my teammates opened the first period of play, and all the while I thought that the fans must have been so disappointed because the build-up for the big fight didn't lead to much of anything—but boy was I wrong.

On my way to the press box to visit with Hoppy, who was broadcasting the game for our local radio station, I must have signed a hundred autographs for opposing fans who practically had to restrain themselves from hugging and kissing me. Some of them were so excited by what had happened that their eyes had welled up with tears. They told me that they had never witnessed anything like that before at a hockey game and how great it was and how glad they were to have come. The reaction to what I thought was a waste of time was a pleasant surprise and another feather in my cap.

Of course I was again rewarded with another two-game suspension and $200 fine, and the team had to pony up another $500 performance bond on my behalf. I don't know what happened to the first performance bond they had to pay for me.

While I sat out the second game of my suspension and Mailhot nursed a broken thumb, the Vito's took advantage of us in their home rink by starting a major skirmish and whipping us 7–3. Two days later, when I was out free, the Vito's had to visit us in our rink and I was waiting for them like a tortured pit bull.

Hoppy had the newspaper greet my return to action with a bold-print **"Packers-Vito's game could be rough tonight"** headline. Even our general manager, Clary Hale, got involved in the hype and was quoted in one of the newspapers saying, "That's been the talk of the town all day. There's a different atmosphere here now, different from what it was in the past three years or so. We expect a capacity crowd...."

The fans packed our house and midway through the third period I stepped out for my second shift of the game to give everybody what they wanted. Daviault was already out there and he wanted a rematch from our first fight when I put him down and took a clear decision with a shot to his forehead.

There was a short break in the action while the officials conversed by the penalty box area about some matching penalties. Everybody in the building knew what was coming, and I certainly didn't have to say anything to Daviault, who skated in a wild, nervous pattern around me near center ice. Mailhot was on the ice as well. He skated around as fired up as Daviault. He first drifted to me and said, "Do it right away, don't make the fans wait." Jacques didn't have to worry about me wasting any time, but I still had the idea he didn't really know what I was truly all about yet.

Mailhot continued his role as town crier, making the rounds to all of the other players on the ice telling them, "Don't even bother to play, the moment the puck is dropped these guys are going at it." Then he said the same thing to the officials after they were done with their business at the penalty boxes.

I made eye contact with Daviault as we floated into the face-off area and we nodded to each other. Like his brother, Alex, Max didn't seem to have much command of the English language, but the funny thing about those two was that they completely understood the meaning of dangled gloves.

The puck dropped, we immediately backed off each other from the wing directly in front of the benches and dropped our sticks and gloves. We took a good hold of each other's jerseys at the neck with our left hands and starting swinging away with rights. Daviault was lively but he wasn't too interested in hanging in there with me toe-to-toe. After taking a couple shots he pulled his head down and away, which sent both of us slowly spinning in a circle. We engaged in a bit of give-and-take, with him bobbing up and down to take his shots and me trying to time the rise of his face for my punches before coming together in a clinch.

Daviault seemed content to call it a day right then. He did his job. He rose to the challenge—and on the road to boot. On top of that he held his own in the fight as it was probably a draw.

But I had other ideas.

I had never been one for wrestling—mainly because of my poor balance—so while we held hands waist-high I worked to grab both ends of his sleeves with my right hand. The refs started to come in to break us up but I yelled at them to stay away. Once I finished switching hands I began to pound away at Daviault with a flurry of roundhouse lefts that knocked him off balance and to the ice for another clear-cut decision.

As I drifted away from Daviault, Mailhot rushed over to me and told me to raise my arms in victory. I had never purposely tried to show up an opponent before because I always had too much respect for anybody I fought for that kind of nonsense. It was just business to me—get it on, get it over with, and go directly to the penalty box. But I also had a lot of respect for Mailhot, so I listened to him and answered the cheers from the home crowd with a half-hearted thrust of my arms.

Reading accounts of the fight in the papers the next day I learned that "Smith immediately signified his victory by skating off the ice with his hands high in the air," and that "Smith pirouetted around with his arms upraised to cheers, claps, and stomps from the fans." After looking at the video, all I really did was throw my arms halfway up for about a second as if I were tossing an empty keg of beer in the air.

I was suspended for four of my first nine games with the Packers but still led the team with 69 penalty minutes in the five games I was dressed. I started four fights, sparked a bench-clearing brawl, and engaged in my first-ever pre-game fight. Add in the fact that the team had gone 7–2 and cornered first place since I arrived and it naturally followed that I became a fan favorite, again.

I was fighting and we were winning. We went to Prince Edward Island and sold the place out for the first time in five years. Everybody wanted to see The Hammer, and at home it got even crazier.

The town had a parade to celebrate something or other, and they put me in the lead car with Miss Miramichi. I was so embarrassed. I wondered if Mailhot was mad or jealous of the attention I was getting, but he never let on. I looked back at the car behind me and there he was looking at me with a big smile. Here was a guy who had played in the NHL, who could probably kick my ass in a fight on the ice, and I'm riding in the front car being cheered as though I had brought home the Stanley Cup. It was as if Mailhot was saying, "Kid, I already had my day, this is for you, soak it up."

Even so, I couldn't help but think Mailhot was irritated having me around, or if he thought I was putting his job as team enforcer in jeopardy. I fully expected him to challenge me to a fight during one of our practices early on, and while I wasn't afraid of him I knew it would be the fight of my life.

Hoppy Dunn: "Jacques, in his mind, thought he was the main fighter, and thought he was taking Doug under his wing. But Jacques didn't know Smitty was willing to take him on in practice. I'd say to Doug, 'I think you're out of your league, and who is going to break it up? You'll ruin practice.' But Doug just wanted to prove a point, to validate why he was there."

The reality was that Mailhot was far more important to the team's success than I. He was probably our best fighter, too, but he could put the puck in the net as well so he was more valuable to us on the ice than kicked out of a game after his one fight. If there needed to be somebody to stand up and fight it should be me because, as I always thought, my value was in being content to be that piece of raw meat thrown to the dogs.

Mailhot: "I didn't really want to come there and be a fighter, I wanted to play hockey, although I eventually did a lot of fighting.

"I was surprised when I heard about Doug. He wasn't the greatest skater, and he knew that. But he had a big heart and that's what you need for the game of hockey. He was the type of player I was, he would do anything for the team to win."

For my part I never gave Mailhot a reason to hate me. I didn't come off as a hard-ass type like that big mouth in the Carolina Thunderbirds' training camp I attacked during an inter-squad scrimmage. I actually idolized the guy. The first time I was with Mailhot in the locker room he must have felt me staring because I never took my eyes off him. I was in awe. I asked him a thousand questions about his career or how to do this and that, and he was more than happy to share his opinions, and then some.

Before long it was clear that Mailhot wanted me under his wing, and he gave me the impression that I was his protégé. It was something I didn't mind, and God help the guy who came along and beat me up because Mailhot would make a point to whip his ass the next time we played. It was as if he were saying, "You're not going to push my little brother around."

After a little while it seemed to me that all the fans cared about was who I fought or who I was going after next. And while I never shied away from the action or attention, a lot of the excitement generated about me had to do with Hoppy.

All the newspaper guys knew that Hoppy was good for a quote. He would say things like, "The upcoming game is going to be a war," or "Hostilities would be resumed," or "The Packers aren't going to forget what happened in the last game." My part of the bargain was to deliver every bit that was promised by Hoppy, and the fans all around the league sopped it up like gravy.

But my coach, Bev Bawn, wasn't playing along. He didn't seem to care much for fighters or the new kind of game I helped bring to the Packers. He could stomach Mailhot because at least he had some skill and could score goals. But it didn't take Bawn long to figure out I couldn't be trusted to play a regular shift. I would start out on the right wing and end up on the left. I

was like a dog chasing a ball in the backyard, or a child's top—pull the string and watch me go.

Bev Bawn: "You have to look at the kind of team you have, and we had a lot of good players so we could afford to carry a guy with Doug's capabilities. Hoppy built Doug up to be this big fighter; it was a public relations thing. The problem was Doug wouldn't be able to stick around very long, because if you looked at him out of the corner of your eye he would fight you and be gone.

"Doug was a real nice kid, he didn't drink. This is a small, quiet town and he didn't cause a problem, he conducted himself well. But he had a very limited skill level. Players tend to improve, he did listen and he had some ambition, but he was extending himself to hold a spot on the team."

Hoppy Dunn: "I think what Bevy's problem was, we were challenging for the Allan Cup, the superiority of senior hockey in all of Canada, and that's a big deal for us. Bev kept telling me that he wasn't going to be able to keep Doug around, that he was looking for a guy with a little more talent who could play the puck. But the fans liked Doug so much that Bev was forced to keep him."

I felt as though there was a lot of tension between Bawn and myself, but I thought a lack of communication was the cause of much of our problem. The situation actually made me a little sad because I knew Bawn was a good man and I liked him, personally. I also respected him as a former standout athlete, excelling as both a hockey and baseball player to the tune of being inducted into the New Brunswick Sports Hall of Fame, so he was no clown. But I also enjoyed what I was doing, knew I couldn't do anything else, and didn't feel like packing up and going home.

Having a coach who doesn't necessarily care for your contribution to the team is a hard thing to swallow, especially for somebody like me with so little hockey ability. Instead I gained all the confidence I needed in knowing that the other powers that ran the club did want me around to help keep fans interested in the team by performing a very particular job, which I did very well.

I wished that Bawn had just talked to me. He could have taken me aside and said, "Doug, I have to play you because the owner wants me to, but we'll both wait until the time is right." That is all he had to do and we would've had a great relationship. I don't know, maybe he didn't want to hurt my feelings, or maybe he thought it would have turned into a bad confrontation. Hell, I wouldn't have cared a lick. Instead he never said a word to me. I sat

at the end of the bench and he ignored me while the fans chanted, "Haaaamer, Haaaamer," the entire game.

When a game was decided one way or another, or if Bawn couldn't stand the howling crowd any longer, he'd send me out to do my thing. It wouldn't have surprised me if he turned his back or left the bench for a hot dog and beer while I was out there. Ultimately, however, I suppose if I were in Bawn's position, I would have also rather had a tough guy who could play hockey better than I could.

After my second fight with Max Daviault I dressed but didn't skate a shift in our next two games, which were both on the road. I didn't really mind because I didn't care about actually playing, and the games weren't necessarily rough so my services weren't needed. I was there just in case, and in a very real sense I felt that merely having me sit on the bench in plain view of the other team worked as an intimidating deterrent to some degree. Understanding that concept alone is like getting an "A" in a Hockey Enforcer graduate course. But the next game was in front of our home crowd, and they would have to be appeased.

The last time the Campbellton Tigers came in to Miramichi I started a brawl. I was left to rot on the bench when we next played Campbellton on the road, but the Tigers figured I might see some ice time at home so they brought somebody along to play with me.

I was pleasantly surprised when I met up with my old pal Rock Derganc in the runway before the game. I had my best fight against him in the East Coast League, a solid toe-to-toe slugfest where we used each other's faces as punching bags. We also were in the Cincinnati Cyclones' training camp and made a pact not to fight each other unless it was absolutely necessary. Now we knew that time had come.

Rock Derganc: "I knew we were going to fight, but you don't prepare yourself for something, you know what your job is and just let it happen. My coach sent me out to fight Dougie, so I had to go after him this time, not like in Cincinnati."

We fought at the start of my second shift, midway through the second period. We lined up on opposite wings, but once the puck was dropped Rock skated over to me and we got at it. I quickly got the upper hand with a series of pounding rights and put him to a knee. But because I had absolutely no animosity toward Rock, and actually liked him, I was just going through the motions of my job and didn't finish him off, which would have entailed wrestling him all the way down to a sprawl on the ice. Instead I let him get up, at which point he went back to work on me and took the upper hand. He was so strong he managed to pull my jersey partway over my head and got a few punches in while I was blinded. When the officials stepped in to break up the fight, Rock leaned in to me and said, "Sorry Dougie, I didn't mean to hit you with your shirt up."

> **Derganc:** "He could've hit me real bad when I slipped on the ice. I was lucky he stopped when he did."

I wasn't upset with Rock, just disappointed with my own performance, especially in front of my home fans. But I learned a valuable lesson in that I couldn't go half-ass into any fight because the other guy may not be going along for the ride.

With my one-fight quota filled I ventured off to the locker room, grabbed a Coke, and sat down alone to relax. All of a sudden Rock wandered in, grabbed a drink and sat down next to me. We talked for 10 minutes about what we'd been doing since being cut from Cincinnati. When the rest of my team came in for the second intermission they were shocked to see us together, as close as two brothers. But as always, our fight on the ice was just business and off the ice we could be the best of friends.

> **Wayne Bernard:** "What many people don't understand about fighters is that you can have a fight with a guy, but after the game you could be in the bar with him having a beer together. We had mutual respect for each other. It was nothing personal, just business."

It was all business for the Packers' management as well. I thought I was a huge bargain for them, and the entire league for that matter, at only $300 a week. I am pretty sure I was on the low end of the payroll, too, with guys like Mailhot and our best defenseman, Lowell Loveday, making much more.

If I had been around a little longer and more comfortable with my place on the team, I could have asked Mr. Gagnon for more money to stick around. He may have even given it me with all of the tickets I helped sell, but I didn't say a word. There was still a very big part of me who was just happy to be around a team being paid at all. Besides, it was hard for me to complain about much because I had it pretty damn easy. I sat on my ass all day in Mr. Dunn's house with a television clicker in one hand and a bowl of popcorn engulfed by the other. I dressed for two or three games a week, maybe getting as much as two shifts a night, if I played at all.

Many of the other players worked full time jobs hauling logs or working a trade. Derganc was a gold miner; Bernard was an industrial engineer who ran his own business. Those were the guys I fought, guys who busted their asses all day and were tired and pissed off when they came to the rink. Sure, most played because they still held a love for the game of hockey, but at this point, in this arena, they were looking to make some extra cash to pay bills and support a family.

In addition to suiting up for the Packers, I felt that another part of my job was to have a good rapport with the people of Miramichi, who in Hoppy's mind were all potential ticket buyers. I didn't play bullshit with them. They would ask me if I was going to fight so-and-so tomorrow night and I'd say, "Hell yah, first chance I get. He's not getting out of our rink until he gets a beating from me." They loved it, they ate it up, and I meant it, too.

> **Hoppy Dunn:** "I got Doug a side job as a bouncer at the Hi-Lo Tavern. Now when Doug was here he wasn't all that big. Sure he was six feet, but he was only about 200 pounds. So if somebody got drunk at the bar they might think, 'What's that guy going to do to me?' But once you told him his name was Doug Smith, the one who played for the Packers, nobody wanted anything to do with him and they just walked out the door."

There was a close-knit rivalry between all of the teams in the New Brunswick League that I didn't experience in the East Coast League. All of the small cities here were about a two-hour ride apart, and the newspapers thrived on fabricating border skirmishes. In fact, the newspapers battled as well, with the Miramichi Packers' *Times-Transcript* squaring off against the Saint John Vito's *Telegraph-Journal*, among others.

Times-Transcript columnist Dave Butler was our booster in the press and he liked me, while all of the other papers serving the opposing teams took their shots at the new-look Packers. I was, rightfully so, painted as a bad guy by the rival sports writers. I was the bully who needed a spanking.

Bill Donovan covered the neighboring Vito's for the *Telegraph-Journal*, and even though he wasn't at my first game against Saint John, he nonetheless pronounced my fight against Max Daviault a draw. Butler, who was at the game, stood up for me and wrote a column detailing the fight blow-for-blow using a video clip for more accuracy, and basically called Donovan an idiot.

That wasn't the last disagreement I had with Donovan, who never liked to give me credit for anything.

I fought another Saint John Vito's toughie, Dennis Vringer. We squared off and shadowboxed for 30 seconds. I stood in a boxer's stance and every time he reached in to grab my shirt I pushed him off. I was looking for a fist-fight but Vringer didn't seem too game for that sort of thing. I finally ended the standoff with a quick right to the jaw that knocked him to the ice. There were actually clips of the fight filmed from different angles broadcast on two different news stations afterward—which of course I copied and mailed home to Gator.

In Donovan's game story he wrote that I "landed just a glancing blow to Vringer's helmet at the same time Vringer was tripping and off balance." Now I'd be the first to agree that I didn't punch Vringer flush, or he would've needed a bed in his locker room, but Donovan's account was simply not accurate. I understood the whole thing about being a homer, but I did expect a member of the media to, at the very least, report the truth.

When I traveled to the Vito's home arena in Saint John a little later, Hoppy introduced me to Donovan and we talked a bit inside the Lord Beaverbrook Rink, which I thought was a great, regal-sounding name. Later I grabbed the morning paper and saw that Donovan basically wrote that their guy, Rene Labbe, was going to destroy me; that it was going to be like a man against a boy.

Labbe had actually won a national championship playing with my Packers a few years earlier, when the team played at a lower level of senior hockey. He was certainly a worthy opponent with a well-earned reputation, somewhat on the lines of a Mailhot, but without the professional experience. Labbe did much of his fighting in junior and senior leagues, and I had watched a video of a solid toe-to-toe war he had with one of the Roberge brothers while play-

Getting set to lower the boom on Dennis Vringer (center right) of the Vito's.

ing in the defunct Republican League. Anybody who had the ability to dance in that manner with a Roberge back then never had to prove their courage any other way again.

During the warm-up I could hear Donovan yelling down at me from the press box, telling me that Labbe was going to kill me. I picked up a puck and threw it, missing him by two feet before it smashed into the wall behind. I thought the whole thing was comical and tried my hardest to stare at him with a straight face so he would think I was really angry at him. Hoppy told me later that Donovan was completely horrified. Donovan actually wrote about the incident in his column the next day, which only added to my growing legend and quite worthy of Mike Chighasola's best East Coast League exaggerations.

What followed in the game was later dubbed "The New Brunswick Senior Hockey League Fight of the Year." We were a few men down and Bawn was forced to play me on a semi-regular shift so I had to try and remain in the game for as long as possible. Labbe and I stared at each other for much of the night and I finally broke down. I had been told the whole season that he was one of the best in the league so I *had* to try him. It was the third period, we were lining up for a face-off and I asked him if he wanted to go. He said in broken English, "Yes, keep it clean."

I didn't know what that meant, "Keep it clean." I didn't like the sound of it because I never fought dirty. I don't pull hair or bite or kick or scratch, so I didn't know what he was talking about. Now that I've had some time to reflect upon it, I've come to the conclusion that Labbe had been around for a while fighting here there and everywhere. He was a veteran of this sort of thing and I was a new guy on the block just now forging a reputation. Labbe was established and he didn't know me, I hadn't earned his respect, so he wanted to be sure I wasn't going to do anything out of hand to try and make a name for myself.

The puck dropped and we immediately dropped our sticks and gloves and squared off. We quickly grabbed each other's shirts at the neckline with our left hands and proceeded to trade short, straight rights. I am a little taller than Labbe so I decided to stand straight up with my chin pressed down toward my thrust-out chest. Labbe bore down and actually pushed me gently backward as he punched, but only a few of his shots landed with any authority because his arms weren't long enough and most of his punches just tapped the end of my chin—thank God.

We were both throwing too many punches too fast to actually put any power behind most of them, but when I noticed Labbe's head down, I switched to uppercuts and nailed him with a couple of beauties. I connected

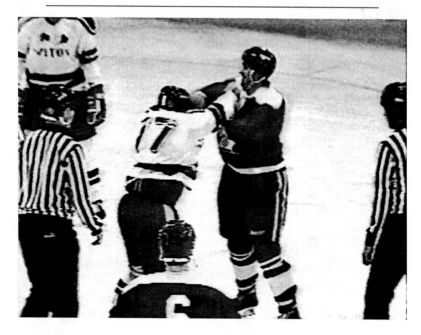

The New Brunswick Senior Hockey League Fight of the Year: me (center right) standing tall against Rene Labbe.

with a series of over-and-under shots that apparently made him decide to call it a night so he pulled me in tight. The officials jumped in and corralled us. I told them to let us go, but I'm glad they didn't listen to me because I was dead tired as well.

I was led off the ice by an official and as I walked down the runway Hoppy, who wasn't broadcasting this game, followed close behind all giddy with excitement. Then there was the click-clack of a second set of skates, and soon there was Labbe waddling toward me from the other end. Hoppy said, "Oh shit, here we go, he wants to fight again." But there was no intention in Labbe's eyes. He extended his hand and we shook right there in the hallway under the arena seats and parted ways with admiration and respect for each other.

My newspaper nemesis Bill Donovan approached me after the game and said he was dead wrong. He told me it was the best fight he'd seen in years. Later on I watched a replay and counted 25 punches landing for him and 27 for me. But while I appreciated the attention everyone gave the fight, it was probably a better show to see in person during the excitement of a game than 20 straight times with the VCR turned to slow motion.

When all was said and done, I now know that I took Donovan's rival comments more personally than I should have, because in reality, Donovan was just playing off Hoppy. It was all business. They worked as a unit to drum up interest for their respective teams and the league as a whole. We were actually one big happy family, even though it was tough for me to make out the distinction at the time.

Through it all Donovan did hit one thing right on the button. He wrote, "Mailhot and Smith have ... made the weak strong and all of a sudden, some players who played the last few years like five-footers are now eight feet tall." That one statement summed up what an enforcer is supposed to do for a hockey team, but he had the final picture wrong when he added, "Unfortunately, the new-found boldness of the Packers won't win them many hockey games, especially on the road." His bias clouded his judgment. Just like the Philadelphia Flyers, the "new-found boldness" of the Miramichi Packers did carry over and translate to wins, as we went on to finish the regular season in first place.

Prince Edward Island's *Charlottetown Guardian* got into the act as well. When we were due in town there was no talk about our leading goal scorers or Jacques Mailhot. The local writers had seen enough of me the first time around when I engaged goalie Wayne Bernard in the pre-game fight, so they keyed on me, The Hammer, the worst player on the ice.

While I was sitting out my suspension from the bench-clearing brawl I started with the Campbellton Tigers, the Islanders beat us 9–4. Now they expected us to come into the Civic Center looking to get some revenge. *Guardian* reporter Garth Hurley opened his pre-game report by stating that the Islanders "were awaiting the arrival of the Miramichi Gagnon Packers and their highly-touted enforcer Doug Smith...."

"If they come here to play hockey, then we will play hockey," said Islanders defenseman Bob Doiron. "But if this guy thinks he's coming over here and running us out of our own rink then he has another thing coming."

I have to admit, Doiron gave me a great compliment without really knowing it when he was quoted as saying, "[The Packers] play tough when he's in the lineup, but they were a little shy coming in here last weekend. Having him here should prove quite interesting." It was yet another shining example of what a tough guy can do for a club and reinforced my confidence as a valued member of the Packers despite Coach Bawn's apparent disdain for my role and place on the roster.

There was another rival writer, Mike Arsenault, who went toe-to-toe in dueling columns against our guy Dave Butler. Arsenault decried hockey violence and took a nice little shot at me after I appeared on a cable television show that Hoppy hosted every week from the Hi-Lo Tavern.

Arsenault wrote, "Hoppy was on the tube a couple weeks ago doing an interview with a fellow named Smith and a classy hockey player by the name of Lowell Loveday." I guess he intimated that I was a classless player. I watched a tape of that show over again to see if I said or did something wrong or classless, but for the life of me couldn't find anything that would be deemed offensive. I just answered questions about where I came from, what my favorite NHL teams were, and what my role on the Packers was.

Arsenault went so far as to lump my role on the Packers along with general violence and a "rash of killings on the river in recent years." He questioned my play as "a matter of moral decency."

I loved all that attention, but what a self-aggrandizing idiot. Talk about taking a sport a little too seriously. And to think Hoppy later told me that Arsenault had played some hockey with a similar role as mine, but had been a bigger asshole than I ever was.

Our paper fought back on my behalf, but I thought it was silly that the team felt it had to "explain [its] approach to hockey," as the headline stated. Coach Bawn, a competent hockey guy who knew the real score, played along and threw some obligatory quotes to show everybody I wasn't a homicidal maniac preparing the Miramichi for my own personal crime wave. He said in part, "Smith is aware how many local kids look up to him and he's made conscientious efforts to see that the kids understand how senior hockey works. Doug has visited many minor practices, he's skated with the kids, and he's sat down and talked with them in the dressing rooms. He points out that players have different roles, like some are scorers, some are back-checkers and so on."

At least I remained popular with the home fans, which is all that really mattered. In fact, even after I played a hand in ruining our playoff hopes the locals still wanted me back.

9

Sunk in Seniors

Away from the United States for the first time in my life while also being paid to play hockey ranked far behind the opportunity to hang around my teammate Jacques Mailhot. He was far and away the funkiest guy I ever played with. Mailhot was the nicest guy in the world off the ice, but when he got to the rink and took his teeth out, he transformed into as mean a bastard as you'd ever want to cross.

I lifted weights, punched the heavy bag, and sparred with guys on the ice and in the gym on a regular basis, but Mailhot did nothing. He didn't do a damned thing except skate. He was the ultimate hockey fighter.

Mailhot was about an inch or two taller than I and weighed in at around 215 pounds. He wasn't overly muscled but he was lean and long, especially in the arms, which he used to straighten out opponents and throttle them.

I took note of Mailhot's type of physical build in many of the players considered heavyweight hockey fighters. I checked them out in street clothes around the various arenas and thought they looked like skeletons in suits. They had obviously melted away most of their body fat from the aerobic effect of all the skating they did. In any event, they all seemed to have long arms and big, meaty fists, and that's what I saw when I squared off with them—those orangutan arms reaching out to me like a 3-D movie.

The patented physical characteristics didn't stop there. Mailhot also owned a huge, rock-solid head with a granite-like jaw for a base. I called it the "Lyndon Byers head." A head like that could absorb a beating, and Mailhot needed the protection because he didn't duck away from many punches.

Mailhot: "My chest and arms are not huge; I do a regular workout on them. But my legs are where I get all my strength. I don't do any boxing at all. Boxing has no association with hockey, they are two different sports. I always laugh at young guys who are working on their boxing skills. Boxing does not make you a good hockey fighter."

137

All I really had to offer hockey was my boxing skills and resulting fistic ability, and while Mailhot may have started out wanting to be a player, in many ways it seemed as though he was born to be a hockey fighter, a natural. But he wasn't, and few if any players are. The fact is, most enforcers grow up emulating the more skilled stars of the game. They dream of becoming the next Wayne Gretzky, Ray Bourque, or Dominik Hasek, certainly not the next hockey barbarian. The same was true of Mailhot and his early draw to gritty and talented New York Islanders forward John Tonelli. But before long, Mailhot's skill level and physical dimensions dictated a different role, that is, if he intended to continue playing hockey at the next level.

Some players recognize the path they must take to play professional hockey. Those who do not are usually delusional, eventually cut loose during training camp and left to get on with the rest of their lives working as teachers, construction workers, insurance salesmen, or uranium miners.

I recognized four distinct types of hockey enforcers while involved in the game over the years. There are guys like me who unabashedly love to fight from the moment they first hit the ice. I think this player is in the rarest category and probably the least valuable to a team.

Former Boston Bruin Jay Miller represented a second type—that of a talented player, good enough to be drafted by the NHL out of high school, who realized later that the only chance he had of forging an appreciable hockey career was to fight. This player has the intelligence to drop most preconceptions of his hockey ability in order to pursue a more successful avenue toward ultimate success, which usually entails making a legitimate living from the game.

A third type is represented by the late, great Bob Probert. This guy is a devastating two-way player who doesn't necessarily adore fighting, but knows a goodly amount of the impressive salary he is paid comes from dropping the gloves, so he continues to do it. This player can score consistently with his stick and fists, and continues to remain one of the most sought-after and elusive talents in all of pro hockey.

Yet a fourth type of enforcer is represented by former tough guy Paul Mulvey, who made it to the NHL as a goon. He had an epiphany, however, copped an attitude, and flatly refused to fight on orders from Los Angeles Kings coach John Brophy during a bench-clearing brawl in the early 1980s and saw his NHL career end from that moment forward. These are the guys who get sick and tired of their job, or maybe they didn't have that much passion for it in the first place, and decide they don't want to do it anymore. I don't know if I would trust this kind of guy to have the mettle to consistently stand up and be counted on when the going got rough.

From my vantage point, it seemed the most important aspect to either begin or sustain a career in hockey as an enforcer was to be able to honestly recognize your role as either the water pump or the bucket, and in only the rarest of instances could one player be both.

Mailhot started out as a wholly unremarkable young player, but when his early fights in juniors were met with cheers from the fans and praise from his teammates and coaches, the path of the goon beckoned and he smartly took it. Ultimately, circumstances partly under his control may have conspired to keep him from enjoying a pension-bound NHL career, but it seemed as though he was still better off playing hockey wherever he could earn a paycheck because he couldn't sing or dance.

As valuable as I thought Mailhot was for the Packers, and we were definitely a better team with him than without, he could strain his relationship with the club. The way I saw it, Mailhot figured that because he had played in the NHL, he should be playing first line, power play, and short-handed for the team. He didn't listen to the coach, he didn't listen to anybody. Nobody could tell Jacques Mailhot anything, and that may have been one of the reasons why he played for 18 different teams during an outrageous 13-year minor-league career. I thought of him as a traveling carnival that everybody was happy to see arrive, and relieved to be rid of following a short stay.

Bev Bawn: "Jacques had been playing with Moncton in the American League and he thought he was lowering himself to play with us. In the dressing room he was a pain-in-the-ass and made it rough on the other players. He thought he knew the game better than I did, and he may have, and he made it known that he should be playing in front of other players. But he put an extra 10 or 20 pounds on some of our more skilled players, so we overlooked the things he was doing, so maybe that was my fault."

Mailhot: "Playing in the senior league was a step down. I mean, these guys were skating twice a week and I was skating every single day. I was just there waiting for a shot back at the American or International League. My only reason for being there was money.

"Bev Bawn was doing some drills I couldn't understand, so I was trying to help him out like an assistant coach. We didn't see eye-to-eye most of the time, but he knew I would come to play every night and play hard so he kind of left me alone. I wanted to win; my desire to win was so strong."

Hoppy made me "The Hammer," but I liked Mailhot's nickname better. He was "The Mailman," and he delivered, but not so much here in the senior league, especially with the injured thumb he was nursing. There were a few other high profile tough guys in the league who also weren't interested in fighting on a consistent basis.

One of them played for the Cambellton Tigers, Gerry Fleming, a 6-foot-5, 240-pound behemoth who was undecided on whether to pursue a hockey career or continue with his college studies. Mailhot told me he had fought Fleming many times in previous senior league games and tuned him up. He said Fleming wouldn't want anything to do with him again, but that he also probably wouldn't fight me because there was really nothing in it for him.

I challenged Fleming anyway and he quickly dropped his gloves, to my pleasant surprise, but he was so strong that he just grabbed me and held tight with a bear-like grip. I am sure if I slipped a punch or two in on him he would've gotten really angry and given me a go, but he didn't seem interested in extending himself in the senior league. Fleming did choose to stick with hockey. His sheer size eventually landed him a spot with the Fredericton Canadians, and three years later he made it up to NHL with the parent club in Montreal.

Darwin McCutcheon was another interesting character. He went 6-foot-5 as well but was a bit leaner than Fleming at about 220 pounds. He was drafted as a defenseman out of juniors in 1980 and played his one and only NHL game with the Toronto Maple Leafs two years later on New Year's Eve, at the tender age of 18.

And that was it.

McCutcheon left his junior team after just 11 games the following season and enrolled in the University of Prince Edward Island, where he played hockey for four years. He came out and gave the pros another shot, signing with the Calgary Flames organization, but toiled in the high minors for four years before settling in for a pair of senior league seasons. I am certain the pinnacle of his playing career was getting that one game in The Show, but I was more intrigued with his suspension for biting a player during a fight in the American League in 1987. He has since gone on to use his formidable brain to become a business entrepreneur and real estate agent.

A few weeks before my fight with McCutcheon, Mailhot engaged him on the island in the best fight I have ever seen in person before or since. The fact my fight with Rene Labbe would be tabbed "Fight of the Year" was a joke compared to this one. It was an absolute toe-to-toe war with both guys using their long arms on each other like a pair of buggy whips. Mailhot got the worst of the early going, but kicked into his second wind and probably ended up with a decision over McCutcheon.

Mailhot: "McCutcheon was a big guy and he was running the show, abusing everybody, and everybody was thinking I was a softy because I hadn't fought yet, so I went after him. I started slowly, like I always do, and he got the best of me. But then I started going and later on people told me that every time I hit him I lifted him off the ice. We scored 30 seconds later and went on to win the game.

"Our next game against the Islanders was at home so I figured to get a shift or two, and sure enough with us ahead 7–2 midway through the third period Bawn answered orders from the fans and sent me over the boards."

Bev Bawn: "A few weeks before we were playing them on the Island and Mailhot and McCutcheon had a great fight, a real toe-to-toe battle. Mailhot wanted at him again the next game but I noticed they sent a second guy out there, so I sent Doug out to be a policeman, to make sure nobody stepped in and ganged up on Mailhot."

I knew Mailhot wanted at McCutcheon again because he had talked about it. But I have to admit to being jealous of their fight on the island. It is not a difficult concept to understand. A good defensive back should get a rise out of going up against the best receivers, and young baseball players are honored to dig in at home plate against the game's great pitchers. It was no different with me. Whenever I played, my goal was to fight the best guy on the ice, and McCutcheon was the best guy on the other team in this game.

But I was also an obedient foot soldier, so I skated down the length of the ice for a face-off in the Islanders' end, looked for the "second guy," and figured he was Islanders winger Darren Murphy. I lined up beside him and voiced my challenge before the puck was dropped but was flatly refused. When he skated away from me I was left alone in front of the net with the puck drawn back to my defenseman at the point, so I stayed there to try and screen the goalie, my old dancing partner Wayne Bernard.

As the play continued I found myself tangled up in the slot with McCutcheon, who had moved over to push me out from in front of his goalie. He came at me from the side so it took me a few seconds to actually realize it was him hovering around me like an octopus. I felt as though I had an opportunity presented to me on a silver platter. In so tight I seized the opportunity to drop my gloves and grab hold of McCutcheon. He had no choice but to follow suit.

We traded punches evenly at the start but he was tall so I pulled him in instead of trying to string him out, as I would have done against somebody my own height. With him in tight I was able to hinder his ability to wind up from downtown with his long arms. I switched hands and landed some nice shots before McCutcheon got pissed off and pushed away from me far enough to unfold those gorilla arms for some good punches of his own.

His last right hand cut me for 10 stitches over my left eye, but I didn't skip a beat and would like to think I pulled off a draw in the bout before the officials came in to break it up. When we were separated from each other and he saw that I was bleeding, McCutcheon raised both arms over his head in a victory salute.

I didn't think I lost the fight, despite the cut, so it took a moment for it to sink in that McCutcheon was showing me up in my home arena. Mailhot got pissed off immediately and made a wild dash toward McCutcheon, but the officials headed him off. While everyone was preoccupied with Mailhot, I did something I'd never done before.

I had always made it a point to march obediently to the penalty box or locker room after a fight. But this time I attacked McCutcheon and attempted to lace him with a flurry of angry right uppercuts and short overhand shots while he tried to cover up the best he could between the two linesmen.

The scene was totally out of character for me because I live by the credo that "fighting angry" is never a smart maneuver whether it be on the ice, street, or in the boxing ring. I always tried to fight using calm faculties so I

Getting socked by Darwin McCutcheon (center left) of Prince Edward Island.

could think about all of my options. Those who fight in anger tend to be out of control and wild; their punches aren't as crisp or on target and usually swing wide in roundhouse fashion. Roundhouse punches, as opposed to a classic straight-on boxer's shot using the hips and back for rotational power, also lead to more broken hands because there isn't as much of the body behind the punch to cushion the impact and support the hand's relatively delicate bone structure.

After I was brought under control and sent to the locker room, I missed the balance of Mailhot's antics. He had blown a fuse for some reason, but it wasn't a stretch to understand what he did with consideration to his previous history. He broke his stick in two against the boards, threw his helmet at a game official, and dove onto the Islanders' bench.

> **Mailhot:** "There was a lot of talk about a rematch between me and McCutcheon after our first fight on the island. Doug wanted him, too, but I told him, 'Smitty, don't even touch the guy, you're not ready for him.' Smitty wanted to do so well but he got bloodied. And then McCutcheon started raising his arms and showing him up, and that made me angry. Here was one of my teammates out there trying to do the best he can and somebody is making fun of him. So that's why I jumped into the bench. That's what got me suspended."

After Mailhot got kicked out of the game, he stomped into our locker room red-faced and furious and said to me, "Are you ready? Let's go."

I thought he meant for me to join him back on the ice for more fighting. Bleeding pretty well from my wound and waiting for the team doctor, I nevertheless followed like a sheep—but instead of walking up the ramp that would lead us to the ice we were headed for the Islanders' locker room. Mailhot was going to beat the shit out of McCutcheon; I guess we both were. The locker room was three doors down and we got to the second one before we were headed off by two policemen and escorted back. I am really glad we never reached McCutcheon because he would have gotten hurt.

During our next game against the Islanders I skated over to McCutcheon and apologized for attacking him as I did. He told me it was okay, that everybody loses his cool from time to time. He was a nice guy and said he'd give me a rematch, adding, "We'll do it again when your eye heals." I appreciated that offer from big Darwin, but we never did fight again.

> **Darwin McCutcheon:** "One thing I left that situation feeling badly about was that Doug asked me for a shot at a fight again and I said, 'Yes.' However, the coach told me to absolutely stay away. The coach wasn't happy

that I fought him in the first place and told me to stay out of fights as I used to log a lot of ice time."

In an incredible twist, one of a few that came out of playing in the senior league, I actually did have an opportunity to fight McCutcheon again—but we were both washed up and in our 50s. Nearly 25 years after our fight I was coaching in a high-level summer league in Massachusetts and out of the clear blue Darwin wandered over to me. He had made the trek east from his home in Colorado to watch his boy, who was playing in the league.

In any case, the Packers left the whole McCutcheon-Mailhot-Smith brawl feeling and playing much worse. My eye did heal just fine, but our team never recovered from the more dire consequences of the incident.

> **Bev Bawn:** "We had a shot at winning the championship but lost the chance against the Islanders. Doug wanted to fight McCutcheon himself, to show how tough he was. So Doug came out and McCutcheon gave it to him good, and that was the end of Doug's role. Mailhot went nuts, got suspended, and we lost him for the rest of the season."

> **Mailhot:** "The night that Doug fought McCutcheon I jumped into their bench and got suspended for 20-some games. At the time the team was in first place and everybody was playing good, but after I left the team they won three of 17 games and lost the run in the playoffs. So maybe I was hardheaded but not exactly a cancer [to the team]. Cancer is something that you want to eliminate."

Losing Mailhot was probably more disappointing for me than it was for the team because I idolized him so much, but his absence clearly rendered the Packers mortal. To make matters worse, we also lost our top goalie, Francois Gravel, to intermittent games with the Rochester Americans of the American Hockey League, as well as another talented and tough kid, Marc LaBelle, who skipped off to the Fredericton Canadiens. A few years later I watched with pride as LaBelle made it up the NHL for nine games with the Dallas Stars.

Even I had a few nibbles. Dave Butler wrote a column listing what some locals might "want or deserve from Santa Clause." The first note right there at the top of his column was "Miramichi Gagnon Packers Doug Smith—a few games with the Moncton Hawks." Dave Farrish, a good friend of Commander, coached the Hawks and talked to me a number of times about the possibility of coming in for a practice or even suiting up for a game "if the timing is right."

But the right time never came. The Packers walked undermanned and wounded through the last two weeks of the regular season into the playoffs.

We were dressing just 12 players, and our best defenseman, Lowell Loveday, was playing through an injury. We were so desperate for bodies that coach Bawn was forced to play me on a semi-regular shift.

Down the stretch I had to pick my spots. I couldn't afford to leave a game too early and further damage my struggling team. Heeding to the needs of my team while at the same time ignoring the pleas of the hometown fans for me to drop my gloves was a little uncomfortable, but it was nothing compared to the most pressure I ever had to deal with as a player.

I had become the most celebrated patron of the Hi-Lo Tavern. I ate almost all of my meals there and the place had a big picture of Hoppy and I hanging on the wall. Bernie Williams, the owner, told me that I "breathed life into the town."

It was incredible how well the locals treated me. I figured any moment I would wake up from this wonderful dream and be back at home with my mother yelling at me to take the trash to the dump.

Williams decided to capitalize on my popularity and announced a donation that he would make to the charity of my choice if I scored a goal in any of the team's final seven games. I hadn't scored a goal all season; in fact our goalie had more points than I did. But the deal was for $700 if I scored in the first game, and the figure would decrease by $100 for each of the six games that followed.

I actually had a breakaway in one of the games. I was floating around the ice looking for somebody to attack when a rogue puck bounced off the boards past a charging defenseman. The puck wobbled free and clear over the blue line, I picked it up and walked in alone, nearly tripping over the tip of my skate blade in the process. I reared back for a wrist shot and followed through, but the puck veered off to the right and came closer to going into the snack bar than the net. The crowd, which was well aware of the deal for charity, responded in unison with a collective groan. I wanted to cut a hole through the rink with an ice-fishing auger and drown myself.

I felt like such a loser, and the publicity surrounding the event in the papers didn't help the situation. After the last game was played, a 7–5 loss to the Islanders, the Transcript wrote in the "Notes" section that "Doug (The Hammer) Smith of the Packers played about a regular shift, didn't take a penalty, but, alas, failed to score, thereby killing a couple of well-publicized wagers that would have benefited local charity."

That little piece really made me feel like a million bucks. Williams pulled my ass out of the fire, somewhat, when he announced that he would donate ten percent of the final game's attendance number in a dollar amount to the Big Brothers/Big Sisters organization in my behalf. Team owner, Mr. Gagnon, agreed to match the figure and the two of them said they'd double the amount if I scored. Of course I didn't.

During warm-ups in the last game, Wayne Bernard and Darwin McCutcheon both told me that they were going to let me score. Bernard started in net and every time I came near him he yelled for me to just shoot at him, but I was so inept that I couldn't even get a handle on one loose puck in order to direct it at him.

We went on to lose six of the seven quadruple semifinal round-robin playoff games. Three of our losses were by one goal to the Saint John Vito's, including two in overtime. We threw in the towel before playing the eighth game, which didn't have a bearing on the rest of the playoffs.

My last fight came midway through the third period during a 9–2 loss in the playoffs against the Islanders. Bob Doiron, a blocky 5-foot-9, 210-pounder who always had something to say about me in the papers, had been running around acting like a tough guy. In the second period he flattened our goalie, who then left the game in a huff.

Doiron had been playing hockey for a long time, he knew the score and he could count. It was obvious we didn't have enough bodies to afford me the luxury of fighting at the drop of a hat, so he grew himself a pair of brass balls and was running around with no care in the world. Finally I had taken all I could of his act and started to challenge him whenever we were on the ice together. He wouldn't fight, and what was worse, he wore a face shield, which made me physically ill. I said to him, "How can you call yourself a tough guy with that motorcycle helmet on?"

Bawn put me out on the ice for what was probably going to be one of my last shifts of the game with nine minutes left in the third period, so I decided to go after Doiron and make him fight. Before I dropped my gloves I thought about how I was going to deal with the face mask.

Because my fights had dried up I really wanted this one and didn't intend to waste time ripping Doiron's helmet off and risk having the officials break up the fight before it had a chance to get started. So I decided to just throw uppercuts and catch him underneath the shield. I threw two or three right uppercuts and caught him with a good one that dropped him to the ice. I wasn't very impressed with Doiran's conduct during the game, especially with him wearing the mask and not wanting to fight, so I stood over him and yelled, "You've got a glass jaw, you phony!"

Needing every single body we had, Bawn was again forced to play me on a regular shift against the Islanders in what turned out to be our final playoff game. For my part I didn't dare fool around and get myself kicked out of the game, and it ended up being the most productive performance of my brief career as I managed to log assists on our first and last goals of the game, and screened goalie Wayne Bernard on another. The Islanders scored an empty-net goal to make it 7–5, and with a minute left, Bawn was nice enough to give me the final shift. Of course I dropped my gloves with Bernard for old-time's sake, but unfortunately the officials moved in quickly and halted my farewell to our great home fans.

Bernard and Company moved on to the national playoffs and eventually won the coveted Allan Cup. I could not have cared less. While I would have rather won a championship than not, and understood and respected my team-mates' enthusiasm, being an American precluded me from sharing in their provincial passion for the Allan Cup. The same has been said about the motivation of many foreign players in the NHL. Weaned more on dreams of playing for their respective national teams and winning a World Championship or an Olympic medal, they have been accused of playing merely with the motivation of money rather than with the fanatical obsession to hoist and kiss the Stanley Cup.

Be that as it may, there was actually some talk around town and in the papers that I was going to stay in the area during the summer to play semi-pro baseball for the Newcastle Cardinals of the New Brunswick Senior Baseball League. They figured all Americans were good baseball players, just like folks in the States figure everybody from Canada plays hockey, or that all Asians know karate. I may have helped spread the baseball rumor as well, but if they thought my skills as a hockey player were poor, they hadn't seen anything until I showed them how I swung a bat or caught a ball. I let the baseball rumor die with the excuse that I was homesick.

I really did want to go home. New Brunswick was a beautiful place, but I missed my family and girlfriend. The Packers asked me to come back the next season but I knew I wouldn't. I had led the team with 16 fights and 170 penalty minutes, but the money wasn't attractive enough to stick around for. After throwing Hoppy and his dad a measly $50 a week—and I'm sure I ate double that—there wasn't much left to pay my various bills and send some home to help out my mother.

The Hi-Lo Tavern threw me a farewell party, which was just another classy move by the people of that wonderful town. Unfortunately for them, however, some really bad times for the team were just around the corner.

Later it was learned that there had been some money missing from the team's coffer. The Packers lost their sponsor and disbanded the next year. The team eventually came back for a short time under new ownership, changed its name to the Maple Leafs, and brought in my old friend Link Gaetz to fill the role I had played.

Hoppy Dunn: "The quality of the league was down and the [Maple Leafs] didn't have as good a team, but they still had a chance for a trip to Nova Scotia for a run at the Allan Cup if they won their final game. But Gaetz blew it on us. He stayed out too late and was throwing up in the locker room. We lost."

There is much more to the brief and dysfunctional marriage between Gaetz, Miramichi, and alcohol, but my favorite episode is about the Miramichi police finding a huge miner, who had been badly beaten by Gaetz, left for dead in a snow bank.

According to a local guy who knew both parties, after a night of drinking the two got into a car and then argued, but "if you're gonna shoot your mouth off with Link, you're gonna get it shut. That lad got his face dismembered. He looked like he was wearing a Halloween mask."[1]

When I learned of this I recalled the special point Coach Bawn made in the newspaper about how I conducted myself and didn't drink. There were only about 18,000 people living in the city of Miramichi when I was there, and I looked upon it as an unassuming, delicate, yet proud community that I would be embarrassed to soil. I guess Link didn't give a damn about that.

A few years later I was at Fenway Park in Boston for a Red Sox game with Gator. We were walking along an isle to get to our seats when I heard a voice clearly within the crowd of thirty-six thousand people yell, "Haaaamer, Haaaamer." May lightning strike me dead if it wasn't a group from the Hi-Lo Tavern taking in the game. I raced up to their seats high behind home plate and shot the breeze. For a moment I could breathe the crystal clean and cool air of the Miramichi, and tomorrow I would fight Big Bad Wayne Bernard for the New Brunswick Senior League Heavyweight Championship again.

But the fact was that I hadn't played a game in two years and was resigned to my new job challenging shoplifters as a full-time cop working the Hanover Mall beat. I was forced to be content with my memories of being a shooting star in a small city tucked away inside another country.

I had nine hockey lives, however, and my best experience in the game was yet to come. As strange as it was to meet up with Rock Derganc again, little could I have imagined that I'd soon end up back in New Brunswick for a date with "The Animal."

10

Hit in the Big Time

It was Christmas 1993, nearly three years removed from playing for Miramichi in the New Brunswick Senior League. I continued to mail my videotaped resume to minor-league teams based about the East Coast, but now I was doing it more out of habit because with my police job there was little chance I could pack up and leave to play for any sustained period of time.

I did have my chances.

I received a number of phone calls from various East Coast League teams inquiring if I'd be interested in coming in for a weekend here or there, or even to finish out the end of a season. But with their low pay scale and zero job security, I couldn't afford to leave my job as a beat copy at the mall, as I was positioning myself for either a better position on the Hanover Police Department, or on the force in a neighboring town. I continued skating, but my hope of playing at least one game in the American Hockey League was growing dimmer with each passing season.

In the meantime, Gator was excited about a surgical procedure he underwent to remedy a condition known by the medical term "gynocomastia," which was caused by his earlier use of anabolic steroids. Called "bitch tits" among the steroid crowd, gynocomastia is a peculiar and embarrassing feminization of male breast tissue. The steroids Gator had used nearly 10 years earlier had supplied his body with too much of the male hormone testosterone. He told me that the culprit was a chemical process called "aromatization" during which excess testosterone was transformed into the less-harmful, primary-female hormone estrogen, which caused his chest to grow something on the order of a 13-year-old girl at puberty. As far as I was concerned, my doctor told me that this condition also afflicts 50 percent of all males naturally, especially during the testosterone-fueled growth sport of puberty, which is when I first began to notice my own excess growth.

I decided to cash in on the few days of vacation time I had accrued in order to go under the knife after Christmas. You could think of this as breast-

149

reduction. The procedure entailed day surgery under full anesthesia. Half-moon incisions were made below each nipple, the skin was stretched wide, and the benign growths were cut out. There were sutures on the inside, and tape-like breathable bandage strips were used to cover the open incisions in order to lessen external scarring. I was also fitted with a tight chest girdle for additional support and told that full recovery time would be on the order of two months.

One day after the operation, my entire chest area over to my armpits was black and blue, and any movement I made that employed my chest muscles was met with a jolt of searing pain. I became so tuned-in to my chest and the inevitability of pain that if I didn't keep busy my concentration would force my chest muscles to twitch, which was like putting my hand on a red-hot stove.

Two days after surgery there was increased swelling and additional pain caused by an interior infection. My doctor removed the tape strips and inserted a thin, three-inch length of clear rubber tubing into each incision. Small bags were attached to these tubes in order to collect a foul-smelling, yellow-, red-, and black-spotted fluid that drained from the wounds.

Shortly after I returned home wearing this contraption I took a phone call from Commander, who arranged for and asked if I'd be interested in playing a game Saturday night, New Year's Day, for the Moncton Hawks, the American League affiliate of the Winnipeg Jets.

Moncton ... the American League. What?

I was in a daze while engaged in some small talk before I hung up the phone. I must have told Commander that I would play.

It finally happened, clear out of the blue, I was going to play a game in the AHL, the second-best hockey league in the world!

For a moment I forgot about the puss dripping into the small bags from the tubes sticking out of the gaping holes in my chest. I twitched my chest muscles and winced.

Of all the time I had in my life to have this surgery I had to have it right before this once-in-a-lifetime opportunity. You had to be shitting me.

But it really didn't matter, I had no choice. There was absolutely no question that I was going to fight in the American Hockey League, no question at all. My chest would have to take a back seat and any further damage done would be dealt with at a later time.

Commander relayed my answer to Moncton and a few hours later, Hawks coach Robbie Laird called me with the particulars. He said that his team's primary tough guy, Kevin McClelland, had been suspended and I was going to take his place for this one game. The Hawks arranged for me to fly out of Logan Airport in Boston that evening, they'd put me up in a nice hotel in town, I'd skate with the team in the morning, and be in the lineup that night against the visiting St. John's Maple Leafs, the top farm club of the NHL's Toronto Maple Leafs.

I checked my equipment in at baggage but carried my skates with me on the plane. I figured that with my skating as bad as it was, especially with respect to the American Hockey League, I couldn't afford to have the skates I'd grown accustomed to end up in Alaska.

While on the plane I noticed Andy Brickley, a Boston guy who had spent some time with the Bruins. He was playing out the end of his career with Moncton now but he was nursing an injury and had gone home for the holidays. When he saw me holding my skates he stared at me but I didn't speak to him.

Once over the Canadian border we landed and were transferred to a small, propeller-driven puddle-jumper for the short taxi to Moncton. Brickley and I were pretty much alone on the little plane so there was no choice for us but to start talking to each other. He offered me a beer from a stash in his portable cooler when I told him I was coming in to play the one game against St. John's for the Hawks. We sat together the rest of the way and he prepped me for my job at hand. He told me that St. John's had a team full of tough guys, but three in particular to watch out for. One was Ryan VandenBussche, who was on the small side at 5-foot-11 and 185 pounds, but game as hell. Another was a kid about my size, Todd Gillingham.

But the most fearsome of them all was 6-foot, 235-pound Frank Bialowas, a 23-year-old goon with two years of mayhem in the East Coast League behind him. He was in the middle of a 389-penalty minute season that would lead to his NHL debut with the parent Maple Leafs at the end of the year—a four-game "Thank You" that Bialowas took full advantage of by fighting two of the baddest names in the Big Leagues, Quebec's Tony Twist and Winnipeg's Tie Domi.

Brickley also told me that Bialowas was called "The Animal." It wasn't a nickname Bialowas made up, others gave it to him. Sometimes they call the fat kid "slim" on the playground for a joke, but in minor-league hockey nobody is called *Animal* for a joke.

"Good luck, kid, do what you have to do, but be careful about fighting Bialowas," said Brickley. "If you fight him you could be in for a long recuperation period."

Great, now I was nervous and I hadn't even gotten to the rink yet. Did I really want to get killed? I hadn't played a meaningful game of hockey in years and I was hurt. Do I take on the smaller guy first and work my way up from there to gain some confidence? I figured, if I couldn't beat VandenBuss-che, I couldn't beat the other guy—never mind the fact that I knew there was no way I could actually skate at this level.

I met Robbie Laird and he thanked me for coming in on such short notice. He thanked *me*. I had to laugh, he didn't get it.

He asked me what I wanted for money and I told him that the airfare and hotel was enough. "You're giving me the opportunity of a lifetime," I said. "If it's not too much of a problem, could I keep my game jersey?"

Laird smiled and said, "Sure."

I walked into the Hawks' locker room and everybody was staring at me; they wanted to know who the hell I was. I scanned the room and through the maze of players and personnel I fixed my eyes on Kevin McClelland.

I expected to see a bigger man. This guy won three Stanley Cups with the Edmonton Oilers. He stood side-by-side with the likes of Dave Semenko and Marty McSorley as part of Wayne Gretzky's bodyguard corps for years, and he was no bigger than I.

McClelland had a very intense appearance; his eyes were wide and wild and crazy looking, a little like those of the comic actor Marty Feldman. Even when he shook my hand to greet me he didn't crack a smile, in fact he looked as though he would just as likely punch me out. The Hawks gave me a stall next to McClelland's. He was Number 24 and they gave me Number 23—a pretty good hockey number for a guy just barging in.

McClelland stayed with me. He hovered over me the whole time and made me feel at home, and I needed it because I was shitting bullets. He asked me if I'd like to wear his gloves because they were well broken-in and easy to drop. I told him it would be an honor.

I sat on my stool dressed in long underwear shivering and biting my nails. Again, just like before my first game for the Thunderbirds I felt as though my entire body was shaking and hoped nobody else noticed it. McClelland did. He took me aside and asked if I was nervous and I told him I was.

"Well you should be," he said. "It would probably be best if you left Bialowas alone. If you fight Frank you could be sound asleep in a matter of seconds."

Great. McClelland winked and gave me a pat on my shoulder. He reminded me of Jacques Mailhot.

Rob Murray was listening. He was one of the Hawks' best players and a pretty tough character himself. "You're going to fight The Animal?" he chirped. "Well, there should be no problem getting that game jersey because if you fight Bialowas you can wear the jersey on the stretcher on your way out the door."

Great.

I went out for warm-ups and meandered around. I didn't dare take a shot because of the immediate pain I knew it would cause in my chest. Then I had a terrifying thought: "What if I got into a fight and had my jersey pulled up over my head and everybody saw those drainage bags hanging off me? I'd be mortified!"

After warm-ups I made a beeline for the locker room bathroom and locked myself into one of the stalls to examine my predicament. I fingered one of the tubes sticking out of my chest and gently nudged it to see how easily it would slip out. It didn't budge. I pulled a little harder and my skin, which appeared to have started to bond to the rubber with the help of some dried blood and puss, kissed the tube and stretched along with my pull. I felt sick to my stomach and broke out into a cold sweat. I thought I was going to faint so I sat on the toilet, leaned against the stall wall, shut my eyes, and tried to control my breathing. When I regained my focus I decided to pull on one of the tubes and not stop until it was out. The tube broke free of my skin with a suction-pop sound and followed one, two, three inches out. Tears of yellow- and black-stained ooze wept from the open wound. Feeling a little nauseous again I pulled the other one out before I lost my nerve. It was done. I reapplied the tape strips and chest girdle and was ready to go.

I took a shift earlier than I expected in the first period and lined up on the left wing beside VandenBussche and said, "Hey, how you feeling tonight, feel like going?"

VandenBussche replied, "Who the fuck are you, where are you from?"

"It doesn't matter who I am. I'm only an ATO player, why are you afraid of me?"

An ATO is a guy on an amateur tryout, a nobody, like me. He wouldn't fight off the face-off so I chased him around a bit. The puck came around to him by the left-wing boards and he got rid of it quickly, but I gave him a little cross-check anyway and backed off to give him a chance to drop his gloves. He responded with a nervous laugh and skated off. Not daring to involve myself in the play I quickly retreated to the bench.

When all was said and done, I had never challenged anybody in a pro game who ended up as accomplished as VandenBussche. He went on to play in 311 NHL games and fight every heavyweight who passed through his crosshairs. Only years later did I find out why he didn't drop the gloves with me.

Ryan VandenBussche: "I didn't fight [Doug] because the game before I hurt my thumb and my hand was taped up. When I got back to St. John's I was told that my ligament was torn completely off the bone. I was out for eight weeks."

The home team is allowed the last line change of players, so when Coach Laird saw Todd Gillingham and Frank Bialowas step on the ice for a shift with 5:25 left in the period he said, "Smitty, jump out on the wing."

The face-off was deep in the Leafs' end so I had some time to think as I slowly skated the length of the ice to take my spot beside the pair. I was nervous and a little scared, but more because I was afraid to embarrass myself. I also felt a little outside my body in a way I could only explain in that it truly was a dream-come-true, and so unreal and exciting that it didn't even seem to be happening.

There was no choice to be made between the two players; Bialowas was the better fighter of the two so he was the guy I would challenge. While waiting for the puck to drop I turned and said, "Hey Frank, are you going to go with me or be a pussy like the other guy?"

Gillingham turned to Bialowas and said, "Coach doesn't want you to fight, don't waste your time."

I told Gillingham to shut up and mind his own business.

Bialowas didn't pay Gillingham any mind, either. "Fuck the coach," said Bialowas. Then he turned to me and said, "Okay, let's go, just keep it clean."

I had certainly heard that request before, but this time, at this level, I didn't mind. I was a new guy trying to make a name for himself and Bialowas

A nice square-off against Frank "The Animal" Bialowas (right)...

didn't want me to do anything foolish in the process. Later I thought more about what this might mean, and I suppose hair-pulling, eye-gouging, head-butting, and biting may be some of the things somebody might do to win a fight at any cost.

The puck dropped, we stood up, flung our sticks and gloves away and squared off. I skated near Frank's stick and motioned to an official to get it out of the ring.

We sized each other up for a few seconds. Frank's arms were very active, as they always were in the videos I watched. His fists bounced up and down in front of his face. I held my hands at shoulder height and prepared to box, but Frank dove into me with his arms outstretched and his head down. We grabbed hold of each other's jersey on the right shoulder with our left hand and began throwing rights.

I started off pretty well and delivered four or five straight right-hand shots. But Frank was strong. None of my punches made good enough contact for any impact and I dropped my head for a moment—long enough for Frank to pop me with an uppercut, and when my head shot up he followed with a sharp overhand right that landed square on the brow above my left eye.

I saw a quick spray of stars and pictured myself as a cartoon character. I lost my grip on his arm and he was able to pepper me with a series of wild rights while I scrambled for something to hold on to and keep my balance.

...but this was the aftermath of my first fight in the American Hockey League.

I begged the officials to let the fight continue when they jumped in to stop things, and I tried to rip my helmet off because it had shifted down a bit over my eyes. When I finally did take it off my performance was over, the officials weren't going to let this one go any longer, there was too much blood. It was done and I was a mess.

As I stood cradled in the arms of a linesman I looked down and watched my blood drip in strips onto my skates and into a small red puddle on the ice. "At least I didn't go down," I thought to myself. That is what Commander always told me, to never let a guy beat you down because it always made things look worse than they were and this was bad enough.

> **Jay Miller, former NHL enforcer:** "I always hid my scars, my cuts. You try to hide your blood so you can come out looking like a rose. If I was bleeding I'd wipe it off on the shirt or on the shoulder of the guy I was fighting. If I was bleeding from my mouth I'd suck it in and spit it out when nobody could see me."

I took solace in the fact that I absorbed Bialowas' best shot and didn't go down, but too much blood to hide from a decisive defeat in the biggest fight of my life continued to spill in front of the home fans. I skated with my head down toward the bench and to the locker room for repairs.

As I walked down the runway a quick memory flashed into my head of Rick Boyd, who I replaced for three games in Johnstown a few years earlier. He was playing his first game in the American League with the Maine Mariners and I laughed when I saw him on television bleeding badly from an ugly forehead gash after a fight against Cape Breton's David Haas. Boyd told me later that his cut was caused by his own helmet digging in to him. Now I wondered who would be laughing at me.

One of the equipment guys followed me into the trainer's room and surprised me a bit when he quickly lifted my jersey off without any warning or instruction. He returned a bit later with no hint of blood on my shirt. Maybe he scrubbed it out with hydrogen peroxide or something, but I recall him saying something about looking professional, and that it would be bush league to return to the game with blood all over my jersey.

The team doctor met me in the trainer's room and was very nonchalant about the whole affair, as I'm sure he'd stitched up many cuts before. The trainer was far more entertained. He took a Polaroid of my face. He had a lot of Polaroids taped on his wall.

"I want to add this to my collection," he said with a laugh. "I've never seen an eye like that before."

Great.

I stretched out on the trainer's table and squinted into the overhead light to watch the doctor's fingers sew my gash closed. I couldn't help but think of all the other players he'd done this for over the years. It was if he were darning an old sock. I can't recall if the doctor shot me up with any pain killer, but I was too numb with excitement, maybe contentment, to feel much pain. I knew I had made it to this level and fought the toughest guy in the league. All I could have asked more for was to have done better in the fight.

Then reality kicked in, and I thought about work. I had to be at the mall walking my beat in two days and my police chief wouldn't be pleased with the way I looked. Presenting a police officer to the public with the appearance of a common street brawler was something the department tended to discourage.

When the doctor was finished with his handy work I got up to look at myself in the mirror. I had never seen a black eye as bad as mine, except maybe in photographs of former Boston Red Sox outfielder Tony Conigliaro after he was hit in the face by Jack Hamilton's fastball at Fenway Park back in 1967. Bialowas had also busted my nose with a glancing blow, pushing it down and off to the right side of my face. I had broken my nose so many times before that it created as much of an inconvenience as missing supper. I simply snapped it back in place.

The trainer asked me if I wanted to wear a shield on my helmet for the rest of the game. I didn't, I was a fighter and only college kids and other pussies wore shields.

Coach Laird came in to check on me. I told him that I was a one-eyed fighter, but if things got rough I'd go out there and do the best I could. Other than that, I told him not to worry about sitting my ass on the bench. I didn't know what Laird thought of me then, but after he left Moncton to coach the Phoenix Roadrunners in the International League, he thought enough to fly me down for a tough, three-game weekend set.

The beating I took from Bialowas, however, may have been matched by the fiasco that dumb-ass Gator endured on his trip to Moncton to watch me play.

Apart from attending training camp, Gator never saw me play a game in person while I was with the Carolina Thunderbirds. During my short stint with the Johnstown Chiefs, he actually drove away from a vacation in Los Angeles in order to catch what was supposed to be a meeting against Troy Crowder in Nashville, Tennessee. When he stopped in Texas to call my mother to make sure I was still with the team, I answered the phone to give him the bad news myself.

There was no way Gator intended to miss my first game in the American

League. With the one-day notice he conducted some quick weather research and found there was no snow expected on the 560-mile route from his house to Moncton. He planned on a solid 10-hour drive at a very conservative 55 MPH to give himself enough leeway. He kissed his wife and four-month-old daughter goodbye and took my car. He left at 8 a.m. on New Year's Day with the goal of reaching Moncton's Maritime Coliseum at 6 p.m., an hour before game time.

With virtually no traffic on the highways through New Hampshire and Maine, Gator had enough confidence and extra time to stop for an hour and enjoy an afternoon lunch. As he crossed the Canadian border, however, the radio clued him in to his first glaring mistake.

It never occurred to Gator that the eastern-most sliver of continental Canada, including Moncton, was in a different time zone. He had crossed from the Eastern Zone into the western-most border of the Atlantic Zone—a full hour ahead of his time calculations. His watch read 4 p.m., but the radio told him it was really 5. He still figured he had things licked. Even a blinding snow squall 100 miles south of Moncton didn't stop him from reaching the arena at 7 p.m., Atlantic time; right on time for the game—and that was his second mistake.

This was a little bit before the Internet took over people's lives; before websites like MapQuest and PornCentral became as part and parcel of the American household as the toilet. If this game had occurred today, Gator may have surfed the Moncton Hawks' homepage and been made aware of a thing or two.

After he parked my car and began to make his way toward the arena's doors carrying his video recorder and 35mm still camera, he thought it odd to hear the crowd cheering so loudly—too loud for warm-ups. Maybe the game started exactly at seven. Mistake Number 2. Because of the holiday, the game's start time was pushed back an hour, to 6. Even I didn't know about that.

Gator picked up the ticket I left for him at the box office and charged into the arena to find the second period half over. In a blind panic he quizzed the usher beside him. Afraid of the answer, he asked if there had been any fights.

"Yes, one in the first period."

Gator asked if he knew who fought, and an older gentleman, a Moncton Hawks fan, joined in on the conversation and confirmed Gator's fear.

"Some new guy, I don't know who he is. He was cut pretty bad, though. He lost the fight."

Gator's heart sank, and not because I lost the fight, although I'm sure that fact bothered him somewhat, but because he missed it. After everything we had been through, all the training, all the hopes and dreams we both shared of me making it to this point, and he missed my fight, *this fight*, out of sheer stupidity.

At least this time I didn't have to go through the trouble of placing an advertisement in the Moncton newspaper looking for a video of the fight. The game was filmed by the television show *Rinkside,* and the cameraman made me a crystal clear copy of my destruction at the hands of Frank "The Animal" Bialowas.

This hockey fight, and some of my others, are part of the world's historical record being catalogued every second of the day on YouTube. And while it makes up only part of a tiny pimple on the ass of an elephant when it comes to the human experience, I still smile when somebody like Ryan Vanden-Bussche vividly remembers such an insignificant encounter and event. If I received nothing else from my experiences in hockey (and I've received far too much), the knowledge of my impact with respect to creating memories and experiences for others must be right at the top of the list—including the following email I received 18 years after the fight.

> **Dave Gushue:** "I spent some of my childhood in Riverview, NB watching the Moncton Hawks.... One game stuck out in our memories in all those years. That game was the one you played in. My father, who is a great story teller, tells of the buildup in the pregame skate and claims you went after a few guys like VandenBussche before going after Bialowas.... I remember, too, how the blood stayed on the ice after the Zamboni passed. It's been a story that my father has told for years as we often relive sports moments. He spent the next day after that game on an airplane with the goalie from that game who retold my dad of the inside details...."

I met up with Gator inside the rink after the game and he laughed at my eye. It was swelling more shut with each passing moment and made it a bit difficult to sign decent autographs for the kids waiting outside the locker room. We went out to dinner with me wearing my damaged face like a hockey badge of courage. After one more night in the deluxe suite the Hawks had provided, I tossed away my plane ticket home and joined Gator for the drive back to Massachusetts.

Gator drove because I had trouble lifting my arms. There was tremendous pain in the left side of my chest because I used my left hand to hold Bialowas while attempting to pull him in during the fight. I was bleeding through the gauze I taped on the incisions and worried that I may have caused more serious internal damage. On top of that my head continued to pound from the tremendous punch I had absorbed. It was a headache that began during supper, kept me from sleeping, and escorted me all the way home to Massachusetts.

When we arrived at Gator's house his young daughter, Adrianna, who was as familiar with me as she was with many of her uncles, met me at the front door. She took one look at my face and screamed. Frightened, she started to cry. I thought it seemed a fitting cap to the whole experience as I turned away and walked out the door.

11

Rent-A-Goon

All of my physical wounds healed, but I was somewhat disappointed at what I knew to be a ringing defeat in the biggest fight of my life against Frank Bialowas. Coach Robbie Laird hinted that his Hawks may need me again, maybe even as a soon as the next weekend, but another phone call didn't come.

Former teammates of mine who had taken coaching positions in the East Coast League began to call me, wondering if I'd want to help them out on a short-term basis. It seemed as though I had developed the reputation of a rent-a-goon. I didn't mind, but while I was still dying to play, I couldn't afford to jeopardize my job on the police department for a weekend of fights in Greensboro, North Carolina, or Pensacola, Florida.

My worst regret came when former NHL fighting great and Stanley Cup winner Chris Nilan, who was coaching the Chesapeake Icebreakers in the East Coast League, called to ask if I'd be interested in finishing out the last half of the season for him. As much as I would have been honored to just skate in a practice session with Nilan, the police department couldn't allow me the extended leave.

Finally, agent Brian Cook paged me at work on a Saturday morning and told me that the Albany River Rats needed a guy that night. The River Rats were the top affiliate of the NHL's New Jersey Devils. It would be another game in the American League for me against the Cornwall Aces, who had a couple of tough guys. I may have balked at leaving work for a night to play in the East Coast League, but another game in the AHL was a different story.

My heart raced. The Cornwall Aces. There was only one guy who played for Cornwall as far as I was concerned, a legend who walked in the same shoes as Jacques Mailhot. I was going to fight Serge Roberge. Fighting Frank Bialowas was special, he was a big name, but he was an up-and-comer. Roberge had already done it all, fought everybody, played in the NHL. He was to minor-league hockey fighting what Rembrandt was to art historians—a Master.

Then my heart skipped a beat. The only flight to Cornwall was in two hours. I didn't have the time to get anybody to cover my shift. I couldn't go. I felt sick, I wanted to throw up.

No doctor could have given me a better cure for that momentous letdown than Springfield Falcons general manager Bruce Landon, who called later on a Saturday night to ask if I'd be interested in coming in to straighten out a fellow by the name of Dennis Bonvie.

Landon explained to me that the Falcons were in the midst of back-to-back games against the Cape Breton Oilers, the AHL affiliate of the NHL's Edmonton Oilers. Bonvie had run around wild and unchallenged during Saturday's game and his unchecked shenanigans embarrassed the Falcons during a 9–5 loss.

The Falcons were actually the old Moncton Hawks that I had made my AHL debut with and fought Bialowas. The franchise packed up for Central Massachusetts when the ancient Springfield Indians moved down the Massachusetts Turnpike to Worcester. The Falcons were sharing a dual affiliation with the NHL's Winnipeg Jets and Hartford Whalers, and the Springfield Civic Center was a mere two-hour drive from my home. For the first time all of my friends would be able to come out to watch me play.

Paul Gillis coached the Falcons. I remembered watching him play with the Quebec Nordiques. The Bruins had his polite brother, Mike, and Quebec had nasty Paul.

The Falcons were short two guys for Sunday because John Stevens was serving a suspension and Brad Jones was injured. I was disappointed kooky Marc Laforge had been traded away from the Oilers. When I was playing with the Miramichi Packers in New Brunswick there had been some talk that I would be brought in by the Moncton Hawks specifically to fight him. Laforge was an established veteran heavyweight goon with some NHL experience, and he would have been my first choice to fight.

Cape Breton did have another big guy on the roster I could tangle with, John Van Kessel, but it was clear I had to zero in on Bonvie.

I knew enough about Bonvie, a 21-year-old, 5-foot-11, 200-pound Bialowas-like character. He went hog wild in junior hockey before making a name for himself in professional hockey by piling up 289 penalty minutes his first season with Cape Breton. Now he was going all out during an eventual 422-minute sophomore year in an attempt to attract the attention of the mother club in Edmonton. His shenanigans did in fact get noticed and he was awarded a two-game call-up later in the season. When all was said and done he'd log 93 games in the NHL over his playing career while also becoming the American League's all-time penalty-minutes leader. Good for him—and I don't mean that half-heartedly; he did it the really hard way.

Bonvie was a good puncher, but he was also a couple of inches shorter and maybe 15 pounds lighter than I, and I was always very confident against smaller guys. That is why I came into the game more interested in fighting the 6-foot-4 Van Kessel.

A group of my friends from the Boys' Club showed up in Springfield to watch me. They brought video recorders, cameras, and "Doug the Thug" banners. There were also many familiar faces in the Falcons' locker room, including Rob Murray, who was in Moncton for my fight against Bialowas.

I had a blast during warm-ups skating around wearing an AHL uniform and taking a few shots on our goalie in front of my friends. They also got a chance to check out a ploy I had fine-tuned over the years.

Whenever I got called in to play for a team I prayed I was going to be the extra guy and not have to skate a regular shift. I didn't want to make a fool out of myself by looking out of place skating on the ice. Well, I viewed warm-ups with some of the same fear.

When you're a new guy everybody watches you—the opponents, your teammates, the press, and the local fans—because they want to know what you're all about. I didn't want anybody to see me screw up trading passes with my teammates, so I'd usually pass up on the drills in favor of cruising lazily between the blue lines and making like I was stretching out. Other times I'd hook up with a teammate and either stand by the bench or coast around talking bullshit with him. If I was skating it would be a nice, slow glide. What everybody else in the arena didn't realize was that I was intently concentrating on making my skating appear effortless and perfect so as not to look out of place.

While all of the other players left the ice at the end of warm-ups I remained out for a few minutes longer to toss pucks into the stands for young fans. I read that Nick Fotiu had done it when he played and the fans loved him for it. I adopted the gesture during my first year pro with the Carolina Thunderbirds, and since nobody told me to stop or that giving away pucks was costing the team too much money I kept doing it everywhere I went to play.

I sat out for most of the first period while the two teams struggled through a scoreless game. Then with a minute left in the period I was sent out for a face-off on the left side of the Oilers' end. Bonvie was already there.

Earlier during warm-ups, while I was stretching by the boards near center ice, Bonvie skated by and I studied him. I never considered myself a huge guy when I played at 6-foot-2 and 215 pounds, but as my eyes fixed on the name "BONVIE" on the back of his jersey it hit me yet again that I was bigger than this guy, which gave me a jolt of confidence. I watched him kneel down on the red line by his bench to stretch, so I moved over beside and stared at him for a moment.

I have never been one afraid to start the ball rolling when it came to saying something to piss somebody off, and I could start a fight in a second with a few choice words. When Bonvie looked over at me I seized on the opportunity and said, "Hey buddy, who's the tough guy on your team?"

Of course everybody in the American League knew who Dennis Bonvie was, and his reaction to my question was equal parts annoyed and incredulous in that either I really didn't know who he was, or I was screwing with his head.

I added, "They brought me in to fight some guy on your team who thought he was the balls last night hitting all the foreign guys."

Bonvie paused and said, "That must be me."

I stood back up onto my skates, looked down at Bonvie and said, "No shit you midget, don't get lost out here tonight."

With that I turned and skated away from him, the table fully set for when I lined up beside him on the face-off and said, "I heard you're a real tough guy picking on all the Swedes."

Bonvie shot back, "Who the fuck are you?"

It is funny to think about all the guys who have said that to me over the years. Undaunted I said, "Want to find out?"

Squaring off against Cape Breton's Dennis Bonvie (center left).

The puck dropped, I bumped Bonvie, made eye contact, slowly backed off, and flung my gloves and stick far behind me while my teammates moved the puck dangerously close to the Oilers' net. Bonvie took the bait and dropped his stick and gloves. I squared right off with my fists held high like a boxer.

My previous encounter with Frank Bialowas was burned into my brain. I wasn't going to let Bonvie thrust himself into me and dictate the fight. I was going to be in control of this one. If Bonvie charged into me like Bialowas with his head down I was going to knock his block off with a right uppercut and make him look like one of those Rock'em Sock'em Robots.

The play continued on in front of the Oilers' net, there was a shot on goal and a scramble for the rebound, but I was oblivious. I was ready for a good one in front of my friends, that is, if Bonvie would ever get down to business. But I was prepared for this, too.

After I got the phone call from Bruce Landon I studied the fight films I had of Bonvie. He was a very good fighter, a puncher, but he was pretty much a one-hander, he threw all rights. What he liked to do after dropping his gloves was to take some time to pull off his elbow pads as well. While Bonvie was fiddling around with his equipment, Rick Bennett fired a backhand shot home to give us a 1–0 lead. As my teammates were raising their sticks in celebration, the two linesmen stepped in between us.

Just then I heard the crowd groan—not because they weren't going to see a fight, but because they figured the goal was going to be called back. Bonvie and I received two minutes each for roughing, and luckily for me the goal counted and I was credited with a plus-1. The plus/minus statistic simply reflects the fact that I was on the ice when my team scored a goal. I would be given a minus-1 if a goal was scored against my team while I was on the ice.

While in the penalty box, Bonvie and I started yipping and yapping at each other. "Hey you runt, why don't you take a little longer taking your shit off," I yelled. "Next time why don't you skate over the bench and get a drink of water and make sure your hair is combed before we go."

Bonvie countered, "You wanna go right now?"

That idea would've been a little slice of heaven for me. I remembered watching Lyndon Byers come out of the penalty box to fight Quebec's Greg Smyth in the Boston Garden and thought it was one of the most entertaining things I'd ever seen in a game. During my time as a player I had started a bench-clearing brawl, engaged in a pre-game fight, and challenged an entire bench. Along with going into the stands to fight with unruly fans, coming out of the penalty box to fight was one of those things that had always been on my wish list.

As much as I wanted to do it, with my lack of experience in the American League I didn't dare take the initiative. I didn't want my coach to hate me for doing something too crazy and maybe never get another chance to play for the Falcons. Even so, I told Bonvie I would do it, but he ignored me and remained in his seat.

"You're a fucking phony," I yelled, and then sat down.

The guy who worked the scoreboard and sat between us turned to me and said, "He was a real asshole yesterday. Are you here to straighten him out?"

I told him I was and that I hoped to live through the experience.

"Why, is he that tough?"

"Yah, the best," I answered, and I meant it. Even though I regarded Bonvie as the enemy I had too much respect for him and the job he did for his team to think otherwise.

I had a lot of time to think of my next move. After spending 53 seconds in the penalty box the buzzer sounded to end the first period and we skated off to our respective dressing rooms for about 15 minutes before the start of the second period.

Giving my sticks away to young Falcons fans.

Coach Gillis told me I did a good job, that I did exactly what he wanted, which was somebody to challenge that son-of-a-bitch Bonvie.

I sat in the locker room and looked around. The Falcons had a big guy I remembered from Moncton, 6-foot-4, 240-pound Mark Deazeley. He was a nice kid with a great nickname, "The Diesel," but diesels don't do well in cold weather and it appeared as though Mark didn't warm up to the job of team enforcer.

The Falcons also had Scott Daniels, who went about 6-foot-3 and 215 pounds. He was property of the Hartford Whalers so I didn't play with him in Moncton. I was told that Bonvie tortured Daniels during the previous game. Bonvie challenged him and challenged him. I am sure they had fought before, either this year or last season. So why did the club have to bring a 30-year-old guy off the street to fight Bonvie when they already had Daniels?

It may have been that Daniels was nursing an injury and couldn't fight. I never knew if that was the case, but I know that a lot of fighters hide injuries. Many tough guys, who boast a limited skill set, are more expendable than other players. There is always another tough guy somewhere on the team's farm system waiting in the wings for a chance to prove himself. For every Mario Lemieux who sits for a string of games because of back spasms, there are multiple tough guys who play through a troublesome shoulder, hairline wrist fracture, or an infected row of knuckles for fear of losing their job.

There are all kinds of reasons why tough guys don't want to fight. With Daniels, it could have been because, after getting a taste of the NHL, he didn't want to put himself out for the Falcons. He would for the NHL Hartford Whalers, but not for AHL Springfield. I knew one former NHL enforcer, a born-again Christian, who had trouble managing the delicate duality of his faith and job description of beating up other people. He actually left NHL contract offers on the table and retired prematurely.

And there are other circumstances that zap the motivation of tough guys. Marriage problems, custody battles, bills, and family illness—things that people in all walks of life battle—can lead to depression, lethargy, and general disinterest. Rare are the players who have the steely mental constitution necessary to dismiss personal problems while on the ice.

I introduced myself to Daniels when I first arrived in the Springfield locker room and felt embarrassed for both of us. Daniels never picked his spots; he had fought all of the toughest guys during his time in the minors and did the same during his 151-game NHL career. Here was an experienced enforcer, who could probably kick my ass, and I was the one tabbed to go with the tough guy on this night.

In any case, I started the second period back in the penalty box along with Bonvie and I made up my mind that I would fight him right after our penalties were up. I felt like just leaving my stick and gloves in the box, and if it were the East Coast League I may have, but I wasn't comfortable enough here to do that sort of thing. This was my NHL, and I was afraid of making a fool of myself.

When Bonvie and I came out of the box at the same time our eyes met in anticipation. He turned toward me as if he wanted to fight, but after I dropped my stick and gloves he turned away from me. He had sucked me in. Feeling lost and stupid with nowhere to go and nothing to do, I took him from the side with a few punches to the head and wrestled him to the ice, where he turtled—a term used for when a player covers up on the ice, as if he were being attacked by a bear. I got off him in disgust before the refs arrived on the scene. I was handed two more minutes for roughing and a 10-minute misconduct. Bonvie received nothing.

I loved the penalty minutes I was piling up but the Oilers scored a power-play goal while I was in the box to tie the game. I looked over at the Oilers' bench and saw Bonvie stand up and wave to me with a big smile. He yelled, "Hey pal, way to go, you just got your first pro assist!" I felt like an ass.

I sat out half the period serving my misconduct and wondered what Gillis and my teammates thought of me. I blew it. When I finally got back to the bench I apologized to Gillis for taking a dumb penalty.

"Don't worry about it Smitty, you did a good job," said Gillis, and he seemed to mean it.

Bonvie didn't make so much as a peep the rest of the way and we ended up winning 4–2. I never shook so many hands as I did after that game, and those were the hands of my coaches and teammates. I got the impression that it didn't even matter whether we won or lost, as long as there was somebody around willing to go after Bonvie, or at least be there to keep him in check. Gillis told me that I did what the Falcons wanted me to do, to stand up to him.

Bruce Landon mailed me a check for $200 and a promise to send me my game jersey at the end of the season. He was going to hold on to it for the time being in case they needed me to come in again later in the year. He also enclosed a small article the Springfield paper wrote about my one-shot deal, and a handwritten note inside a Falcons greeting card that read, "You did what was asked and we appreciate it. I have your number in case something comes up. Again, my apologies to your mother for calling so late."

These guys still didn't get it. It would have been one thing if he were a telemarketer calling at midnight on Christmas Eve trying to sell me a vacuum cleaner, but Landon's call gave me my second game in the American Hockey League and I would have paid *him* $200 for that honor.

A week later, Bonvie was chosen to participate in the AHL All-Star Game as an injury replacement. Commander was there to scout the game when he bumped into former Boston Bruins player and head coach, Mike Milbury, who was preparing last minute notes as the color commentator for the cable telecast. He asked Commander for some information on the new kid, Bonvie.

I watched the game on television. During the first period intermission, Milbury started to talk about Bonvie, who had scored a goal. I decided not to go to the bathroom.

Milbury told a story about a game that occurred the previous weekend in Springfield, where a local cop was brought in by the Falcons to challenge Bonvie, who had run around unchecked the game before. He said that Bonvie was challenged and turtled. Milbury went on to say that if Bonvie intended to move up to the NHL he had to fight all comers.

A month later I watched Bonvie play his first game in the NHL with the Edmonton Oilers. While I was disappointed he wouldn't fight me back in Springfield, his deserved promotion made me proud; it gave me a little bit more of a connection to the game.

Years later, when I was working as a fight coach in the Boston Bruins organization, Bonvie picked me out of the stands at the Providence Civic Center while he was on the ice during a morning skate with his latest minor-league team. I was at the same time stunned, taken aback, and honored that he remembered me from one no-account AHL game years before. We got together after his practice and shot the shit like two re-united brothers. It was like being in the locker room with Rock Derganc in Miramichi all over again.

When Bonvie eventually signed with Boston, we spent a lot of time on the ice together sparring and wrestling. I can't explain how proud and happy I was for Dennis when I watched him with a Bruins jersey on score the first and only goal of his 93-game NHL career.

Springfield didn't call me for another game that year, but with a month left in the season I received a phone call from another agent I had come to know, Jay Fee, who told me that the Phoenix Roadrunners contacted him asking if he had a tough guy in his stable of players who could come in on short notice for three games on Friday, Saturday, and Sunday. Fee asked if I was still playing, but more importantly, if I would still "do it." Then he told me that the Phoenix coach was Robbie Laird, who had given me my first American League game in Moncton. After a series of crisscrossing phone calls, Laird phoned to offer me my first game in the International Hockey League.

With the Phoenix Roadrunners of the International Hockey League.

At the time I played in it, the International League shared the distinction, along with the American League, of being the top farm system of the NHL. It was considered Triple-A hockey, but it wasn't always so. I had some friends who played in the "I" back in the late 1970s and early 1980s when it was more of a Double-A circuit. In the mid–1980s there was talk of it morphing into another major league on par with the NHL, but the dream never came to fruition. What really seemed to happen, and I based this on comparing the rosters of all the teams, was that while the American League carved out a reputation as a holding pen for younger prospects, the International League carried more free-agent veterans who had logged time in the NHL and were more or less resigned to their fate as career top-tier minor leaguers.

When the Moncton Hawks left for Springfield, which was already under the control of the Hartford Whalers and coach Paul Gillis, Laird was shuffled to the Phoenix Roadrunners, which had a dual NHL affiliation with the Winnipeg Jets and Los Angeles Kings.

It is funny how things work out sometimes. I was brought in by the Roadrunners because I was the last domino standing. The Kings had injuries to a couple of outstanding players, including Robert Lang and the great Jari Kurri, so they reached down to grab a couple of Roadrunners, including center Yanic Perreault, who had 51 goals at the time and was on the cusp of starting a productive 913-game NHL career. In a panic to flesh out the roster, the Roadrunners fell back on Mark Straub, an East Coast Leaguer who happened to be in town to watch his brother play, and then there was me.

I certainly wasn't brought in to replace Perreault, or Roadrunners winger Kevin Brown, but according to an interview with Brown in the Arizona Republic newspaper, the two games against the Las Vegas Thunder on Friday and Saturday "could be a real blood bath."

That meant it would be right up my alley.

Las Vegas had already clinched a playoff berth along with the Roadrunners. Both teams were playing out the Southwest Division string, but Las Vegas had a tough club and wouldn't think twice about beating the hell out of us in its home rink—if only to leave a calling card for the upcoming playoffs.

Las Vegas was flush with veteran goons and had two legitimate heavyweights on the roster in 6-foot-5, 210-pound Jim Kyte, who played in more than 500 NHL games, and 6-foot-2, 212-pound Kerry Toporowski, who had the reputation of a complete madman. Las Vegas coach Chris McSorley had a reputation as a madman as well. McSorley, who took over as coach of the Carolina Thunderbirds after my rookie year, was a defenseman in the International League when he bit off the tip of an opponent's nose during a rumble.[1] He later claimed that forward Marc Magnan had bit his cheek first.

It was the first road trip I'd ever been on with a financially secure team. Instead of taking an old beat-up bus through the icy roadways of New York or a two-prop engine into the wilds of Canada, the Roadrunners put me on a jet to Phoenix in time to catch their America West flight to Las Vegas.

"Road Trip #17" was the title of my two-page itinerary and it was first-class all the way. After landing at McCarran International Airport in Las Vegas we were picked up by a transportation service and whisked away for a noon meal at a nice place called Battista's Hole in the Wall. Our rooms at the Imperial Palace were waiting for us a short walk away, and that was about the only walking we ever had to do. At 4:45 p.m. we were again picked up by a service and transported to the arena for our 7 p.m. game at the Thomas & Mack Center, which was where the University of Nevada–Las Vegas basketball team played.

I skated in the Friday night warm-up and couldn't keep my eyes off Kerry Toporowski. Jim Kyte was huge, but Toporowski looked like a cartoon character. His head was so big that his helmet didn't fit properly. He couldn't even fasten the chin strap of his helmet, which sat on his huge squash like a yarmulke. I wondered how anybody could hurt this guy. How could somebody punch him in the head and do any damage?

I could ponder the thought from the stands because I didn't dress for the game. A guy who had been injured tested himself during warm-ups and pronounced himself fit to play in my place. I sat with some other players and watched us lose, 7–5. I desperately wanted to get credited with playing at least one game in the International League. I couldn't imagine the team would fly me across the country for nothing, I was somewhat confident I would probably get the chance to play during the balance of the three-game stretch, so I didn't mind sitting on my ass watching—besides, I had a blast simply drinking in the life. I had read and heard stories about the pampering of professional athletes at the higher levels, but until you're actually the one being fawned over it's just a daydream.

We were picked up after the game and taken back to Battista's for a late dinner. It sure beat the microwave pizza and Snickers bars I lived on during my time traipsing through the Adirondack Mountains with the Thunderbirds. The Roadrunners picked up the tab for the meals and even gave us a handful of spending money, which many of the players just poured into the hotel's slot machines.

Saturday presented more of the same, except we were taken for a morning skate before hitting Battista's for our noon meal. I skated in the warm-up again, but this time I was inserted into the lineup for the game. Oh boy!

I stared at Kyte and Toporowski; they knew why I was there. A pre-game report was printed for each game and it contained all the latest news about the teams including injuries, transactions, statistics, streaks, and trends. Everything anybody needed to know about newcomer Doug Smith was also on the page: "Doug Smith signed a 25-game tryout contract yesterday, he played one game and had a fighting major in Moncton last year, and racked up 14 penalty minutes in one game with Springfield this season."

Gee, I wonder what Doug Smith is going to do here?

As it turned out, not much. It was a close game and I didn't get to play a shift.

There was one fight the night before, which is probably why I was dressed for the second game. But nothing much happened in this one until near the end when a skirmish involving all 10 skaters on the ice broke out in front of the benches, which were situated side-by-side and separated by a piece of Plexiglas.

After contributing nothing to the Roadrunners' effort up to then, I wanted to do nothing less than jump over the boards and start a full-fledged, bench-clearing brawl. With thoughts of maybe being asked to play again down the road, however, I managed to behave and restrain myself.

I dutifully stood at my usual position at the end of the bench beside the back-up goalie and Plexiglas separator, and leaned over the boards to get a good look at the madness. All of a sudden I felt a light tap on my helmet. It was Toporowski, who was basically beside me at the end of his bench, and he had just rapped me with the blade of his stick. I couldn't believe what was happening; it was almost as if he had read my mind.

I held my stick like a pitchfork and feigned a move with the blade at Toporowski. He then slid his stick down to his side as if he were thrusting a sword back into its sheath and took a swing at me from around the Plexiglas. I slid my stick down as well, and while the scrum continued on the ice, Toporowski and I took turns trading wild punches. The on-ice officials were preoccupied with the larger mess and didn't even notice us fighting on the bench, but Laird saw the duel and cheered me on as he yelled, "Smoke him Smitty, smoke him!"

Laird hoped that I'd catch Toporowski with a lucky shot, but I was dealing with a guy who had a cinderblock for a head. I probably wouldn't have hurt him if he let me have a clean shot with his hands tied behind his back. Nevertheless, it was fun, and something I would expect a goon of my caliber to do in this very situation.

Because I didn't take an actual shift, I knew I wouldn't be listed "in the books" as playing a game in the IHL, but the thing that disappointed me more was that we didn't go back to Battista's for dinner. Instead we ate on the flight back to Phoenix, where Kevin Evans and the Kansas City Blades awaited us for Sunday's matinee at our Arizona Veterans Memorial Coliseum.

Evans had become an instant hockey celebrity when he amassed a ridiculous 672 penalty minutes during his first year as a pro with the IHL's Kalamazoo Wings during the 1986–87 season. For his efforts and notoriety, Evans was rewarded with nine games in the NHL with the Minnesota North Stars and San Jose Sharks. The sickest part of his achievement was that he was listed as weighing 180 pounds at 5-foot-10, and rosters always inflate those numbers.

I was given my opportunity to go into the official record books as having played in an International Hockey League game with a couple shifts against the last-place Blades. I came out on the fly on my second shift and went right after Evans. I slammed into him along the boards in his end, hard enough for any tough guy to know my intentions, but Evans just skated away uninterested.

It was the same old story. I had watched hours of Evans' fights on video, I knew what he could do and he did it against every tough hockey player in North America. He was just a tired warrior now, going through the motions in a meaningless road game at the end of a losing year. He knew he'd probably be right back with the Blades next season if he wanted to be. But me, a simple rent-a-goon taking time off from a cop's beat at the Hanover Mall, where could I go?

12

One More
Shot at the Animal

The 25-game tryout agreement I signed with the Phoenix Roadrunners sounded so much better than what it turned out to be, which was nothing more than a standard, at-will contract for free agents who weren't expected to be around very long. My contract was basically terminated after the three-game weekend. Coach Robbie Laird said the team would probably use me again and that he was going to keep my name on the playoff roster just in case, but as I had become accustomed, nothing more came of it.

The Roadrunners gave me the home shirt I wore against Kansas City, and the Los Angeles Kings cut me a check for $600, which wasn't bad dough for a total of two insignificant shifts.

I went back to work at the Hanover Mall and daydreamed for months about the pampering I received during that one weekend in heaven with the Roadrunners. I thought of how great it would be to play five years there with a contract. I fantasized about traveling back in time so I could start skating at the age of four or five and learn to play hockey like all of the other guys.

One of the worst parts about my venture into professional hockey wasn't the pressure of showing up every game expecting to fight the toughest guys on the other team; that was fun for me. What really sucked was the knowledge that I could've had a career in this game, maybe even an NHL career, if I had only started skating when everybody else did. It sucked to get so excited by every phone call, every conversation, and every nibble that some team might want to take a chance on me. It sucked to play one game, one lousy AHL game, and the guy beside me, who had played 500 games, and could play 500 more if he wanted to, would rather be playing golf.

I continued to send out my resume and I received some promising bites, but I didn't play in any more games for two years after the Roadrunners experience.

A friend of mine in the neighborhood back home married a girl whose dad worked in the front office for the tough Portland Pirates, the AHL affiliate of the Washington Capitals. He knew as much about hockey as I did about brain surgery, but his daddy-in-law fudged him a job in the front office.

He told me he would get me a few games with the Pirates, maybe even an invitation to training camp just to do some fighting. But the closer the date for training camp approached the less and less I heard from him. He finally confessed that it wasn't his call to get me on the ice. All he had done was try to impress me. He had married a paycheck and must have been an inside joke within the organization.

I was also a victim of shit luck after Providence Bruins coach Bob Francis called me on Friday for a Sunday game. There was nothing more I wanted to do than wear a hometown Boston Bruins jersey, and the P-Bruins were the next-best thing.

Not only was I going to play, but Francis said he planned to start me on the wing with toughies Martin Simard and Marc Potvin. Francis wanted to open the game with a bang against the Albany River Rats, and the plan was for me to fight veteran NHL goon Darin Kimble, who was playing in the New Jersey Devils' system at the time.

Complete and utter disaster struck on Sunday morning, however, when I heard on the radio that the Bruins had traded winger Steve Leach to the St. Louis Blues for tough guy Kevin Sawyer, who was to report to Providence in time for Sunday night's game. That was the end of the promising Providence gig for me. To make matters even worse, I attended the game as a spectator and Sawyer didn't even play. He was a late scratch when it was discovered he had an injured hamstring.

With those defeats eating at my flesh I jumped at the chance to go back down to the East Coast Hockey League when Louisiana IceGators leading scorer, Don Parsons, gave me a call the week before Thanksgiving during the 1997–98 season. Parsons was a Boston-area kid who skated shinny hockey with me for years. When his club needed a fighter in a pinch for a rough, three-game weekend, he told his coach, Doug Sheddon, that I was his man.

The IceGators didn't play in the prehistoric East Coast League I was weaned on during my stay in Winston-Salem with the Thunderbirds years before. This current version was like the difference between riding a bike and driving a car.

I was flown down to Southern Louisiana and taxied to the IceGators' new home arena, the Cajundome. The team was averaging more than 11,000 fans a game, almost as many as the Boston Bruins were drawing in The Garden. The IceGators were affiliated with the Detroit Red Wings, and most of the players were either under contract to Detroit, or had been the property of another NHL team at some point during their careers.

Henry Brabham's future vision of the old East Coast League that he founded had come true, and I felt as though I was brought back for this brief return visit to witness first-hand what kind of butterfly had emerged from the ugly cocoon I began playing in nearly a decade earlier. I was 34 and the third-oldest guy to ever suit up for the IceGators at the time, and way out of my league in the skills department, but I was just there to fight, and I knew I could still do that.

I didn't dress for Friday night's game against the Birmingham Bulls, which was unfortunate because the Bulls were loaded with tough guys. The IceGators instead went with their resident enforcer, 6-foot-3, 215-pound Ryan Pisiak, a former LA Kings draft pick who was splitting time between here and the Fort Wayne Comets of the IHL. With Pisiak scheduled to be away with Fort Wayne over the weekend, I took his place for Saturday's game against the Mississippi Sea Wolves, and then again in Sunday's return home engagement with the Bulls.

But first I had to survive a little embarrassment.

There was a jersey hanging in my locker room stall before the start of Saturday's game against the Sea Wolves. It had the number "98" on the back with no name, and I thought that the quality of the jersey was a little poor for a team that seemed to be so financially secure and successful. But what did I know?

I also thought that 98 was a strange number to give me. Hockey numbers are usually allotted to players by their position. In general, goalies tend to wear 1, 30, and 31. A quality forward may have 7, 9, 12, or 16, and a goon had historically taken such numbers as 21, 24, 27, 29, 34, or whatever extra number was hanging around the equipment room. Ever since Wayne Gretzky began wearing 99, it seemed only superstars wore high, double-digit numbers such as 77 for Ray Bourque and Paul Coffey, Jaromir Jagr's 68, Sydney Crosby's 87, and Alexander Mogilny's 98.

I wrote "98" on my three sticks and gave them to the trainer to put in the stick rack. I was too interested in skating around slowly and looking cool while checking out all of the fans filling the arena, so I didn't pay too much attention to my teammates during warm-ups. It's too bad I wasn't using all of my senses to their full potential because if I had, I may have noticed that everybody else on my team was also wearing Number 98, which simply stood for the current year.

I didn't know that the shirt was only used during warm-ups. When Parsons discovered my gaffe he alerted everybody in the locker room and made a point to create a scene by yelling, "Hey, look at retard over here, he put 98 on all his sticks!"

Great, like I needed that. All I wanted to do was slide in quietly and fit in. Damn sticks. I didn't even need a stick. All I did was hold it for a few seconds before dropping it to fight.

I retreated to the safety net of the bathroom to prepare for the game. One thing I always did before going out for battle was lubricate my face with Vaseline. I spread it over my eyebrows and cheekbones, which were places where a punch could rip skin. It was a routine I carried over from my boxing days. If you catch a punch flush, right on the money and your skin is dry, the fist can stick like it's on sandpaper and the resulting friction can cause a cut. The grease helped the fist slide off the face with less skin-ripping drag.

Guys would always walk by me and ask what the hell I was doing and I'd usually just smile and ignore them. I didn't feel like getting into it because only another fighter would understand.

On the flip side of the Vaseline was a trick I was told about during my days with the Thunderbirds but never opted to use. It was said that some guys had worn clear rubber surgical gloves with the fingers cut off. They would leave only an inch or so of the rubber visible between the top knuckles and wraps of tape used to protect the wrist and the bones on the meat of the hand.

The plan called for the "punching" knuckles to be covered with rubber so they would stick to dry skin on the face and rip it during the follow-through of a punch. In the movie *Slap Shot*, the crazy Hanson Brothers wrap their hands with tin foil. The rubber-glove thing was something to do if you really wanted to mess somebody up, but I never dared do something like that because I never hated another player that much, not even Ron Aubrey. I also didn't want to risk getting suspended or blow further opportunities to play. I was lucky to be playing in the first place.

Another technique I was taught and did use was to take a hacksaw to my helmet. While all my teammates were shaving and taping their sticks, I ran the hacksaw every which way over my helmet so that sharp and abrasive plastic shards stood up everywhere. If a guy punched my helmet, he'd cut up his hand. It was like punching a rock-hard briar patch. I thought it was funny to sit in the penalty box and look over at the guy I just fought. He would be examining his cut-up and bloody hands and looking at me, wondering why my face wasn't damaged.

I didn't consider this act hypocritical. While the rubber glove worked as an offensive weapon, my thorn-bush helmet was more of a defensive gesture, sort of in the same vein as anti-tank structures set by the Germans on Omaha Beach.

Back in the ECHL with the Louisiana IceGators.

I was slated to start on the wing against the Sea Wolves, who employed my old friend Kevin Evans, the same guy I couldn't draw into a fight in Phoenix two years earlier.

While Jacques Mailhot may have been the funkiest guy I ever played with, Kerry Toporowski the funniest looking, Kevin McClelland the most intense, Alex Daviault the scariest, and Frank Bialowas the meanest, Evans was the freakiest of them all. He also had the most celebrated reputation of anybody I ever went up against, but I feared him the least because I had four or five inches on him.

Because of all the practice I had against 5-foot-6 Gator, smaller guys never worried me much. So despite Evans' lofty reputation, which was well-earned, I was on an incredible high skating around before the start of the game because I knew in my bones I would have a good showing against him. I was going to grab him and throw all uppercuts.

I skated into the opening face-off, gave Evans a little bump and said, "Hey, let's start this game with a bang."

He was crouched over in position with his stick on the ice and looked at me with a slack-jaw and open mouth. He reminded me of the kid from the movie *Deliverance*, the young kid who played the banjo. I didn't know if anyone was home there.

When the puck was dropped I squared up with him, put my stick behind his knee and pulled him in, but he just pushed my stick away and skated off into the play. What was I going to do, chase him down? I figured I did my job, he knew there was a guy here with the IceGators who wanted to fight, who wasn't intimidated—and I guess that was good enough. I quickly got off the ice and Evans did nothing out of line the rest of the way.

Sunday's game against the loaded Birmingham Bulls held more promise of some serious action for me. Kerry Toporowski had ended up with them, and they also boasted Dennis Pinfold, Kevin Popp, and another kid with the great-sounding name of Garry Gulash.

The Bulls also had a familiar face coaching them, Dennis Desrosiers, who made me one of his last cuts in Cincinnati years before. I skated over to him for a nice little chat during warm-ups. He certainly knew why I was there.

At the end of the pre-game skate I hung around until all of my guys were off the ice. Toporowski was the last guy off for the Bulls. He hadn't changed; he still couldn't strap that helmet onto his huge squash.

As we filed down the runway to our locker room, I noticed Steve Carlson walking toward me outfitted in the Charleston Chiefs uniform like the one he wore in *Slap Shot*. Steve wasn't coaching the Johnstown Chiefs any longer, but he kept busy during the hockey season with his brother, Jeff, and former

Tossing pucks to IceGator fans in the Cajundome.

minor-league teammate Dave Hanson, reprising the roles they made famous with "Hanson Brothers Night" performances staged in minor-league rinks across North America.

"Hey Smitty, what the hell are you doing here?," asked Steve with a knowing smile.

"Oh, they just brought me in for a weekend to do my thing, you know."

Carlson laughed. "So you're still up to the same old, same old. Good luck!"

While sitting in the locker room waiting for ice to be made, I talked to one of my teammates about Toporowski. I asked why he was down here and if he would fight. While we were engaged in this conversation I noticed that another player curiously listened in. Suddenly, the guy I was talking to said, "Why don't you just ask his brother what's going on with him?"

The kid listening in was Toporowski's younger brother, Brad. Here I was talking about fighting this guy and his brother was listening to the whole thing. It served me right for not even looking at my own team's roster.

Brad told that his brother had come down to the East Coast League on more or less a rehabilitation assignment for a bad shoulder, and that he wouldn't fight. Truth be told, the big guy was really about done. He sat out the following year and then finished out his playing career with five seasons in the Single-A-or-so United Hockey League and three games in Russia.

Regardless of his physical condition, Kerry Toporowski's shoulder woes didn't stop him from playing like a jerk here. Kerry had the reputation of a hatchet man who would swing his stick a lot. He was a defenseman, and if you set yourself set up in front of his net you were screwed because Kerry had the uncanny ability to find the smallest area on your body that had no protective padding and he'd slash, cross-check, and hack you to death right there. Aiding and abetting these armed assaults were the officials, who let him get away with it all.

I watched this go on for half a period before I got my first shift. When I hit the ice I made a beeline for Toporowski in front of his net and challenged him. He put his stick up into my face in a defensive posture like barbed wire and said, "Fuck off," but he wouldn't drop his gloves.

Kevin Popp noticed this going on and came right over. He was a young kid out of juniors, a Buffalo Sabres draft pick about my size. He started the game for the Bulls and ran around sticking everybody during his first few shifts as well, and I originally thought he'd be my first guy, a good warm-up before going after Toporowski.

Popp gave me a little elbow, we pushed each other, dropped our gloves, and squared off in close quarters near the Bulls' bench. Popp charged in and pinned me up against the boards. I held him off as best I could and tried to throw some punches.

While I tangled with Popp, the players on the Bulls' bench right beside us were yelling, "Hey cop, hey pig, where's your mace? Spray him pig, hit him with your billy club."

I looked over at the bench for a familiar voice. I couldn't see him from the crowd of players but I knew the ringleader was Desrosiers. When the linesmen pulled Popp away from me I found Desrosiers and winked at him. He winked back and gave me a friendly smirk.

And that was it. I received the seven penalty minutes I was looking for—two for roughing and five for fighting—and not another shift. I was on the next flight home.

That would have been a fitting end to my unlikely venture into minor-league hockey, a full-circle journey closed in the league where it all began. But I was given one last opportunity as a player, one last chance to fight the guy I'd held a candle for since he split me open, spilled my blood, and closed my left eye on New Year's Day in Moncton four years earlier.

Dave Farrish, the Moncton coach who said he'd call me up if the time was right during my senior league days in Miramichi, had taken over the

Springfield Falcons from Paul Gillis and found that right time. The Philadelphia Phantoms were arriving for a Friday night game, and Frank "The Animal" Bialowas was coming in with them.

I took my first and only shift early in the first period. Bialowas came off
the bench after a whistle and was setting up on the left wing. We had the last
line change as the home team and Farrish told me to hop out and get on the
left side.

That is what I loved about my job. All the coach had to say to me was,
"Take the left side," which was really code for, "Smitty, go out and challenge
Bialowas."

I pulled up beside the mean-looking bastard, turned to him and said,
"Remember me?"

Bialowas gave me a little peek and said, "No," without any emotion.
Good for him, touché.

"Yes you do, Moncton," I said. "How about a rematch?"

I don't really know if Bialowas remembered me or not because he probably had 150 fights since our encounter, but I've found that most fighters have
an astounding memory and are able to recall all of their battles.

Here I was, 34 and ready to take on the world, but Frank was old. He
was only 28, but the four games he played for the Toronto Maple Leafs after
punching me out in Moncton was four long seasons of fighting ago, and the
only taste of the NHL he'd ever get. He may have had an idea, but he likely
didn't know for sure that this would be the last full season he'd ever play as
a pro.

"Not tonight," said Frank flatly. "My hand is sore from a fight last night."

"Oh come on," I whined. "What are you, a one-handed fighter?"

"No, not tonight," Frank said again.

What a waste. One of the things I took pride in was my willingness and
desire to come back. You could beat me five times in a row but I'd be front
and center for a sixth go-around, and that might be the one time I knock
your teeth down your throat. Bialowas wasn't going to give me that opportunity.

I thought about grabbing him and making him fight, but I had a lot of
respect for the tired warrior. There is an honor code, an unwritten rule amongst
tough guys, and if somebody said they were hurt that was the end of it.

"All right, but I'm going to be watching," I said. "You do any fooling
around tonight and I'm coming after you, bad hand or not."

The puck dropped, I stood up, squared myself off with him and made
eye contact to make sure he didn't have a change of heart. He turned away
to get into the play and I skated off to the bench.

Asking Frank Bialowas (center right) for a rematch in Springfield.

Farrish and a bunch of the guys disregarded the play and rushed me. I felt like a teenage boy who'd just taken a dare to talk to the prettiest girl at the dance and now all my friends wanted to know what she said.

"He said he didn't want to fight, he said his hands hurt and he didn't want to fight tonight," I announced.

Farrish smiled. The guys nodded knowingly and swore. It was good news. There would be no Frank Bialowas to deal with on this night.

I did my job. Other than a shouting match he had with our big defenseman, Sean Gagnon, Bialowas did nothing the rest of the way and we won the game.

That was the subtle beauty of what I did during my scattered career as a minor-league hockey fighter. In the end, in my last piece of action, I didn't even have to fight. Just being there, being in a position to stand up to the toughest guy on the block and protect my own people was enough.

Career Statistics

Doug Smith—Forward
Born December 27, 1984—Quincy, MA
Height 6.02—Weight 215—Shoots R

Season	Team	League	GP	G	A	Pts	PIM
1988–89	Carolina Thunderbirds	ECHL	28	0	1	1	179
1989–90	Johnstown Chiefs	ECHL	3	0	0	0	29
1990–91	Miramichi Packers	NBSHL	23	0	3	3	170
1993–94	Moncton Hawks	AHL	1	0	0	0	5
1994–95	Springfield Falcons	AHL	1	0	0	0	14
1994–95	Phoenix Roadrunners	IHL	1	0	0	0	0
1997–98	Louisiana IceGators	ECHL	2	0	0	0	7
1997–98	Springfield Falcons	AHL	1	0	0	0	0
Totals			**60**	**0**	**4**	**4**	**404**

13

More Than a Goon

I never had any problem with what I did on the ice during my short excursion as a hockey player, never any illusion that I was anything more on the ice than a goon—a hired bodyguard and hitman. I only wish that I had been a better skater back then so that I could have played more and maybe built a little hockey career, but I did what I could and succeeded in my simple quest despite long odds.

What I never expected was to parlay my limited hockey experience into the roles of professional hockey fight coach and linesman. Yet again it took the right pieces of the puzzle to line up for me, but once the opportunities were presented I took my best shots.

My pal Commander ended up joining the Boston Bruins organization in 2001 to work in the scouting and player personnel department. The vice-president and general manager at the time was Mike O'Connell, a friend of Commander, who grew up in the next town over on Massachusetts' South Shore.

In the meantime, I had dabbled a little bit on my own as a half-assed fight coach for kids who were planning on attending pro tryouts. An agent would call me and ask if I'd be willing to meet with a client at a local rink, or a college player would approach me and ask for some guidance on what the hell to do if faced with a guy who wanted to drop the gloves in training camp.

Along with being very flattered that anybody would think enough of me to want my advice and instruction, I actually enjoyed the coaching aspect and thought I was fairly knowledgeable and competent in what I was teaching. With some prodding from Commander, I had Gator help me cobble together a fighting program proposal to present to O'Connell and the Boston Bruins.

Gator thought that the key manipulation early on was to sell my program as more of a "defensive" package rather than straight-out fighting. He thought it would be more palatable to the higher-ups if I stressed the importance of protecting the team's valuable investments, especially the European and college kids the Bruins signed, for the times they may find themselves involved in a fight on the ice. I would be instructing the players on how to defend themselves rather than just teaching them how to fight.

The people at the meeting were impressed with the detail of my outline for the program. I offered my services as an unpaid volunteer to get my foot in the door, and they bit. After a few years I went on the payroll and had an absolute blast working with various Bruins farmhands who were playing with Boston's top affiliate in the AHL, the Providence "Baby" Bruins.

I started out working under the approving eyes of P-Bruins head coach Bill Armstrong, a 6-foot-5, 220-pound tough guy during his playing days in the AHL. I would drive 45 minutes from my home to the Dunkin Donuts Center in the middle of Providence two mornings a week and at the end of practice I'd get out there and teach anybody who was interested the same things I worked on with Gator for so many years.

I showed guys the benefits and drawbacks to grabbing different parts of an opponent's shirt, how to block punches with the shoulders and arms, angle the head to avoid catching a clean shot to the face, and how to utilize the entire body to support and protect the hand while throwing a more effective punch.

I wore boxing target training gloves for the guys to hit, put on head gear and fought with them, and sometimes hung a heavy bag from the rafters at center ice for the guys to wallop. I even bought a half-figure dummy, the kind used in self-defense classes, that could be fit with a hockey jersey and filled with water to weigh about 250 pounds. The guys would practice grabbing hold and beating the shit out of it on the ice.

Sometimes the Dunkin Donuts Center wouldn't be available and we'd have to practice at Providence College, and when the schoolboys wandered around the rink and saw this shit going on it blew their minds. Imagine— there'd be Scott Metcalf over here working on his wrist shot, over there would be Kevin Dallman, Andy Hilbert, Milan Jurcina, Matt Herr, and Carl Corazzini going through the power play with Tim Thomas in net, and at center ice Colton Orr and Brendan Walsh were taking turns fighting me. It was an absolute freak show.

For the first few years with Armstrong I didn't get paid, but Mike O'Connell took care of me in other ways, including giving me his luxury box in the Fleet Center for one Boston Bruins game a year. I was able to cram 15 or so people in the box and it worked out well as a nice way for me to thank some of my supportive friends and act like a real big shot at the same time.

As usually happens in the coaching ranks, especially in the minors, Armstrong was let go by the Bruins and replaced by his assistant, Scott Gordon.

Working with Czechoslovakia native Zdenek Kutlak (left) in Providence.

Gordon had been a goalie during his playing days, which I first thought would be the death knell for my services, but he surprised the hell out of me by actually appreciating the need for tough guys in the game. Gordon left to eventually make it all the way up to the NHL with the New York Islanders, and was in turn succeeded by his assistant, Rob Murray, a big penalty-minute guy with whom I had played in Moncton and Springfield. More than anything else, having these kinds of hockey guys watching over and appreciating what I did kept me involved within the Bruins organization for an eight-year ride. The end was bittersweet, however, as a year after I was let go as part of a cost-cutting measure, my hometown Boston Bruins won their first Stanley Cup in 39 years. If I had still been in the fold I probably would have been given a Stanley Cup ring. The thought still makes me want to throw up.

The players I worked with came and went as well, but there are some who made lasting impressions.

Probably the hardest worker and best success story I was involved with was Saskatchewan native Steve MacIntyre. At 6-foot-5 and 250 pounds, Big Mac had already had what he figured was his best shot at making it to the NHL, and found himself floundering in the lower minor leagues during his sixth year of professional hockey.

After the NHL's spring player draft, the Bruins, like every other team, would fill up the rest of its open spots within the organization with whatever role players they needed. If they had need for a fighter in Providence, sometimes I'd be asked for my opinion. Knowing I could put my two cents in from time to time, I made it a point to contact and stay in touch with various fringe or otherwise available and accessible tough guys. I wanted to know how their health was, what their plans were or where they were going. I wanted to get inside their heads to find out if they were still willing to fight.

Big Mac was one of the guys I called. His size always interested me and I liked what I saw of his fights on tape. I asked if he was still interested in fighting and he was a bit noncommittal. He seemed to be fed up with the game. He had gotten himself a bit of a shot in the AHL with 30 games over the span of a couple years, but the last two seasons saw him fall back full time to East Coast League, and then the new United League with something called the Quad City Mallards. I even remember asking Nicky Fotiu about him, and he had the same impression that he just didn't want to do it anymore.

MacIntyre had the height, strength, chin, and balls. He *almost* had it all. I felt that if I could get a hold of Mac on the ice I could work on his head; I could pump him up and get his confidence and desire back so that he could kick ass and in the process open up some eyes at the higher levels.

Sure enough, we got MacIntyre in Providence and he took to me like gasoline to a match. Mac couldn't get enough of the training, and the guy could do it all—he was quick, could throw heavy punches with both hands, go over and under—I just worked a bit on his stamina. I would have him punch himself out on the hand targets, maybe 25 punches each hand, and then I'd wrestle around with him until his entire body felt like melting into the ice.

I couldn't believe there wasn't a place for this nightmare in The Show. Only special players could deal with his size and fighting ability. Sometimes we'd get going pretty well during a sparring session and I'd get the upper hand or pop him a good one by accident, and after that I wouldn't want to stick around. I could literally feel MacIntyre's persona snap as he'd try to get back at me. At that point it was like wrestling a mountain lion in a phone booth.

I couldn't believe the Bruins let him go the next year. That was okay, because the very next season MacIntyre skipped the AHL completely and went straight to the Big Leagues with the Edmonton Oilers, where he solidified a reputation as one of the best and most-feared fighters in the NHL. He went on to play with the Florida Panthers, and was signed by the Pittsburgh Penguins to help protect none other than the great Sydney Crosby.

Another intangible MacIntyre had that couldn't be taught was meanness. MacIntyre was mean on the ice. He was angry. When he dropped his gloves and got to fighting he was pissed off.

I don't want to think what John Scott could do to me if he got angry and really wanted to fight. Scott, who won a Stanley Cup with the Chicago Blackhawks, packed 260 pounds on his 6-foot-8 frame, but when I worked with him he didn't seem to have a mean bone in his body. Veteran NHL tough guy Sean Thornton might disagree with me on this point, especially after suffering a concussion after a one-sided, brutal beating issued to him by Scott during the 2012–13 season.

The Thornton fight aside, the difference between Scott and MacIntyre was striking—but for good reason. MacIntyre, who could skate pretty well for a big guy, was nevertheless doing what he had to, literally fighting for an NHL roster spot because his other skills weren't *that* great. Mac couldn't afford to be an affable guy. On the other hand, Scott used nearly 150 games in the NHL with the Minnesota Wild and Blackhawks to at least present the potential of being a top-six defenseman on a team.

The position that Scott found himself in didn't necessitate that he fight— but his size did. Scott, just the nicest of guys, made no bones about it when he admitted to me that he didn't really want to fight, but his employers demanded, somewhat, that he drop the gloves when the opportunity presented itself. So when I watched Scott playing for Buffalo, he was patrolling a wing, and not for his offensive prowess.

I couldn't blame Scott for his attitude. Fighting in hockey isn't what most of these guys grew up dreaming to do, but to make a six- or seven-figure salary playing hockey, sometimes a guy has to do what he doesn't really want to do.

Nobody holding target gloves had to guess which one of these guys relished his role as a hockey fighter. I could train for hours with Scott, but MacIntyre punished the bones in my hand. He punched *through* the gloves.

Before working with a player I watch his fights, which is easy because most fights, from the NHL down to the lowest minor leagues, are broadcast on YouTube a matter of hours after the game ended. I like to get a handle on what a guy's strengths may be, but more importantly I try to gauge weaknesses to help them improve upon. The one thing I noticed about Scott was that, while he won most of his fights, he did so because of his sheer size advantage. He would grab a guy by the neck, hold him fully outstretched and pummel away with rights. It was so unfair. All of the guys he fought were smaller and a lot of them couldn't reach his face with their fists, so I thought he fought with a measure of impunity.

I worked with Scott on throwing punches with his left hand, because two fists are better than one, and switching hands when one arm got tied up was always good medicine. I also introduced the idea of grabbing different

Giving NHL All-Star John Scott a target for his long rights.

parts of the jersey. If a guy he was fighting was right handed, it made sense to grab the sleeve of that arm to stunt the power. Many guys who fight because they have to, and aren't necessarily students of the fight game, grab in front of the neck while their opponent's punching arm fires away unimpeded. It's silly—and dangerous.

Colton Orr was another of my prized pupils. The Bruins signed him as a free agent out of juniors and I got to mess around with him on the ice right from the get-go in 2002. He was eager to accept and learn the craft that would eventually put many loaves of bread on his table. He was only a little bigger than I, but was he ever strong. He had a great grip, like a bear. He would grab hold of me and I couldn't break away. He was a pretty good puncher, too. He caught me flush during one session and closed my eye, I couldn't see out of it for a week.

Unfortunately, Orr was another tough guy who didn't last long with the big club. After 21 games over two years in the NHL he was put on waivers by the Bruins. Fotiu, who was working for the New York Rangers, got hold of me and asked if I thought Orr could fight in the NHL. I told him that he could definitely hold his own, and a few hours later the Rangers picked him up.

Orr wasn't happy, but I was glad to see him go. He didn't know what he was in for with Boston, with the way they historically treated their fighters. Some of the guys in New York, like Fotiu, had clout and would help him out. Sure as shit, he established himself as one of the NHL's top heavyweights over the next four years, and cashed in by signing a four-year, $4,000,000 contract as a free agent with the Toronto Maple Leafs; another of the few millionaire hockey players who earn their money with their fists.

I got to work with Aaron Downey late in his career. He had bounced around between the AHL and five NHL teams when he landed in Providence for a second go-around with the organization during the last half of the 2006–2007 season. I didn't know him personally, but because I knew he had played about 200 games in the NHL, I was apprehensive about approaching him. Maybe I was a little intimidated, so I decided to try a different tactic with him. I pretty much ignored him and continued to work with my group of regulars. Maybe it was something like ignoring that pretty girl all the other guys were fawning over. Downey would watch what I was doing with the other players from a distance. I dangled our fighting drills before him like a steak in front of a hungry hyena. Before long he wandered over and asked, "Hey, can I get in on this?"

Downey wasn't a huge guy but he was solidly built at six feet and 215 pounds. His value as a pro was that he was actually a decent player while also being game as hell to fight. Continuing a predictable pattern, the Bruins let him go the next year and he ended up with the Detroit Red Wings, where he earned the right to have his name engraved on the Stanley Cup. Great for him.

A guy who never made it to the NHL but made me look pretty good to some within Bruins management was Matt Goody. When the P-Bruins needed somebody to fight down the stretch during the 2005–2006 season, I recommended the 6-foot-2, 230-pound Goody, who had been wallowing around the lower minors. He delivered three quality fights during his six-game AHL career, none better than the showing he had against 6-foot-8, 260-pound behemoth Mitch Fritz.

Even Colton Orr didn't look forward to fighting the Frankenstein-like Fritz, telling me after a battle with him in the minors, "I hate fighting that guy, I can't get in on him." Goody took on the impossible task with a heart as big as his balls. Going in with the knowledge it may be his last opportunity to shine at this level, he flung caution to the wind and hung in there toe-to-toe with Fritz, earning him an improbable tie, and me some instant credibility.

The delivery of Goody directly lent me the ability to get a guy like Jonathan Tremblay to the Providence Bruins, but not before I had to dance around some loyalty issues.

I traveled up to Maine with Commander to watch the Portland Pirates play the Worcester Sharks. I liked to tag along with Commander on his trips to scout out talent on the other AHL teams. While visiting down in the locker room area I was asked by a friend of Commander if I would help out the Sharks' 6-foot-3, 240-pound Tremblay, who would be called upon to dance with Portland's similarly sized resident enforcer, Trevor Gillies, another former P-Bruins toughie who would eventually make it to the NHL.

I pulled Tremblay aside and told him that Gillies was strictly a left-handed fighter, so he should change his stance and go as a lefty as well. That would not only allow him to lead with his right hand as a jab, but more importantly be able to reach out and grab hold of Gillies' dangerous left, effectively shutting him down. While in front of the open locker-room door practice fighting with Tremblay, a Boston Bruins employee who knew me stopped by the door with a stunned look, staring in disbelief.

Tremblay fought Gillies early in the game as a southpaw and did very well. I on the other hand scrambled to find the Bruins employee to explain that, while my loyalties were certainly with Boston, which was paying me by then, I was just doing a favor for a friend by helping out Tremblay. The employee was great about it, he didn't give a fuck, he just didn't expect to see somebody he knew in street clothes fighting with a uniformed player. Regardless, at the time I was thankful the story never got back to management. A few years later Tremblay was working with me in Providence. The 41 games he logged during the 2008–2009 season with the P-Bruins were the most he ever played in the AHL, and his last experience as a pro.

I didn't work with goalies, for obvious reasons, but I had some fun with Hannu Toivonen while he was in Providence. Hannu was a Finnish goalie drafted by Boston, and after practices in Providence he liked to hang around and watch me work with his teammates. I would bait him a little, give him shit, call him a pussy and get him to come out every once in a while and wrestle around with me. I would say, "Ah Hannu, you're never going to have to do this in a game."

Well, one night in Providence, two guys fought but didn't have enough time in the period to serve their penalties so they were escorted off the ice toward their respective locker rooms. When they started to continue their battle under the stands, the benches cleared to join in on the fracas. Only Hannu and the opposing goalie were left on the ice.

Brendan Walsh, a tough little bastard and one of my favorite pupils with the P-Bruins, was up to his old tricks in the middle of the mayhem when he heard the crowd going crazy. "I knew it wasn't for us because the fans couldn't see and didn't know what was going on underneath the stands," Walsh told me later. "We knew there had to be something going on out on the ice, so we all rushed out and there were the goalies going at it."

I had no idea why, they weren't mad at each other, but all of a sudden I looked out and it was just the two goalies on the ice, and for whatever reason, maybe to get in on the fun and atmosphere of the charged building, they skated toward center ice taking off their masks and gloves. They squared off and fought. Hannu did a great job. He knew where to grab and hold, and he threw some punches. What hockey fan doesn't want to see two goalies slugging it out? Hannu was so proud of himself after that. He was just another one of the team's tough guys now!

I got a little work in with the St. Louis Blues as well. Larry Pleau, the Blues general manager, hired me for some attractive money during a two-week rookie camp one summer when the club was affiliated with the Worcester IceCats. I got to work with a couple of great kids, including D.J. King, a 6-foot-3, 228-pounder from, where else, Saskatchewan, Manitoba. He wore his hair in a sort of big afro that made his huge head look even bigger, if that were possible.

I found that most hockey fighters share one of two characteristics— either they have great balance and are soft punchers, or they have a big punch but lousy balance and end up falling down. King had good balance, *and* he punched my hand targets so hard he bruised me to the bone.

Right after working with King that summer I got to watch him fight my boy, Colton Orr, in Providence. It was incredible. It was one of those fights where everyone in the arena was silent and you could hear the punches landing, "thwack, thwack, thwack." Either player could have knocked out the other, and in the end they were both cut and bleeding. King ended up making it to the NHL with the Blues and then the Washington Capitals, where he was able to renew acquaintances with Orr a number of times.

I still take on clients to train; it's a good way to hang on to the game and great for my ego. But having my hands pounded black and blue by the Mac-Intyres of the hockey world gets old. They ache down to the bone and when I hold them out a day later they shake like I've got a case of the DTs. I am also getting a little on in years to be wrestling with some of the monsters who put on skates nowadays. A few years ago I found myself grappling with a youngster out of Boston College, Brian Boyle, who was getting himself ready for training camp with the Los Angeles Kings. The damn kid was 6-foot-7 and nearly 250 pounds. Are you shitting me? My fingers were sore for two days from grabbing hold of his jersey. The end is clearly in sight. In time I'll just rest on my laurels and ego-building stories like the one where, before Colton Orr and Steve MacIntyre fought for the first time in the NHL, they talked before the game and asked each other if they had talked to me recently. I thought that was pretty cool.

The fight game, the one I used to play and then coach with these guys, is all but gone, so I'm even more appreciative of these memories. Those who think they know better, the button pushers, figure fans don't want to see fighting in hockey anymore. Only future attendance will prove if they were correct.

In the meantime, I smile broadly at the old lightbulbs burning their brightest before dying out. One such moment for me came when John Scott received the most fan votes for the 2016 NHL All-Star Game—much to the dismay of the league brass. In the inaugural 3-on-3, four-team tournament format, Scott looked anything but out-of-place. Not only did he score two goals for the Pacific Division's semifinals victory, but he was on the winning side in the 1–0 championship game and pronounced, legitimately, MVP.

It was so nice to watch the NHL have that one shoved up their ass.

* * *

Fully aware of the physical limitations I had to endure as a fight coach, I needed to carve out another niche to remain in the pro game in some capacity, so I decided to pursue the goal of becoming an on-ice official.

There are two kinds of on-ice officials in the pro game, a referee and linesman. The referee is the top guy, the overseer, the foreman of the game. He wears an orange arm band for identification and basically supervises the flow of the entire contest. A large part of that includes calling penalties. If a ref calls a game too tight it can stymie the flow, like a car running with a bad carburetor. If he just puts his whistle away and lets the guys play, sometimes things can get out of control and players could get hurt. He walks a fine line. A linesman does whatever he can to support his ref, including calling offside and icing, and providing extra eyes for penalties and goals. They also drop the puck for face-offs and of course break up fights, which is the main thing I wanted to do.

Once again I found myself in the right place at the right time, and had somebody in position to help me keep my head in place after I stuck my neck out.

Eugene "Geno" Binda sped up my learning curve. At the ripe age of 44 I had no desire to start out officiating 10-year-olds on Saturday mornings, so Binda, a supervisor of game officials throughout New England and Eastern New York, ushered me right into local junior hockey leagues.

I learned on the fly, made my share of mistakes, and worked with some quality partners who taught me right from wrong without discouraging me. The funny thing was, for the first time I could actually skate my position on the ice pretty well, and my size was a huge advantage in not only the presentation of an authority figure, but my ability to break up scuffles at the junior level, which housed players up to 21 years old.

My goal all along was to officiate in a professional game, and in my area the only possible venue was the American Hockey League, which would be a very tall order. In the first place, regardless of who I knew, it was one thing for me to have a fight in the AHL—hell, I was a fighter—but quite another to try and officiate a pro game. Who would have the balls to give me that chance to screw up?

The opportunity came along as if I placed the order myself.

From out of the sky dropped on my plate a brand-new, Single-A hockey circuit called the Federal Hockey League, a name taken from the fictional league in *Slap Shot*. The league opened its inaugural 2010–2011 season with six teams, including four in New York State and one in Brooklyn. The franchise in Danbury, Connecticut, would be my baby.

Geno set me up for my first professional game as a linesman on November 26, 2010. The contest pitted the Danbury Whalers against the Broome County Barons of Binghampton. The Danbury Ice Arena gladly accepted an unexpectedly large crowd of 1,849 fans, and shortly into the first period I broke up my first fight and escorted my man to his penalty box.

Between periods in the officials' dressing room I was bouncing off the walls as excited as a little kid. I felt like I did after my first fights for the Carolina Thunderbirds. The other two guys I was working with thought I was mental. These guys were just doing it for the money, which was pretty good, but I was having a genuine blast for myself. It was absolutely everything I wanted, and more. After another fight, as I was escorting a player off to the penalty box, I told him that "if somebody grabs you by the neck in a fight, don't throw overhands, throw uppercuts!" The kid looked at me in disbelief, like I was crazy, like, "Who the fuck *are* you?"

I saw it as a player, but in my short time as a linesman I've experienced a little bit more of the banter that occurs between the officials and players and coaches before and during a game. Conversation and lines of communication between the parties can be healthy and help a game progress smoothly. When officials, players, and coaches share a good rapport, an atmosphere of respect, understanding, and even forgiveness improves the dynamics and flow of the game.

I enjoy talking to each team's heavyweight fighters in warm-ups and even during the game. Sometimes they'll tell me what they're planning to do, like if they're going to fight right away, off the face-off. I have had guys tell me what shift they intended to fight. I appreciate the heads-up, as it's always best to be prepared. I also thought that if the tough guys had a good relationship with me, when it came to breaking up their fights they would be more apt to listen to my instructions. There would probably be nothing worse than for me to end up wrestling around with a guy who wouldn't stop fighting, and maybe we'd end up going at it. Actually, that's what I secretly wanted.

Relationships with coaches are a bit different. Some coaches have a built-in repertoire of questions and complaints about every whistle directed at their team. Their team never goes offside and never commits a penalty. They are forever yelling at me, telling me that I missed the call or the face-off is *over* the line, not inside. I understand, it's all about intimidation. You see it in baseball all the time. The players and coaches chirp about this pitch and that pitch, and before you know it the umpire is giving the pitcher an extra inch off the plate. I think even veteran officials can be molded and manipulated by criticism in a game—it's only human nature.

I hadn't been around long enough, certainly as an official, to know everything about managing the flow of a game, but it's certainly not in my constitution to take *too* much shit from anybody. If I blew a call, and I had, many times, I had no problem wandering over to the bench and apologizing to the coach—at least to let him know that I realized I made a mistake. Again, if an official has a good rapport with the coach, the simple acknowledgment of the error should suffice to blunt excessive abuse.

If the coach continues to call me a fucking idiot, and of course the players then follow his lead and chirp in, I have to stand my ground. I make them fully aware that they're not in the Show, that we're not in Madison Square Garden so fucking relax. You want to keep badgering me, complaining that your guys are getting shoved around? I'll tell you that your players are a bunch of pussies for not answering the other team's challenges and they deserve everything they get. Don't look at me to be your fucking nursemaid. Want to keep killing me about a bad icing call? Don't worry, I'll blow a big call later that you can really cry about.

I'm not a player anymore, but you can't just take the animal out of the jungle. I had a feeling that the longer I continued to be on the ice, even as a linesman, the better chance there was that I would end up squaring off with somebody—and it didn't necessarily have to be on the ice.

In a classic twist of lower minor-league hockey fate, the Barons folded in Binghampton and magically appeared on Cape Cod, where I officiated my second pro game at the Tony Kent Arena in South Dennis, a mere 45 minutes from my house.

It was the first minor-league hockey game on the Cape since 1982, when owner Vince McMahon, he of television wrestling fame, had his one-season-old Cape Cod Buccaneers of the defunct Atlantic Coast Hockey League fold a month before the start of the playoffs. I got three fights to break up servicing the new Cape Cod Barons, but the real fun came from a two-pound cod.

Every time the home-team Barons scored a goal, a fan tossed a frozen fish in the direction of the opposing goalie. The second time he did it I just happened to skate between his cross-hairs and the cod hit me; its frozen and rock-hard fins tore a slice on the back of my left hand that later required a tetanus shot and five stitches.

I thought I acted pretty professional in that I didn't flinch and make a scene. While the arena's maintenance crew scraped the fish off the ice with a shovel, I covered my wound with a maze of Band-aids and closed out the first period.

Of course Gator was at the game taking photos of me, and during the first intermission from in front of the officials' locker room I yelled for him. He ran over thinking I wanted a drink or something, but instead I asked if he saw what happened. I was actually amused because I thought it was such a perfect scene for minor league hockey. It was something right out of *Slap Shot* and I was glad at least one of my friends saw it. After telling me I smelled like rotten fish, he told me he was sitting in the first row with his son and the guy ran right past him both times to build some momentum in order to hurl the fish all the way to the goalie. Furthermore, he pointed the guy out to me. He was 30 feet away, right in front of the rink's front doors.

I couldn't believe it. This jackass who ripped my hand open was getting pats on the back from three other fans telling him how great he was for throwing all the fish.

I was going to have myself a chat with the guy. Gator cautioned me about getting into a fight with a fan and getting into trouble with Geno, but I tugged at the Federal Hockey League patch Velcroed to my shirt and said the league could fucking have it.

I walked over, standing about 6-foot-5 on skates, and approached the fish thrower, a stocky 5-foot-10 working stiff with a scraggly beard, maybe in his late 20s, wearing a Harley-Davidson leather jacket. At this point I was pissed off that Gator didn't have his camera; he left it with his son in the stands and didn't want to run after it for fear that I might get jumped by the three other fans still milling around.

I placed a hand heavily on Harley Boy's shoulder, parked my face two inches from his and said with a straight face and calm but stern voice, "Hey buddy, if you throw one more fucking fish on the ice I'm taking this patch off my shirt, climbing over the glass and punching you out." Then I glanced at the three other guys with him and said, "If you want to do anything I'll be glad to knock you out, too."

The other guys were horrified and froze, but Harley Boy didn't really know how to read me. I thought he took me a little light-hearted, as if I wasn't really serious. So I showed him my hand and said, "Getting hurt doing this is not worth $140 to me, and this game isn't worth getting your teeth knocked down your throat."

The guy made a little smirk as if to test my resolve and I asked if he'd like to go out into the hallway right now. At this point Harley Boy knew I was serious. He cowered and admitted his mistake, and promised he wouldn't do it again. I thanked him for understanding and walked away to finish my job on the ice, and maybe get called back to work another game.

But it didn't matter, I was done. Sometimes you have to realize when you're over your head, and I was. I do have some personal pride, and I didn't like some of the mistakes I was making—like anticipating an icing and blowing the whistle too early, not thinking that a player was actually fast enough to reach the puck in time, or that a goalie would play it. I had a feeling some people just wouldn't say anything critical to me out of respect or fear or just wanting to be nice to me. So to keep respect for myself, in the end I was con-

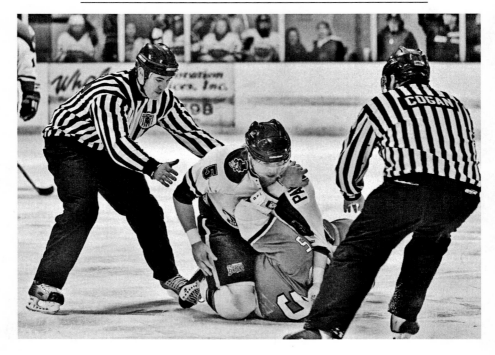

Moving in to grab Brad Pawlowski of the Cape Cod Barons while officiating in the Federal Hockey League.

tent that I was able to realize a goal of being an on-ice official, and then walk away.

That isn't to say I walked away without regrets. One was that I didn't knock out the fish-throwing asshole. Another is that I didn't have a fight on the ice while wearing the stripes.

I thought it would be a wonderful experience, something so fantastically different and unique and ESPN-worthy to get into a fight with a player while officiating a game. But the problem came with how to pull it off without actually instigating the fight myself. I mean, the mistakes I was making as a linesman were bad enough, how much more of an ass would I look like if I went out there and just challenged a kid to fight? I needed somebody to come at me, so that it would appear as though I had no choice in everybody's eyes but to defend myself. I still take pride in the fact that nobody ever had to ask Doug Smith to fight; that nobody ever had the chance to challenge me because they could never get the words out of their mouth fast enough to beat me to the punch, so to speak. The moment I came out on the ice I was asking a guy if he wanted to go.

But this was different. I thought I had a glimmer of a chance down in Danbury one night. I was in the process of breaking up a fight when out of the corner of my eye I noticed a player skating toward me as if he were going to jump in on the melee. I just instinctively held my arm outstretched with my fist clenched—a position necessitated more out of personal preservation than anything else—and the kid ran his face right into it. He wasn't too happy and we both swore at each other. I was still engaged with the main fight, so I wasn't able to square up with this kid, but I suppose he got the message that he was being a bad boy and skated off without pursuing the issue any longer. That was my best chance.

I did have an outstanding plan that dropped into my lap, but the window of opportunity didn't stay open long enough for me to capitalize. Somehow Billy Tibbetts finagled or maneuvered his way onto the local team, the Cape Cod Bluefins.

Everybody in pro hockey knew about the *notorious* Billy Tibbetts, who grew up a few towns over from me. A peculiar and talented kid, his trip into professional hockey was temporarily derailed by a significant stretch in

Coming full circle: escorting Danbury's Matt Caranci to the penalty box.

prison. Before heading off to the pen, Tibbetts gave a solid hint of his appreciable hockey ability during a stint with the Johnstown Chiefs during the 1995–96 season. Playing in a much-better East Coast Hockey League than I dipped into, Tibbetts scored 37 goals to go along with 31 assists in 58 games, and also logged a nice, even 300 minutes in penalties. He was truly a dual threat, and yet another one of those guys I could only dream was me.

Tibbetts sat out the next four hockey seasons, but almost immediately after getting out of lockup began impressing scouts with his 6-foot-2, 215-pound frame and solid play in the same local summer league I had been spotted in years earlier. Despite the fact Canadian law barred him from playing in that country, Tibbetts was nevertheless signed by the Pittsburgh Penguins, and had to skip playing in the AHL All-Star Game because of his first call up to the big club. Nobody can argue that this accomplishment was anything short of amazing.

However, despite realizing his dream of making it to the NHL, the trouble that came with the talent didn't relent. While both the Philadelphia Flyers and New York Rangers would also give Tibbetts games in the NHL, his behavior eventually led him to no fewer than 12 different minor-league teams in seven leagues, including Europe. During this nomadic stretch, his longest time with any team was 46 games with the Chicago Wolvers of the AHL (20 goals, 22 assists, 249 PIM). His shortest was three games with the Danbury Mad Hatters of the fledgling and lowly Eastern Pro Hockey League (1 goal, 4 assists, 9 PIM).

So here he was again, somehow and for whatever reason, at 37 years old and two years removed from 12 games with the Huntsville Havoc of the Southern Pro Hockey League. He could still play, that was for sure, especially against the college kids in this league. He racked up 40 points in 15 games, and he didn't become shy on the ice, as he ran around enough to log 109 penalty minutes.

Oh yah, I thought, Tibbetts could help me out here.

I knew Tibbetts from the various rinks I frequented. I liked and admired—his ability. He was in great shape, had a great build, like a bodybuilder, and he had such a sincere desire and willingness to fight. We worked out a bit on the ice together practice fighting.

Tom Sullivan (Northeastern University): "Doug Smith was the only guy who challenged [Billy Tibbetts] ... well, he didn't really challenge him, it didn't get to that point. I used to skate shinny hockey in Quincy with Doug. I was about 12 or 13 years old at the time, and Tibbetts hit an older guy into the boards, hard enough that the guy went down. Doug came right off the bench. Tibbetts looked up and saw Doug coming, so he turned to the older guy and tried to console him—like he didn't mean to do what he did."

I knew Billy was a loose cannon and would probably be game for just about anything, so I figured we could stage a fight, a real fight. He'd do it. Maybe I'd call a penalty on him. It certainly wouldn't be out of his nature to argue. Maybe he'd charge at me, give me a bump or shove—then we could square off and really go at it. It would be a thing of beauty. It would probably end up on ESPN.

Alas, Tibbetts didn't last long enough in this league for my plan to hatch. There were a few rumors why he disappeared this time, but suffice to say they all hinted at him wearing out his welcome, and since that aborted 2012 season he hasn't laced them up for any real play again.

14

GOON: The Movies

On Tuesday, June 27, 2006, I received an email from a young man by the name of Jesse Shapira. Finally I had come across somebody who wanted to do more than just *talk* about turning my story into a movie.

Maybe it was the classic underdog theme, but despite what you may think of my unlikely journey, when the book was first published my story attracted attention from a number of different Hollywood types. Some of them sounded big and impressive, like the guy from Sony Pictures or the agent of a well-known television sitcom actor. But others seemed like wannabes from the fringes of the movie-making scene.

These folks from seemingly all corners of the Hollywood world would send emails every couple of months asking if the movie rights were still available, and of course I said they were. While the courtship went on like this, from a distance, without much more than preliminary questions being asked and answered, it was still at least somewhat exciting that there was this sort of interest from the movie world.

Then the 2004 NHL strike occurred, and like the flick of a switch the emails stopped. When the strike was settled the emails started up again, but by this time I was aggravated with the emotional rollercoaster. My initial excitement of a possible movie was replaced with being annoyed by what I now perceived as nothing more than tire-kickers, and soon I began responding to their emails that the movie rights were in fact still available, "but not to you." In other words, leave me the fuck alone unless you're really interested in doing something.

At the time he contacted me, Jesse Shapira was a 29-year-old Pittsburgh native living in the Los Angeles area with some friends and acquaintances involved with the entertainment industry. He had grown up a Pittsburgh Penguins fan and struggled along with the perennial NHL losers before the maturation of Mario Lemieux and Company produced a pair of Stanley Cups in the early 1990s. Shapira loved Super Mario and the championships, but he also took an interest over the years in the Penguins' tough guys like Troy Loney, Jay Caufield, and Dan Frawley.

Upon graduating from Colgate University, where he played football and competed with the track and field team, Shapira worked in Los Angeles as an intern for Fox Sports Net and then back East as a scout in the Buffalo Bills organization. Moving back to L.A., seemingly out of the clear blue sky, Shapira decided he might want to make a hockey movie about a goon. Who the hell would do that? He proceeded to conduct an Internet search for any stories about enforcers, and my book punched him in the face.

That, folks, is how at least two movies based on this book came to be. Of course there is more to the story of the initial movie, which took even more luck and five years to complete.

What separated Shapira from all of the other interested parties was that he almost immediately negotiated a renewable, one-year option on *GOON*. I told him he could have the option for free, but he demanded I take at least a little money. I don't know, maybe money needed to exchange hands to make the option binding, but in any case, this guy proved to me he was serious.

Shapira ended up with an "Executive Producer" credit on *GOON*. The executive producer, in general terms, is the money man, the person who secures funding and makes sure the movie is shot on schedule and resides at least somewhere around the stratosphere of the planned budget. He also strikes up relationships with people like me, and the standard option he secured allowed him the legal freedom to shop my story to screenwriters, actors, directors, financiers—anybody and everybody who could help in cobbling together a motion picture. That is some of what an executive producer of a movie does—he gathers up the pieces of the puzzle, the ingredients that can be mixed together to make or "produce" a movie.

Armed with the option, Shapira set to work on getting a screenplay written that was based on my story. He told me about an up-and-coming, but relatively-unknown writer who was going to be a big deal in future years. Shapira's childhood pal and working partner in L.A., David Gross, had a connection to Canadian-native Evan Goldberg, who had penned the script for *Superbad*, which had yet to be released, and had just finished writing *Pineapple Express*. As things turned out, both movies eventually combined to gross nearly $300,000,000 worldwide.[1]

In the guise of a favor, Shapira tagged along with another producer to a meeting with Goldberg to pitch a movie idea about a guy who runs a privatized prison out of his California home. I still think that idea could make for a fun movie, but Shapira said that Goldberg hated the concept. With the meeting winding down and nothing left to lose, Shapira acted on *his* plan and broached the subject of *GOON*.

Goldberg admitted that he didn't know much about hockey, but that he had wanted to do something with his hockey-crazed friend, Jay Baruchel, a rising Canadian-born actor with the films *Million Dollar Baby, Knocked Up,* and soon *Tropic Thunder* under his belt. Goldberg told Shapira that he would run the idea by Baruchel and get back to him. Thinking he was probably being given the slip, Shapira was bowled over the next day when Goldberg actually called to tell him that Baruchel loved the idea, and a deal to write a screenplay was soon struck.

Throughout the early process, Shapira reiterated to me that he wanted to tell a realistic story of the relationship between a hockey enforcer and his team, but cautioned me that the movie he had in mind was going to be at least a light comedy—not slapstick, but funny, violent and vulgar. He encouraged me to see the newly released *Superbad,* and probed me to find if there was going to be a problem with a comedic aspect to *GOON.* I agreed that the movie had to be funny, in the same way *Slap Shot* was funny, and I didn't give a flying fucking shit how many swears were in it.

With a screenplay written by two burgeoning Hollywood heavies, Shapira shopped around for actors and a director. Illustrating his uncanny foresight once again, Shapira mentioned the name of Seth Rogen to me. Like the names Goldberg and Baruchel, I had at the time never heard of Seth Rogen—not many people had—but soon he would be such a successful movie star he may have become too expensive with no extra time on his schedule for *GOON* and was scratched off Shapira's shopping list. Baruchel, who was Rogen's pal, also grew in stature with lead roles in *She's Out of My League* and *The Sorcerer's Apprentice,* but after writing himself a juicy role based on Gator, *GOON* became Baruchel's baby and he wasn't about to jump ship.

Early in the game, Shapira tossed around other possible names to play the goon character. Beyond Rogen, an agent for one major action movie star inquired about the lead role. I really liked this guy in everything he'd been in, but he was too short. I know Sylvester Stallone isn't very tall, either, and filming angles and such have made him look bigger on screen than he really is, but I wasn't even partly sold on this other guy, no matter how big a star he was. As it turned out, the guy's price tag precluded him from being involved with *GOON* anyway, thank goodness.

Other actors were added to and subtracted from the lead-role list until Shapira managed to snare Seann William Scott to play Doug Glatt. This created a little bit of a stir because Seann was rumored to be the top choice as the lead in director Kevin Smith's hockey project, *Hit Somebody,* based on the Warren Zevon song about an enforcer in the WHA back in the 1970s. Seann seemed a lock for this role because he had worked with Smith in the film *Cop Out.* I believe Seann decided on *GOON* because it was further ahead as a project than *Hit Somebody,* which didn't yet boast a script.

I didn't take a shine to the choice of Seann, initially. I remembered him as the character "Stiffler" in the *American Pie* movie series, where he came off as a cocky but likeable goofball. And while he had a lean, muscular build, I didn't think he was big enough nor had the physical presence to pull off a believable heavyweight hockey enforcer. At least the goofy Seth Rogen was beefy.

Shapira, whom I had come to trust, assured me that Seann had the requisite height at six feet, was bulking up to 200 pounds, and had also transformed his boyish look with some tattoos. Shapira had been right about everything else, so I settled in for the ride.

Another most important piece of the puzzle was the choice of director. While a producer gathers together the ingredients for a movie, what ultimately ends up on the screen, the filmed presentation of the screenplay, is much the vision and child of the director. A director puts his fingerprint on his movies. Those who know film much better than I can watch a movie and guess who directed it. I suppose the same can be said for the visual characteristics of a particular painter's work, which would be recognizable to the trained eye.

Shapira had to get the right director for the job, which is no different than getting just the right actor for the job. Can you imagine anybody else but Marlon Brando playing the lead in *The Godfather*? Hell, Orson Welles and Lawrence Olivier were around; they were big, burly guys and great actors who could have physically replaced Brando, but I don't think they would have pulled it off as well. Why did Mario Puzo's book *The Godfather* translate into movie gold while Sidney Sheldon's runaway *New York Times* best-seller *The Other Side of Midnight* turn into celluloid crap? Sometimes it's the fault of the director's vision.

Like the choice of Rogen early on, it was likely through the guiding of Baruchel that Shapira concentrated his energies on landing Canadian director Michael Dowse, a hockey fan and ex-college football player who garnered a cult following Up North for his *Fubar* movie series.

With the screenplay, lead actor, and director in place, one of the toughest roles to cast proved to be the goon's chief rival, written as a briny and battered veteran finishing off a legendary two-decade run of pounding opponents at every level of professional hockey. Dismissed from the NHL for yet another brutal attack, he finds himself in a disciplinary swan song, squaring off against the lead character during the climax of the movie.

The choice of actor for this part seemed to drive Shapira crazy, and also appeared to place a drag on pre-production. Shapira told me that he didn't think Hollywood offered many choices for this role. Some names were bandied about, including Kiefer Sutherland, a well-known hockey enthusiast, and Keanu Reeves, who was in the hockey movie *Youngblood*. Shapira was initially excited about both prospects, and I recall him noting that Reeves had bulked up, grown a beard, and "looked mean."

I thought it would be great to have the star of *The Matrix* in GOON, even if I didn't think Reeves looked tough enough to be a fearsome heavyweight hockey enforcer. I felt the same way about Sutherland. Everybody knew Kiefer Sutherland and I thought he would be great for publicity, even if his boyish facial features didn't strike fear in me.

The name that received a bit more play from Shapira, however, was Viggo Mortensen. I didn't recognize the exotic name right off the bat, but I sure knew the face. I liked this guy the first time I saw him on screen in *A Perfect Murder* with Michael Douglas and Gwyneth Paltrow. He was very handsome, at once cultured and dashing as well as rough around the edges and pedestrian. I researched him on the Internet and found he was a Montreal Canadian fan, a big Guy Lafleur guy, and he worked as a translator for the Swedish National Hockey Team during the 1980 Winter Olympics in Lake Placid, where he watched in person the "Miracle on Ice" game between the U.S. and Soviet Union. I searched and searched, but the biographies I read didn't mention if he could skate. Over the years I noticed that Mortensen landed a big role in the *Lord of the Rings* movies, and the lead in a small, personal favorite of mine, *Hidalgo*. But he was old now, too old to play a hockey player, even one at the end of a long, punishing career. I knew Hollywood makeup artists could work miracles, but shit, he was 50, with a ruggedly weathered face like Clint Eastwood. I didn't like him for this.

Again from out of the blue, Shapira excitedly mentioned that a fellow by the name of Liev Schreiber was in the running as the big rival enforcer, but that he would be a long shot to hammer down. Again, I didn't recognize the name, but when I rushed to my trusty Internet image search I immediately remembered him from *Scream, X-Men, The Manchurian Candidate,* and one of my wife's favorite movies, *Kate and Leopold*. I was also surprised that he had won a Tony Award for the play *Glengarry Glen Ross*, but I was even more impressed that he was married to Naomi Watts, whom I had just seen reprising Fay Wray's role as the heroine in the new *King Kong*. To my surprise, and in short time, Schreiber was on board, and knocked everybody for a loop with his creation of Ross Rhea, a Dave Schultz–like character complete with a Saskatchewan accent.

There were many impressive "name" actors mentioned as possibly taking roles or making cameo appearances in the movie, including Tim Robbins, Bruce Willis, Michael Myers, and Steve Carrell and Craig Robinson from the television series *The Office*. I was also told that the agent for Robert Duvall inquired about the role of the goon's coach. After landing the long-shot Schreiber I thought there was a chance Shapira could pull off Duvall, one of my very favorite actors, but nothing more came of it—if there was anything there to begin with.

I don't know how close any of these actors came to being in the movie, if there were any real inquiries versus wishful thinking, but in the end there weren't any surprise cameo appearances—except for Georges Laraque, one of the greatest NHL hockey fighters of all time. Laraque, a monster of a man at 6-foot-4 and 250 pounds, had only been retired for a year when he agreed to square off with Seann in front of the cameras. I am guessing that this may have been the role originally envisioned for Craig Robinson from *The Office*. Thank goodness it went to Laraque. After getting up close and personal in the rink, with Laraque on skates being even more physically imposing—if that were possible–Jesse couldn't fathom the concept of having to fight a guy like this on the ice. I think Laraque gave a lot of people on the set a reality check and at least a partial clue of the gonads it must take to be a hockey enforcer.

I always asked Shapira about the female lead. Being the father of two daughters and somewhat a feminist, I was a bit disappointed that the female lead didn't really matter. I did understand, however, that in this male-driven film, the female lead was definitely of secondary importance, and that there was a far larger pool of attractive and available women to play the role. Over the years Shapira mentioned a few strikingly beautiful actresses on his radar for the role, but I think as the screenplay evolved, the female lead did as well, and the emphasis switched from drop-dead gorgeous, to either just plain pretty or even simply cute.

One of the first names mentioned who encapsulated the latter was Canadian actress Ellen Page of *Juno* fame. The production was even considering filming much of the movie in Page's hometown of Halifax, Nova Scotia. But GOON ended up with a different cutie I wasn't familiar with but a face I recognized in Alison Pill, who had been the female lead of *Milk*, for which Sean Penn won an Oscar. She looked like she could have been Ellen Page's sister, and she had been nominated for a Tony Award for her stage work in *The Lieutenant of Inishmore*.

The metamorphosis of the female lead character, Eva, was interesting. The decision to hire a lead actress like Pill was made because it was rightfully surmised that few Victoria's Secret models would care to strike up a meaningful relationship with an ex-bouncer with no education who played minor-league hockey. In fact, the production went a step further, as after many re-writes, Pill's role as a young, sophisticated career woman was shifted toward a less professional, more approachable and far more *willing* woman. In fact, there is a scene in the movie where Pill calls herself a "slut." In today's parlance she'd be known as a "Puck Bunny."

Baruchel, for a time, appeared to be the person most affected by the hiring of Pill. The pair met for the first time on the Winnipeg set in October 2010, began dating almost immediately, and announced an engagement by Christmas. The initial plan was to marry in September of 2012. When I finally met Pill at the *GOON* premier in Toronto, I told her it was pretty neat that my little story was the vehicle that helped them get together. Unfortunately, their affair was grounded when their breakup went public in early 2013.

Romance aside, I was certainly impressed with the quality of the cast Shapira and company had managed to piece together, and that was before popular character actor and comic Eugene Levy appeared from out of the sky to play the goon's father, and Kim Coates signed on to play the goon's coach. I remembered Coates from his little roles in *Waterworld* and *Battlefield Earth*. He always seemed to play offbeat characters, usually scumbags. He had also made his mark on the little screen as well, including recurring roles on the television shows *Sons of Anarchy* and *CSI: Miami*.

In the movie *GOON*, the title character is brought in to a high-level minor-league team to protect a young superstar who had become timid and otherwise uninspired because of the physical beatings he had taken from opposing tough guys—in particular, the lead villain Ross Rhea played by Liev Schreiber. Sound familiar?

French-Canadian heartthrob Marc-Andre Grondin was hired for this role of fancy Francophile superstar Xavier LaFlamme. The 27-year-old was one of the better skaters and hockey players on the set, but his importance to the production meant he couldn't afford to get hurt during any of the body-checking scenes, which helped create yet another job for a stunt man. The stunt doubles for Grondin, as well as Seann William Scott, landed nice positions with the production and were invaluable to the authenticity of the hockey scenes.

Financing was, of course, always an issue, especially in the heart of a recession. Shapira told me that because of the tough economic times, major studios were taking fewer chances with fewer movies. Rather than risk tens of millions of dollars on a hockey movie, an underserved but decidedly fringe market, the major studios would rather make something like *Alvin and the Chipmunks*, which already had a target audience that the box office could count on for a satisfactory return on investment.

Even so, Shapira did have at least one deal on the table from a big independent movie company. To his credit, because the deal didn't give a definitive time table for shooting and would allow the company to shelve the project, Shapira chose to leave some money on the table and walk away.

Shapira also wanted to make *his* movie *his* way. Giving up creative control to a large production company would have definitely cut into anything he had to say about what would eventually appear on the screen. In a way, Shapira was trying to keep a hold of what I had tossed away when I signed my option deal with him.

From the get-go, Shapira recognized that because of the major movie studios' aversion to taking risks, there would be a lack of movie product available for theaters to show during what appeared to be an inevitable recession. He was going to make *GOON* the way he wanted, beholding to no one, fashioning an attractive collection of screenwriters, actors, and director into a film he could strut like a smoldering Hollywood starlet and drop into the lap of the highest-bidding studio or distribution company.

Shapira and Company's desire to control nearly every aspect of production included me as well. During one of my initial conversations with Shapira, I read him a list of requests I wanted included in the original option agreement. I wanted to have a say in casting, dialogue, and the choreography of fight scenes. I also wanted to have some of my friends who supported me over the years in the movie. I could almost feel Shapira's neck twisting on the other end of the phone, but he pulled himself together and said, "Doug, what do you think will happen if I walk into a studio looking for millions of dollars and say, 'I have this great property here, *GOON*, but this guy you never heard of and don't know wants to pick the actors and write the screenplay and do this and that.' What do you think they're going to say to me? They're going to tell me to get the hell out."

Then Shapira asked me the simplest of questions: "Do you want the movie made?" I said, "Yes," and basically backed off, giving him a green light to do whatever he needed to get the movie done. The reality was that I was very, very fortunate to have anybody even consider making a movie based on my experiences, but I think I would have kicked myself later if I didn't at least attempt to get some of the things I wanted.

All that being noted, Shapira did ask me to write a treatment based on my book. I penned a tale with the basic premise intact—a guy who couldn't skate just wanting to fight in minor-league hockey. I had him playing in the minors and getting involved in a love triangle. The daughter of the club's owner used to date the star of the team, but now she falls for the new guy she finds so different from all the hockey players she's been around. There is of course resentment and jealousy between the goon and the star, but eventually the star comes to respect the goon after realizing the value of being protected on the ice by him.

I don't know how much if any of my treatment was read by or influenced the screenwriters, but I think there are some strong similarities between it and the movie. Another thing I *may* have had a hand in changing was that early on, Shapira said the movie was going to be based on the junior hockey circuit. Knowing that all of the players are mandated to wear facemasks in juniors, I told Shapira that this may affect the recognition of the star actors, and he seemed to agree.

As far as production money, Shapira ultimately eschewed studio money and finagled to secure much of the production money himself. Final financing was still being worked out while the movie was being filmed and right through post-production. In any case, the heavy Canadian flavor of the movie coincided with some of the funding coming from the Canadian Government, which brought with it some attractive tax-break benefits, as well as certain unattractive rules and regulations.

When money is taken from such an entity, even in the United States, there are strings that come along. It certainly made sense. Hell, when anybody puts money up for a project there usually comes with it a proportionate say in some decisions. In this case, the production had to employ X-amount of Canadians. I was also told that only two of the actors could be non–Canadian (Scott and Schreiber), and that the second-highest paid actor had to be Canadian.

These restrictions pretty much took Gator and I completely out of the picture as far as being actors or technical consultants, which I thought sucked, big time. Considering all of this, it came as no surprise that one of the main hockey consultants hired was former NHLer and three-time Stanley Cup winner Mike Keene, who was from Winnipeg, where the movie was being filmed. I was disappointed the consultant wasn't me, which would have been a very logical and natural choice, but was at the very least glad that somebody of Keene's stature was involved in trying to make the hockey scenes look realistic. A brother of Keene was also hired as a consultant, and snagged a role as an opposing coach.

I was further disappointed when Shapira called from the *GOON* production office in Winnipeg and told me that the production crew was playing shinny hockey as a way to bond. His production office was inundated with mountains of sticks and hockey equipment sent to him from various companies, and he sounded genuinely proud of his own improvement on the ice. He invited me to come up and play, and of course I wanted so much to be up there with him, but there was no way I could take such a leave of absence from the police department, my working wife, and our two young daughters.

There was talk that the production was going to include filming locations in Montreal as well as Halifax, but Winnipeg, Manitoba and some surrounding locations proved better logistically and financially. Much to the relief of everybody involved, principal photography of *GOON* finally began as scheduled on the morning of October 18, 2010. Shapira was so excited that he immediately (and secretly) emailed me the first shot of the day he pirated with his cell phone—a 10-second clip of Scott working in a bar as a bouncer going after a drunk patron on orders from his boss. It was surreal; this thing was really happening!

Shapira ended up securing in the neighborhood of $11 million to make the movie—no small feat during a recession. To put that production figure into perspective, *The Wrestler* was filmed for about $6 million independent dollars, while Disney's *Sorcerer's Apprentice,* in which Jay Baruchel played the apprentice, sopped up $150 million production dollars. Shapira's money woes continued with a late music squabble, and he also had to pony up more dough when a Glatt Family home dinner scene was scrapped in favor of a Toronto shoot of the outdoor Glatt Family synagogue fiasco.

Our cast was clearly representative of a much higher budget, but the thing with many independent productions is that many of the actors take the job for the role, not necessarily the paycheck. I am sure most or all of them worked for the neighborhood of scale. There are also less frills and coddling on an independent set. Gator brought a couple of his kids up to the filming in Winnipeg and he said that Seann William Scott used one of the rink locker rooms for his dressing room. There was no excessive ass-kissing, there were no divas on set demanding fresh flowers daily and water bottled from the edge of a glacier.

I originally thought that the shooting schedule of late fall into early winter was short-sighted and would experience problems because it ran into the Canadian hockey season. Initially it was in fact a problem because few rinks around Winnipeg were willing to forfeit their ice times for the *GOON* shoot. Undaunted, the production instead filmed hockey scenes overnight in various rinks from 11 p.m. to 11 a.m. The most impressive venue they rented was smack in the center of Winnipeg, the ESL Center, which was then home to the Vancouver Canucks AHL affiliate, the Manitoba Moose. It is now host ice for the NHL franchise Winnipeg Jets.

Director Michael Dowse appeared to run a tight but comfortable ship. The set was laid back, but there was very little wasted time—there was no budget for waste. Despite his reputation for filming many takes, everything seemed to run very organized, quick and smooth on the ice, with one scene and set-up gliding one right after another. Various assistants brought the actors and extras drinks, sandwiches, and snacks in between takes, with a more formal one-hour break taken at about 6 a.m. for "dinner" right inside the arena.

When I came across the first still photograph of hockey action from the movie, which was released on MTV's website, I thought it was a stock shot from an actual minor-league hockey game. It took me a moment to realize it was in fact Seann William Scott going toe-to-toe with another actor. I was relieved to see Scott using a solid, wide base with his skates, and that his right elbow was cocked high to set up a technically sound, straight right-hand punch. I was impressed and very excited that everything looked so realistic.

The goon is supposed to be from Massachusetts, maybe even from the Boston area, and the writers created the fictional hometown of Orangetown for Doug Glatt. I wondered if Baruchel or Goldberg knew there really is a town in Central Massachusetts by the name of "Orange."

While I'm Irish, Baruchel, whose mom is Catholic, said that some of the inspiration for Doug Glatt came from his late Jewish father, a gritty player in his day on an all–Jewish hockey team. He also said that the goon is partly amalgamated from former minor-league tough guy Mike Bajurny, whose grandfather and father are doctors, and brother is the producer of the fine hockey documentary *Les Chiefs*. In that film, Bajurny is badgered by his parents, who would like to see their son do something more with his life than continue to pursue his love of dropping the gloves. This scenario is clearly paralleled in the movie, as Glatt's gay brother and dad are doctors, and both parents wholeheartedly disapprove of Doug's chosen path as a hockey fighter.

I was excited that some of the reviewers of *GOON* tabbed it as the "*Slap Shot* of my generation." That's a heady comparison. My own opinion is that *Slap Shot* has a lock on the greatest characters—the three Hanson Brothers—but *GOON* has the better story. In any case, it is surely the *Slap Shot* for a new generation.

Unfortunately, for many of those associated with the *GOON* production, this new generation brought with it some serious piracy issues that put a beating on our film almost from the get-go.

GOON leaped out of the blocks and was the highest-grossing film in Canada during its first week of release. Beating out all Hollywood competition was pretty heady stuff for a Canadian production—but the money take declined precipitously from there. I learned what had apparently happened by following the irritations of veteran movie-maker Don Carmody, a co-producer on *GOON*.

Hashing it out with actor Seann William Scott (left) at the *GOON* world premier after-party in Toronto.

One thing Carmody heard was that, because of the R rating, younger kids were buying tickets to *The Muppets* and then sneaking into *GOON*. Well shit, I've done that as a kid, too.

But Carmody wasn't sold on that being the major problem.

GOON was first released in Europe, and while Carmody worried that somebody might film it with a video camera and then sell pirated copies in North America, it didn't happen.

But VOD happened.

Video-on-demand was a fairly new marketing and distribution strategy employed by Magnolia Pictures, the United States distributor of *GOON*. For a $30 fee, people could pay to watch *GOON* on television before it hit the theatres. The day after *Goon* opened in Canadian theatres, a decent copy of *GOON*, probably taken from VOD, showed up on the Internet. Even I had no problem finding streaming copies of the movie after a 30-second search on my computer.

Carmody had seen nothing like this extent of piracy in his four decades in the industry. He figured the movie lost millions in ticket and DVD sales.[2] Even in Portage la Prairie, where some of the movie was filmed, a resident was selling DVDs on Facebook for $10. And just like at the Portage la Prairie cinema, the movie theatre in my hometown of Hanover had high hopes for GOON after a decent first week—before a startling plummet of ticket sales ushered the movie away with a black eye.

But like most things of quality, GOON was able to survive its somewhat dubious unveiling, and as the years roll on, it continues to grow in stature as a cult classic.

* * *

Bruised and Battered

While GOON was being filmed in Winnipeg, I watched Kim Coates, who played Halifax Highlanders coach Ronnie Hortense, being interviewed and asked, to my surprise, if he would be interested in a sequel.

A sequel? Quite a bit premature, I thought, considering the first movie was still being filmed. But I stored that little interview in the back of my mind, along with a quip from Jay Baruchel that he envisioned GOON as a trilogy.

Then it started happening. In the summer of 2013, Baruchel announced he was joining with a pal, Jesse Chabot, to write the sequel. Two years later GOON 2: Last of the Enforcers was being filmed in and around Toronto with Jay as the director. Are you shitting me?

Pretty much the entire original cast was back, minus Eugene Levy, who was deftly killed off, and there were some great, and I mean GREAT additions. There was the introduction of Eva's boozing sister, the beautiful Elisha Cuthbert, who was married to Dion Phanuef of the Ottawa Senators. The production also nailed down a prince of Hollywood royalty with the son of Kurt Russell and Goldie Hawn, Wyatt Russell, who had played some college and minor-league hockey.

I was most interested by the stream of former and current players brought in for cameo roles. There were a few in the original, most notably big Georges Laraque, but GOON 2 brought guest appearances to another level—and I would finally be part of it.

First there were publicized appearances of superstar scorer Tyler Seguin and Flyers defenseman Michael Del Zotto. I figured, hell, anything for publicity, anything to generate interest in the movie is a good thing. Then I was notified the production was interested in bringing me in for a shoot. Holy Shit!

They sent me the script. I was going to have some lines with Seann and fight Liev Schreiber. Holy Shit again!

The production had a car service pick up Gator and I at our respective homes to bring us to Logan Airport. I told the production folks that we could share the same car, but the *GOON* people wouldn't have it. I told them we could share a room at the Toronto Hyatt, where they were putting us up, but they told me "that's not the way we do things." Fine, great, whatever you want to do for us. The thing is, I'm a cop and Gator is a teacher in jail—we're just not used to this kind of treatment.

We were picked up at the Toronto airport and run up an hour-and-a-half to the Molson Center Arena in Barrie where the Major Junior Barrie Colts play. Our driver, who had worked for other productions, told us he had never seen anything like the *GOON* set. It was the production everybody wanted to be involved in. He said guys would finish filming, but instead of packing up and going home they'd come back just to hang out with the crew for a beer or burger after midnight. I saw it myself; it was like summer camp. One little group sipped beer and smoked cigarettes, another fired up a barbecue, and a few people just wandered around together talking under the summer moonlight. There was absolutely nothing untoward going on—simply people soaking up and enjoying each other's company, like a close-knit community. Of course this was all in stark contrast to the first movie, much of which was filmed overnight in brutally cold, late-fall Winnipeg.

This camaraderie transpired within part of the arena's parking lot that was transformed into something of a trailer park, where Gator and I were given our own Hollywood-style honeywagon. Ours was a double-long, I guess, split into two separate apartments with a television, fridge, sink, microwave, couch, and full bathroom. Kim Coates took the other apartment. Seann and Liev had their own trailers adjacent and across from ours. Next door there was a food trailer with a cook; all-you-can-eat and made-to-order breakfast, lunch, and dinner. For more elaborate meals, like dinner, the arena had its own little pub that the production had catered for us. Being part of a movie crew—especially an actor—seemed like the same kind of pampered life a pro athlete lived. Gator and I just looked at each other with a broad smile and shook our heads. We tried to keep our excitement tempered enough to be able to actually enjoy what was going on.

We arrived early, maybe nine or ten in the morning. Call time was around eleven or so, and the transportation guys were dropping off actors. Baruchel, ever full of energy, bounded over to see us. We just missed a monster, as 6-foot-9 former minor-leaguer Lane Manson was up for a few days of filming. But as one player left another wandered in for his cameo, and Gator spotted Brandon Prust, recently with Montreal and now with the Vancouver Canucks, chatting with the affable French-Canadian actor Marc-

Andre Grondin by his trailer. Grondin is flat-out wonderful, but they all are, really.

We had a large table with chairs set up under a canopy in the middle of our trailer community for eating and hanging around, and I was made giddy by the company I got to keep. Liev sat with us—shirt off and hockey pants on, complaining about pain in his knee and hip. After watching the extraordinary effort he put in on the ice, I wasn't surprised he was hurting.

Coates plopped down for 20 minutes before going into the rink to film a scene. He was from Saskatchewan and we talked about *Waterworld*, the 1970s Philadelphia Flyers, and everything in between. Being a parent myself, I thought it great that he was most exited and talked glowingly about one of his daughters, an aspiring actress. Seann stopped by and we talked a while. I told him that I was very impressed with his physical condition—lean and muscular with biceps bursting from his shirt. He looked like a male Olympic gymnast. Not bad at all for a guy in his late 30s.

While I was talking with Seann, a younger guy approached. He was probably in his late teens or early 20s and he had been an extra, playing a hockey player on an opposing team. The production had finished with him but before going home he wanted Seann to autograph something. He actually had to get permission to approach Seann and ask for an autograph. I don't believe this was in any way directed by Seann, but rather the rules or ways of production etiquette, where extras are not allowed to fraternize with the actors—unless the actor specifically makes the overture. I have to admit to thinking this rather odd and petty.

Other things like that, rules or points of etiquette on a movie set, included not taking unauthorized photos or video of the filming. Gator, very much like the Jay Baruchel character in the first film, is into documenting everything on film—and I mean everything. He does it on family vacations, his kids' sports, and on the set of *GOON*. Of course the production tolerated Gator, and he took advantage of his almost complete and free access to take a goodly amount of behind-the-scenes photos and video during the production of both movies. Gator, who documents events for personal posterity, is also somewhat of a Neanderthal when it comes to social media, so the vast majority of his material doesn't go public—I'm sure much to the relief of the production.

All of these experiences and revelations were exciting for a guy like me, just as getting into my first professional hockey fights were such a rush. I almost feel spoiled by it all, to the point where I wondered then if there was anything left to get excited about.

There was.

Practicing with a stunt man for a scene in *GOON 2: Last of the Enforcers*.

A production assistant gave me a schedule for the day. Expected in were Colton Orr, Georges Laraque, George Parros and…. Mel Angelstad? Are you shitting me?

Now Orr and Laraque were popular, long-time NHL enforcers, and tough guy Parros won a Stanley Cup with the Mighty Ducks. But Angelstad, while he only played two NHL games with the Washington Capitals, was a minor-league legend, a shadow-like figure known only by those who monitored far-flung events on YouTube or frequented games in places like Portland, Maine, or Kalamazoo, Michigan. Angelstad's nose, which had previously been plastered nearly flat to one side of his face, was now fixed pretty well— but what couldn't be fixed was the size of his freakish fists, which seemed twice the size of my fairly meaty mitts.

And I also have to say that, after standing next to Laraque, I'd love to fight him if for no other reason than the challenge and notoriety. But damn, my strategy would just be to try and land one big knockout punch because he's too fucking big—all over—to even dare to engage in anything long and drawn out.

These cats, along with friendly ex-minor leaguer Neil Clark, were brought in to join me in the "Bruised & Battered" sequence, which was supposed to be an outrageous, 10-man, winner-take-all hockey brawl. I have a strong feeling that the idea for this came from the 2005 "Battle of the Hockey Enforcers" event staged in British Columbia, where a group of hockey fighters battled it out, two-at-a-time, toward one standing champion for a cash prize.[3]

Once on the ice I was let down—big time—when, without even a consultation, my original role was given to my old Providence Bruins student Colton Orr. I was not going to have lines with Seann and no fight with Liev, after all. I was almost despondent but tried my best to hide my disappointment and complain only to Gator. But what could I do? Nobody really knew who I was, but Colton was a bona fide and popular NHL star around these parts who would certainly be far more recognizable to movie-goer hockey fans. So at this point I grudgingly accepted my apparent fate as a fill-in amongst the group who would be relegated to the periphery of this massive rumble.

But things got better, much better, slowly.

After painfully having to watch Orr get my lines with Seann, I got my facial close-up, along with everybody else, but for some reason they had me howl out a scream into the camera—a yell that I actually had trouble holding for a couple seconds so they had me do it twice. Ok, it wasn't really a line, but it was a little something extra to set me apart from the other guys.

The individual fights were filmed one at a time, seemingly in short fashion, but in the end the entire shoot took about 12 hours. There was Schrieber fighting Laraque and Angelstad, Parros matched up with Orr, and then Seann doubling up against Parros and Orr. Lastly, I filmed a nice, short tilt with the minor-leaguer, Neil Clark, finishing him off with an uppercut and a squirt of corn-syrup blood.

Then, for the first time since high school, I did a little math. The "Bruised & Battered" sequence started with 10 players. Two stunt players were knocked out early, Liev sent Laraque and Angelstad down for the count, Seann took care of Parros and Orr, and I dispatched Clark. That left three fighters standing: Liev, Seann, and me. Oh Boy.

Stunt coordinator Dan Skene, who also doubled for Seann in both movies, had whispered to me that I was going to square off against Seann. I had been let down before, so I didn't fully buy into it, but now it was at least mathematically clear why they gave my original role to Orr. I was going to be sticking around. Yah, this was going to be cool.

Baruchel called it "The Two Dougs" (Doug Smith vs. Doug Glatt). Maybe in time movie viewers who don't know me or my significance to *GOON* will come to realize the meaning of us fighting, but the intelligent Baruchel does

The Players from the "Bruised and Battered" scene in *GOON 2: Last of the Enforcers*—**Seann and I kneeling in front; back row, left to right: Liev Schreiber, Georges Laraque, Mel Angelstad, George Parros, Colton Orr, Neil Clark.**

The Two Dougs square off in *GOON 2: Last of the Enforcers*.

appreciate historical significance, which is why he also had former celebrated and notorious NHL rivals Parros and Orr square off with each other.

In the end I finally got my scene with Seann, and Baruchel even had me improvise a couple lines. I wished it were more of a drawn-out fight, but I was dispatched quickly with a single headbutt.

However my scenes look on the screen, if they don't end up on the cutting room floor, I assure you it didn't look all that great in real life. I punched Neil Clark for real by accident during one of our many takes, and my reaction to Seann's head butt was always late, no matter how many takes were filmed to capture it. Even the blood I spat was late. I suppose it would be left up to the editor to make me look good. In any case, with that final head butt scene I was done. Somebody from the wardrobe department asked for my jersey, but that wasn't going to happen. It's now hanging up on my basement wall with all of the others.

Chapter Notes

Chapter 1

1. Bak, Richard. "Gordie's greatest hits: The night Howe took apart Lou Fontinato." Detroit Athletic Co. Blog. November 01, 2014. https://www.detroitathletic.com/blog/2014/11/01/gordies-greatest-hits-the-night-howe-took-apart-lou-fontinato/.

2. Pelletier, Joe. "John Ferguson." Montreal Canadiens Legends. May 2006. http://habslegends.blogspot.com/2006/05/john-ferguson.html.

3. SmashMouthHockey. "NHL Enforcers: Dave 'The Hammer' Schultz." YouTube. January 26, 2009. https://www.youtube.com/watch?v=qEPEy7B1STU.

4. TheBadQuality. "HBO's Broad Street Bullies." YouTube. October 28, 2012. https://www.youtube.com/watch?v=IJgMQDkyJH0.

5. "Flyers Heroes of the Past: Dave Brown (Part 1)." NHL.com. April 02, 2007. https://www.nhl.com/flyers/news/flyers-heroes-of-the-past-dave-brown-part-1/c-435735.

6. Starkman, Randy, Kevin McGran, and Mark Zwolinski. "Former teammates and opponents remember Derek Boogaard. Thestar.com. May 14, 2011. https://www.thestar.com/sports/hockey/2011/05/14/former_teammates_and_opponents_remember_derek_boogaard.html.

7. Hockeyfightsdotcom. "Ivanans vs. Laraque Nov 30, 2006." YouTube. February 05, 2007. https://www.youtube.com/watch?v=6UYqkEzmeFI.

8. Northlands. "Staged Hockey Fights." YouTube. January 21, 2007. https://www.youtube.com/watch?v=HfdOEp35ql4.

Chapter 2

1. ECHLAAHockey. "Henry Brabham." YouTube. November 29, 2010. https://www.youtube.com/watch?v=Pk7ZRRMHkws.

2. ECHL AA Hockey. "Pat Kelly." YouTube. November 29, 2010. https://www.youtube.com/watch?v=2t5C8vYOVGI.

3. Jbabik. "Home Page." The ECHL—Premier 'AA' Hockey League. http://www.echl.com/.

4. "Rampage may come running. After roof cave-in, ECHL move possible." Tribunedigital-baltimoresun. March 18, 1993. http://articles.baltimoresun.com/1993-03-18/sports/1993077046_1_echl-roanoke-valley-rampage.

5. "Class of 2008." ECHL Hall of Fame. http://www.echlhalloffame.com/class-of-2008.

Chapter 4

1. Solloway, Steve. "Former Cape hockey star has big plans for a birthday bash." *The Portland Press Herald*. September 27, 2014. http://www.pressherald.com/2014/09/27/former-cape-elizabeth-hockey-star-has-big-plans-for-a-birthday-bash/.

2. Murrell, I.C. "Cook steps into ring." *Stillwater News Press*. August 12, 2010. http://www.stwnewspress.com/sports/cook-steps-into-ring/article_bc183598-032c-55d4-a4c2-7c1558a6bccb.html.

3. "Samuel Peter–Ron Aubrey. KO." YouTube. September 28, 2014. https://www.youtube.com/watch?v=v-mm7q-LAPU.

Chapter 6

1. Emmons, Mark. "Tracking down the Sharks' 'Missing Link.'" *The Mercury News*. August 13, 2016. http://www.mercurynews.com/2011/05/16/tracking-down-the-sharks-missing-link/.

2. Urstadt, Bryant. "The legend of Link." ESPN. March 25, 2013. http://www.espn.com/nhl/story/_/page/Mag15thelegendoflink/hockey-scariest-man-link-gaetz-remember-most-mayhem-espn-magazine-archives.

3. "Let's watch John Stossel get slapped!" YouTube. December 29, 2008. https://www.youtube.com/watch?v=M0q44ALM7jo.

4. "Jim Rome vs. Jim 'Chris' Everett." YouTube. August 10, 2010. https://www.youtube.com/watch?v=p8pAZ75WKh8.

Chapter 8

1. "SIHR | History of the Allan Cup." SIHR | History of the Allan Cup. http://sihr.ca/new/p_allan_cup.cfm.

Chapter 9

1. Emmons, Mark. "Tracking down the Sharks' 'Missing Link.'" *The Mercury News.* August 13, 2016. http://www.mercurynews.com/2011/05/16/tracking-down-the-sharks-missing-link/.

Chapter 11

1. Robinson, Doug. "New twist to 'lend me your ear'" DeseretNews.com. July 02, 1997. http://www.deseretnews.com/article/569908/New-twist-to-lend-me-your-ear.html.

Chapter 14

1. "Evan Goldberg." IMDb. http://www.imdb.com/name/nm1698571/?ref_=tt_ov_wr.

2. McClearn, Matthew. "Movie studios fighting Bit Torrent, but can they win?" *Canadian Business.* March 12, 2013. http://www.canadianbusiness.com/technology-news/battling-bit-torrent/.

3. CBC Sports. "Hockey goon competition given green light." CBCnews. June 29, 2005. http://www.cbc.ca/sports/hockey/hockey-goon-competition-given-green-light-1.562198.

Index